Driven to change

Published in our
centenary year
≈ **2004** ≈
MANCHESTER
UNIVERSITY
PRESS

Driven to change

THE EUROPEAN UNION'S ENLARGEMENT VIEWED FROM THE EAST

edited by Antoaneta L. Dimitrova

Manchester University Press

MANCHESTER AND NEW YORK

distributed exclusively in the USA by Palgrave

Copyright © Manchester University Press 2004

While copyright in the volume as a whole is vested in Manchester University Press, copyright in individual chapters belongs to their respective authors, and no chapter may be reproduced wholly or in part without the express permission in writing of both author and publisher.

Published by Manchester University Press
Oxford Road, Manchester M13 9NR, UK
and Room 400, 175 Fifth Avenue, New York, NY 10010, USA
www.manchesteruniversitypress.co.uk

Distributed exclusively in the USA by
Palgrave, 175 Fifth Avenue, New York,
NY 10010, USA

Distributed exclusively in Canada by
UBC Press, University of British Columbia, 2029 West Mall,
Vancouver, BC, Canada V6T 1Z2

British Library Cataloguing-in-Publication Data
A catalogue record for this book is available from the British Library

Library of Congress Cataloging-in-Publication Data applied for

ISBN   0 7190 6808 8   *hardback*
        0 7190 6809 6   *paperback*

First published 2004

13 12 11 10 09 08 07 06 05 04   10 9 8 7 6 5 4 3 2 1

Typeset in Minion
by Action Publishing Technology Ltd, Gloucester
Printed in Great Britain
by CPI, Bath

Dedication

This book is dedicated to the people of Central and Eastern Europe who have lived through a remarkable period of change and especially to those who believe that it is leading them to a better future.

Contents

    integration process
    Iveta Reinholde   163

11 Conclusions: the 'end of history' of enlargement or the beginning
    of a new research agenda?
    Antoaneta L. Dimitrova and Bernard Steunenberg   179

    Select bibliography   194
    Index   207

Tables and figures

Tables

Figures

Contributors

Antoaneta L. Dimitrova is Associate Professor at the Department of Public Administration of Leiden University, Leiden, the Netherlands.

Richard A. Baldwin is GIS/LIS Project Director for Eastern and Central Europe, BloInfo A/S, Bath, United Kingdom.

Călin Hințea is Lecturer at the Public Administration Department of Babeș Bolyai University in Cluj Napoca, Romania, and President of the Romanian Association of Schools and Institutes of Romania.

Veronica Junjan is Lecturer at the Public Administration Department of Babeș Bolyai University in Cluj Napoca, Romania.

Darina Malová is Associate Professor of Political Science at the Department of Political Science, Comenius University in Bratislava, Slovakia.

Klaudijus Maniokas is former Deputy Director General, European Committee under the Government of Lithuania, former Deputy Chief Negotiator; Lecturer, Institute of International Relations and Political Science, University of Vilnius, Lithuania.

Ewa Popławska is Assistant Professor at the Institute of Law Studies, Polish Academy of Sciences, Warsaw, Poland, and Lecturer at the Cardinal Stefan Wyszyński University, Warsaw, Poland.

Janno Reiljan is a member of the Estonian parliament (RIIGIKOGU) and head of chair for International Economy, University of Tartu, Estonia.

Iveta Reinholde is teaching associate, Eurofaculty, University of Latvia, doctoral student, Department of Political Science, Faculty of Social Science, University of Latvia, Riga, Latvia.

Marek Rybář is Assistant Professor at the Department of Political Science, Comenius University, Bratislava, Slovakia.

Sorin Dan Șandor is Lecturer at the Public Administration Department of Babeș Bolyai University in Cluj Napoca, Romania.

Bernard Steunenberg is Professor of Public Administration, Department of Public Administration, Leiden University, Leiden, the Netherlands.

Kristina Toming is doctoral student and Research Associate at the University of Tartu, Estonia.

Andrej Udovč is Assistant Professor of Agricultural Economics at the Biotechnical Faculty at the University of Ljubljana, Slovenia.

László Vass is Professor and Director General, Budapest School of Communication Budapest, Hungary.

Gallina Andronova Vincelette is Consultant at the World Bank (Europe and Central Asia Region), Washington, DC, USA.

Acknowledgements

Above all, I would like to thank the contributors to this book, many of whom, while actively engaged with the changes in their countries, found time also to write about them. This book would not have existed without the efforts of Bernard Steunenberg who designed the initial research project from which it arose and the financial support of the Dutch Scientific Council (NWO). I am grateful for NWO funding which allowed us to organise the conference 'Changing Rules: Enlargement Driven Institutional Change in Central and Eastern Europe', the contributions for which made the basis of this book. For their hospitality and invaluable help with the conference organisation (and the lovely flowers!), I would like to thank Zuzana Stefanikova and Barbara Kolarova from AI Nova. Thanks are also due to Karen Anderson for reading and helpful suggestions. Last but not least, I am grateful to the anonymous reviewers whose suggestions helped improve this book.

1

Enlargement-driven change and post-communist transformations: a new perspective[1]

Antoaneta L. Dimitrova

The enlargement of the European Union (EU) to include the former communist states of Central and Eastern Europe has been the Union's most challenging and complex enlargement so far. A formal end to this process, at least for some of the initial twelve applicants[2] was reached when in December 2002 the Copenhagen European Council agreed to welcome ten new members in 2004 and Bulgaria and Romania in 2007. However, the moment of entry is only one stop along a long road of transformation for the new members. Enlargement has been a process requiring tremendous adaptation from the candidates and the European Union. Even the teams who have had to complete the complex work of negotiating the final deal of terms of accession and all separate chapters of the European Union *acquis* may not be aware of the extent and range of changes, which have been taking place in the context of enlargement.

The lack of awareness of the changes taking place in the context of a momentous process, which affects institutions and societies all over Europe, creates mistrust in the West and uncertainty in the East. This volume aims to contribute to a better understanding of the patterns of governance and institutional change linked to the EU's enlargement to the East, an enlargement that has been in preparation for more than a decade and is soon to become a reality.

The first ten candidates: Estonia, Hungary, the Czech Republic, Latvia, Lithuania, Poland, Slovakia and Slovenia, as well as Cyprus and Malta (outside the scope of this book), completed their negotiations in December 2002 and are joining the Union in 2004 while Bulgaria and Romania, still some way from finalising their negotiations, aim to join in 2006–7. Turkey is recognised by the EU as an official candidate and has embarked on its own transformation in order to fulfil the criteria for starting negotiations. Croatia, Serbia, Macedonia and other states are knocking at the door, drawn by the magnetic pull of the EU as an example of prosperity and resolution of conflicts through integration started by the EU founding states after the Second World War. The enlargement of the European Union is seen by policy makers in the West and East of Europe as another step towards peace and stability in Europe, a way to achieve the final unification of the continent and rectify the historical injustice which placed countries in Central and Eastern Europe (CEE) behind the iron curtain.

Precisely because it is difficult to argue with this enlargement's broad historical rationale and the hope that it will bring stability, security and prosperity to the whole of Europe, there has been so far limited critical examination of the tremendous changes enlargement brings to institutions and societies in CEE.[3] This volume strives to present such a critical examination in a broad overview of the wide range of sweeping changes, which the EU's enlargement has set in motion.

Supporting this enlargement and its goals and nevertheless taking a critical look at its potential effects and the changes it brings about, is a difficult task. It is difficult, and perhaps unnecessary, to distance oneself from the basic assumption, shared by all the authors of this book and many others, that enlargement will indeed bring peace and prosperity and stabilise the new democracies in Central and Eastern Europe. For many, joining the EU has no alternative, in economic and geopolitical terms. This does not mean, however, that we should not scrutinise and try to evaluate the changes which enlargement brings, the new institutions, policies and patterns of rules. An important contribution of this book is to link the enlargement process and its adaptational pressures to the post-communist transformations in Central and Eastern European candidate states, transformations that in themselves represent multiple processes of change.

The approach of this book: post-communist transformations and the role of the European Union

The 1990s, when the former Soviet bloc states of Central and Eastern Europe embarked on their path of accession towards the European Union, marked the most important period of transition from the communist regimes, which was 'a distinct period of organizational change'.[4] The pace of this change has been breathtaking and the scope and consequences are yet to be fully understood by participants and evaluated by observers.

A 'bird's eye' perspective which has become fairly widely accepted by most scholars views these changes as multiple processes of political, economic, societal and state-administrative transformation, affecting at least the spheres of national identity, orientation and (sometimes) statehood, of the system of property ownership and the economy and of the foundations of the political system (constitutional change).[5] Scholars of these post-communist transformations have stressed that they involve the making of numerous crucial institutional choices more or less simultaneously as well as dealing with the communist legacy of the previous regimes.[6] The difficulty of simultaneous transformations and the problems of mutual obstruction which have occurred between the processes of establishing democracy, the market and sometimes new states have led some analysts, such as Claus Offe, to make the pessimistic prediction that the transformations would not be successful without an external guiding power.[7] However, despite the high profile case of the disintegration of former Yugoslavia, which seemed to confirm fears that ethnic politics would be unleashed in the aftermath of communism, Offe's pessimistic prognosis did not come true.[8]

While the prediction that the multiple transformations would be impossible to complete successfully has fortunately proven to be false, the rebuilding of weak, discredited or inefficient institutions remains a major challenge of the post-communist period. In some cases these have been institutions inherited from the previous regime which have to be given new meaning and legitimacy, recreated to serve society and not the party state (such as parliaments, the administration, the judiciary), in other cases there are institutions which have to be re-established after a long time (market institutions) or yet in others institutions that had never previously existed have to be created (constitutional courts, ombudsmen). The precariousness and difficulty of institutional design 'on the move' has been captured by Elster, Offe and Preuss' comparison to 'rebuilding a ship while at sea'.[9]

In the context of the tremendous challenge of rebuilding post-communist institutions and societies, the European Union presented an example for emulation and hope for support. It is difficult to determine whether the elites and leaders in the CEE states in transition were led by an awareness of the enormous task that lay ahead of them or the desire to 'return to Europe' where they felt they belonged, when they applied for EU membership soon after 1989. Evidence from numerous empirical accounts of the motivation in Central and Eastern Europe (and, one expects, Turkey) of elites striving to join the EU suggests that these elites 'have been driven by a sort of synthesis between "value rationality" and "instrumental rationality"'.[10] Early on in the democratic transitions, EU membership was already seen as a way to help secure the emerging democracies and liberal values, similar to the role it was seen to have played in the consolidation of democracy in Spain and Portugal.[11] The general public in Central and Eastern European states also perceived a link, at least initially, between democratisation and accession to the EU. Public opinion surveys in Poland and the Czech Republic, for example, showed that accession to the EU 'was perceived as a sequel to the grand democratic transformation'.[12] The European Union focused the aspirations of post-communist elites and populations by providing a model of prosperity and democracy to be emulated and thus became the closest thing to an external guiding power. In the words of Vladimir Tismaneanu, 'the magnetism of united Europe (or perhaps the political myth of unified Europe) has thus played a decisive role in preventing anti democratic forces taking the lead and subverting democratic institutions'.[13] This provides one possible explanation to the paradox of the relative success of the multiple transformations, declared impossible by Offe, as by and large, there has been a successful completion of most transitions to democracy in Central and Eastern Europe despite the multiple challenges they faced.

The European Union has been part of the CEE elites interactions in several ways: ideologically, by influencing ideas about the future and providing an example of stability and prosperity, and strategically, by setting the conditions for membership and using various instruments of governance in the enlargement process to spur reforms and modernisation. In terms of ideas, the 'return to the Europe' has been the closest thing to an (albeit weak) guiding ideology of the post-communist transformation, serving to unite the closely associated processes of democratisation, marketisation and European integration.[14]

The European Union member states, however, have been, to say the least, apprehensive about the challenge of diversity which the candidates presented.[15] Therefore joining the EU did not turn out to be the quick process envisaged by post-communist reformers in the first years after the collapse of the Soviet bloc. The end of euphoria came in 1991–92 when the candidates negotiated association agreements with the EU, but did not receive the hoped-for promise for accession. Even though this promise came with the decisions of the Copenhagen European Council of June 1993, these decisions also set the barrier of a number of criteria, which the candidates had to fulfil before they could join.

Studies of the EU's decision making related to this enlargement[16] provide ample reason why the EU chose to delay enlargement and to create sets of conditions and criteria to be fulfilled by the candidates. Not only, as Preston has suggested,[17] has the Union always favoured its internal agenda over external demands, but also, in this enlargement, this tendency has been exacerbated by the mistrust among the EU member states towards the twelve states knocking at its door, states with poorer populations and weaker economies and institutions. EU member states had little confidence in the candidates' ability to function in the Union's multi-level system of governance and, as aptly pointed out by Grabbe, saw enlargement as 'a medieval crusade in which the barbarians had to be taught the superior Western ways of doing business and politics'.[18] In a less extreme form, the view of enlargement as a process in which the candidates adjust to the superior standards of the West is reflected in most of the literature about it, which has focused on the challenge for the Union, the diversity of the candidates, and the potential for paralysis of the Union's institutions.

An equally important question, which has hardly been addressed so far, is how enlargement affects the candidates and in particular the processes of post-communist institutional design, which make this enlargement different from all previous enlargements. The relative lack of attention for this *problematique* can be explained by the fact that the adaptation and changes linked to enlargement are still under way, yet a similar obstacle does not prevent scholars from studying transitions to democracy or European integration, the latter an area in which change and adaptation are a mode of existence. A more important unacknowledged reason is that scholars from Central and Eastern Europe have by and large not been well represented in the enlargement literature or when they have, they have joined the majority of analyses which simply show how far or how close the candidates are from the EU standards. To address the question of how enlargement would affect the post-communist transformations, one would need a link with the literature on the processes of transition and transformation from communist regimes,[19] state ownership and planned economies to democracy and the market. Scholars researching these processes have focused mostly on domestic factors and for quite a while neglected to see the importance of the European Union for domestic processes.[20] More recently, work which has explored the post-communist transformations from domestic perspectives emphasising state weakness, privatisation and networks[21] has also failed to register the influence of the EU on its sensitive radar. Not only are scholars focusing on domestic reform often underestimating enlargement's significance and impact on domestic political processes,[22] but also more importantly, no theoretical framework has been so far developed to take into account the effects of the European Union on polities and policies in states undergoing transitions to democracy and market economy. It is therefore important that these effects and the process we can call pre-enlargement Europeanisation, are explored with the help of a suitable theoretical framework linking transformation research and the recently ever more prominent Europeanisation literature.

This book tries to bring the research agendas of these literatures closer together by addressing both the post-communist transformations and enlargement related changes. It also brings together a number of contributors from the CEE states that have focused on explaining how and to what extent enlargement matters in the post-communist transformations. The contributions in this volume are a first step, which endeavours to stimulate a broader debate between scholars about this enlargement evaluated in an institutionalist (post-communist) transformation perspective. The chapters that follow also present a not too often seen perspective evaluating the enlargement changes 'from the East'.

Key questions

The suggested debate on enlargement from an institutionalist perspective would have to address important questions such as: How does the process of acceding to the European Union interact with the multiple processes of post-communist transformation which are only partially completed in Central and Eastern Europe? Is the ongoing enlargement of the European Union to the East, with all its demands and complexity, creating incentives for the completion of the post-communist transformations? Are the potential effects of enlargement for democracy, markets and states in CEE mostly positive, as many proponents of enlargement have assumed? How will the institutional design in CEE fare subjected to the multiple changes required by the transformations and soon thereafter, if not simultaneously, by the enlargement adaptations? How do the new rules promoted by the EU interact with patterns of behaviour influenced by tradition or the communist legacy?

When thinking about these questions, we need to distinguish between on the one hand, the overall direction of development of the post-communist states – the macro level, at which ideas of European integration still play an important role and, on the other, the stability of institutions defined as structures and (constitutional or lower level) rules affecting behaviour. Even if we accept the widespread assumption that accession to the EU will prevent CEE democracies from lapsing back into authoritarianism through a number of incentives and constraints,[23] this does not necessarily mean that it will ensure stability in the new institutions established as part of the transformation/enlargement processes. Whereas ideas of democracy and the market underpinning the post-communist transformations and enlargement are broadly the same, when it comes to structures and rules, the adoption of 'external' rules creates several risks, which have not been discussed by proponents of enlargement but which deserve careful consideration.

One potential risk relates to the link established in popular perception between enlargement and democratisation. This means that a failure of enlargement may be perceived by many as a failure of democracy and makes it imperative that candidates such as Bulgaria and Romania are not indefinitely kept at the door by the EU after years of painful adjustments. Indefinite delays make enlargement a risky form of democracy promotion.[24] Another rarely acknowledged risk is presented by the sheer volume of reforms and adjustments[25] that the EU requires from the candidates. The adoption of the EU *acquis* will in some cases inevitably result in too much tinkering with newly established institutions. Constant change may weaken the acceptance of (especially constitutional level) rules, something which new institutionalist accounts such as the ones by Offe, Elster and Preuss[26] warn against, claiming that endless rounds of rule making in the new democracies are not likely to produce stable institutions. Last but not least, Scharpf has been calling attention to the risks associated with 'the Commission's role in imposing the *acquis* on new Member States that had no voice in its definition and whose economic and social conditions differ fundamentally from those of the Member States from whose self-interested bargains these rules have emerged'. Scharpf warns that imposing the *acquis* on the candidates in a strict and legalistic manner has the potential to have detrimental effects on their economies similar to the effects on the East German economy after unification.[27]

The only way to evaluate how real both the assumed benefits and potential risks are is to engage in more empirical research studying how the governance extended from the EU to the candidates, the bargains struck in the negotiations for accession and the bargains struck in the past by existing member states affect the institutions of the new members. Keeping the 'grand transformation' perspective as a starting point, the contributions in this volume focus on a broad range of changes in institutions and areas linked to the EU conditions and requirements for accession. Institutions are defined as 'the rules of the game in a society or, more formally, the humanly devised constraints that shape human interaction', the 'systems of nested rules with rules at each successive level being increasingly costly to change'.[28] Given that institutional changes linked to both enlargement and post-communist transformations are still comparatively recent, most authors have focused on changes in formal institutions, such as constitutional rules, democratic procedures, administrative systems, currency board arrangements and others. Most chapters, however, share the assumption that such changes would have to be followed by changes in norms, attitudes and practices before they can create stable institutions. But it is too early yet to tell whether the outcome of the critical juncture of change will be translated into a long lasting legacy.[29]Addressing this issue will be beyond the scope of this book and an important task for future research on the effect of European Union enlargement.

Defining enlargement governance

The enlargement process clearly matters and has significant impact on the candidate states but how does it matter? This simple question is difficult to answer, as the new Europeanisation research agenda, which deals with the effects of European integration on EU member states' domestic arenas, is only recently beginning to produce theoretical frameworks to help us understand how states react to 'the emergence at the European level of distinct structures of governance'.[30] A shared finding of much of the Europeanisation literature is that the pressures from EU level do not produce convergence in national policy structures, domestic institutions and other patterned relationships, but, rather, result in 'domestic adaptation with national colors'.[31] The lack of convergence and the persistence of diversity are important conclusions to be drawn from Europeanisation research and borne in mind when dealing with expectations that the EU will manage through the enlargement preparations to reduce significantly the diversity between it and the candidate states.

However, analysing the impact of the EU on the candidate states as simply a form of Europeanisation would be misleading and contrary to the enlargement and transformation approach advocated in this book. Apart from the interaction with post-communist institutional design, the governance in the enlargement period has several other important features which distinguish it from governance inside the EU and which must be taken into consideration when assessing the impact of the EU on the candidates. Defining the main features of enlargement governance[32] can help us anticipate its effects on the political, economic and administrative institutions of the candidates and establish the similarities and differences between the impact of enlargement and Europeanisation inside the EU.

The governance extended to the candidates in the enlargement period by the EU differs from the bargaining or network modes of governance existing inside the Union in several important respects. In the first place, the enlargement process has an executive bias[33] and involves a relatively small number of societal actors. Interactions are based on meetings of various Councils and committees in the framework of the candidates Association Agreements with the EU and later the negotiating teams and the Commission. Thus enlargement governance involves a relatively small range of societal actors – the Commission and the enlargement task force on the side of the EU and the negotiating teams and the executives in the candidates. This presents a contrast with 'new' modes of governance in the EU, which involve a multiplicity of state and non-state actors in polycentric and non-hierarchical relationships.[34] Whereas in the EU, governance is increasingly produced in the interaction between actors at various levels who share power in a network or bargaining configuration,[35] in the enlargement process governance flows from the EU to the applicants and is channeled mostly through the Commission and the Council, on the EU side and the executive, on the candidates' side.

Enlargement is explicitly defined by the EU and accepted by the candidates as an 'asymmetrical process' of taking over the rules of a club. The enlargement negotiations are, as stressed by many officials and experts involved in them such as Avery and Cameron and Mayhew, strictly about the conditions for joining the club.[36] The asymmetry between the EU and the candidate states also means that political elites in CEE have limited control over the institutional changes they have undertaken to effect. This raises a whole set of questions related to democracy and the potential for the EU to export its own democratic deficit.[37] One remedy is suggested by Klaudijus Maniokas in the first chapter of this book – a politicisation of the enlargement process which may let the public be better informed about the bargains and deals made by governments. Governments have been, however, very reluctant to make negotiations more open and transparent as this exposes them not only to public scrutiny but also to the participation of affected interests who may wish to veto them. Examples are the pressure from Polish farmers for a better deal secured at the last minute in December 2002 in Copenhagen or the debate around the EU requirement to close the nuclear power station, Kozloduy, in Bulgaria. Even if they are more open, negotiations for entry in the EU remain asymmetric and this creates a 'democracy' problem for governance before, during and after enlargement.

Linked to the asymmetry of the process is another characteristic of enlargement governance, namely, the emphasis on the transfer of the *acquis* of the Union, representing the institutionalised rules and norms, which allow the Union to function as it does. From the first enlargement onwards, it has been well established that the EU has projected its formal and informal rules by insisting that new members take up the *acquis communautaire* (later the '*acquis*' of the Union) in full – a norm which has become institutionalised as the EU's 'classical method of enlargement'.[38]

The changes required for adaptation to the *acquis* are very extensive in this particular enlargement. According to Alan Mayhew, 'the adoption of the *acquis* in the internal market area has been an extremely long process even within the Union; certain of the directives have not yet been transposed into national legislation and implementation has in some areas been slow. The work, which the

associated countries will have to do to adopt and implement the same legislation, is far greater in that they are starting from a lower base of market economy
legislation. In the associated countries each peace of legislation adopted does
not mean a marginal change to existing legislation but usually a major policy
choice'.[39]

Despite the potentially far-reaching and yet understudied effects of adopting
the main part of the *acquis* before accession, the norm of the immutability of the
acquis has shaped enlargement preparations and determined the content of
negotiations in a way that has overshadowed enlargement's proclaimed historical rationale. In the words of former Romanian foreign minister Andrei Plesu,
'an exclusive emphasis on legal and fiscal integration transforms Europe into a
scheme, a strictly technical framework, a simple managerial recipe. "Europe"
develops the regrettable appearance of a set of criteria that must be passed and
loses the aura of an attractive model, of a project that inspires emulation'.[40]

The most prominent feature of enlargement governance, which makes the
EU's influence ever more strongly felt in the candidate states, has been the
employment of conditionality. The EU started to use conditionality in the first
(Trade and Cooperation, later Association) agreements it concluded with the
CEE states, by including suspension clauses which made the operation of the
agreements conditional on respect for human and minorities' rights and democratic principles. Conditionality was and remains strong in the PHARE
programme, the main vehicle for financial support for Central and Eastern
Europe. The next chapter by Klaudijus Maniokas, shows how the EU's criteria
for accession developed into the most complex and extensive set of conditions
the Union has ever used towards third countries.

Remarkably, EU conditionality goes far beyond ensuring that the Union's
institutional rules and norms are established. For this purpose it would have
been sufficient to ensure the transposition of the *acquis*. Instead, EU conditions
have been partially designed to address transformation problems and weaknesses of the candidates. This is evident from an examination of the so-called
Copenhagen criteria, introduced by the Copenhagen European Council in June
1993, which have been the linchpin of the enlargement governance mode. These
are:

- the stability of institutions guaranteeing democracy, the rule of law, human
  rights and respect for and protection of minorities;
- the existence of a functioning market economy, capable of coping with
  competitive pressures and market forces within the Union;
- the ability to take on the obligations of membership, including adherence to
  its aims of political, economic and monetary union;[41]
- administrative capacity, a criterion added by the European Council
  decisions in Madrid in 1995, defined as capacity to implement the '*acquis
  communautaire*'.[42]

How enlargement governance matters: from procedural democracy and constitutions to administrative systems

The Copenhagen criteria have remained central in the enlargement process and have been developed in subsequent enlargement instruments such as the Commission's Opinions on the candidates, the yearly Progress Reports and the accession partnerships, leading, as is shown in the next chapter, to increased and more complex conditionality.

A proposition which can be formulated given the predominance of conditionality in enlargement governance is that few actors have the possibility of becoming veto players, as institutionalised veto points matter less in candidate states than in member states.[43] Yet this does not necessarily mean that the stronger potential for impact of the EU on the candidates always translates into more uniform effects than witnessed by the Europeanisation literature. The chapters in this volume present a variety of domestic responses to EU enlargement governance, from which the puzzles of future research are already emerging. Variables such as reform fit, domestic configuration of preferences and domestic tradition and legacy, are shown by the authors to matter for the extent to which EU institutional rules are adopted by the CEECs. Some cases show the EU-driven process of change substitutes almost completely domestic reform and domestic reform consensus is replaced by EU conditionality – as is the case of administrative reform in Latvia or Romania. Others, such as the chapters on Bulgaria and Poland, present a more complex picture of interaction between domestic institutional arrangements and the anticipation of EU requirements. And in some cases, as in shown by the chapter on Hungarian administrative reform by Vass, the EU's impact is minimal due to factors such as good reform fit and stability of existing institutions.

Following the discussion of the features and impact of enlargement governance developed in this and the subsequent chapter, the rest of the chapters, presenting different aspects of the enlargement driven institutional change in CEE, are grouped into sections, corresponding to the Copenhagen criteria dealing with: (1) changes in constitutions and the set-up of the political system; (2) changes in the economy; (3) changes in administrative arrangements.[44] The case studies discuss various ways in which the EU is driving this successive round of institutional change.

As mentioned above, Maniokas's chapter makes an important contribution to the debate on enlargement governance by asking the important question how this enlargement process has differed from previous ones. Maniokas discusses and illustrates the emergence of the new principles of enlargement with reference to the accession experience of Lithuania and highlights their implications for the candidates' democracies and institutional stability.

The following chapter by Rybář and Malová picks up the theme of conditionality and shows how the EU's conditionality and the instruments of enlargement governance have affected democratisation and consolidation in

Slovakia. The case of Slovakia where conditions existed for institutional instability to be affected by a pro-active EU policy appears to be a more or less rare example of a successful EU intervention in support of democratisation. In contrast to the Slovak case, others, such as Maniokas, point out the potential negative effects the technocratic style of enlargement governance may have on domestic political institutions.

When referring to political institutions defined as rules we distinguish two levels of change: the level of changing the rules (policy change) and the level of constitutional change (changing of the rules about the rules). It is desirable that citizens accept constitutional-level rules in a democracy as the foundation of the political system. Constitutional-level rules – and correspondingly, constitutions, are generally designed in such as way as to be the most costly to change. Constitutions contain in themselves high threshold requirements for amendment because 'being able to embody certain agreements in presumptively unchangeable rules allows us to make commitments to one another that are credible'.[45] Enlargement governance, however, has the potential to overcome the high threshold for constitutional change – at the very least in the provisions that deal with deceptively 'simple' issues such as the sale of land to foreign citizens.

The chapter by Ewa Popławska, examining the Polish constitutional changes preparing Poland for EU membership, addresses the important issue of constitutional change in the context of enlargement. Her analysis has interesting implications for the scholarly debate discussing whether changes in basic rules are a response to conditionality or a process of emulation of EU norms and forward looking adaptation. Popławska's chapter also suggests the limits of potential adaptation, as she discusses the various arguments in the legal debate regarding the general acceptability of EU norms such as the supremacy of EC law in Poland.

The extent to which enlargement affects the economy and society of the candidate states is illustrated by the next chapter's overview of the key problems of accession for Estonia. Janno Reilan and Kristina Toming present a broad and balanced review of economic advantages and disadvantages of enlargement from the perspective of a small candidate state. Their discussion of Estonian preparations for accession highlights the ambiguity of EU conditions and the need for a careful evaluation of the economic and social adjustments this enlargement will require.

In the next chapter, Gallina Andronova Vincelette addresses one important aspect of economic adjustment, monetary policy, in the case of Bulgaria. She shows how Bulgaria's currency board arrangement can serve as a stabilisation tool which advances the financial system in the country and facilitates its joining the eurozone. Similarly to the Polish chapter, the chapter on Bulgaria discusses adjustments that are made in anticipation rather than as a response to conditionality.

In another chapter dealing with market institutions, Andrej Udovč and

Richard Baldwin analyse the problems of developing the agricultural land market in Slovenia and the influence of the accession negotiations on this process. Starting from the perspective stressing post-communist transformation, the authors identify key institutions that still need to be reformed to support the agricultural land market in Slovenia. They highlight a number of constraints, which make the opening of the agricultural land markets a difficult issue in Slovenia – a finding that is relevant for several other candidate states as well.

Following the discussion of democracy and political changes and market institutions in the first two parts, the final chapters deal with a theme that became more and more prominent in the late 1990s as the EU required candidates to develop sufficient administrative capacity to implement the *acquis*. The chapters by Vass, Hinţea, Şandor and Junjan and Reinholde are united by the theme of the reform of post-communist administrative structures, which has also acquired prominence in the transition literature. Evaluating administrative change is important from both a transition and an accession perspective. Weak states and inefficient bureaucracies are seen to hinder the consolidation of the new democracies, threaten security, create mistrust in the citizens and hinder countries in absorbing EU funds.

Finally, the concluding chapter summarises the various scenarios of interaction between enlargement-driven changes and domestic transformations revealed in the case studies. Some general conclusions regarding the impact of enlargement governance on democracy, market institutions and the institutions of the state are drawn and, based on these, the chapter suggests a rich and exciting agenda for future research.

The increased complexity of the enlargement process has meant that its societal impact has been very difficult to predict. There are, however, already some indications that not all the changes linked to enlargement will be beneficial to the post-communist societies. It is important for both societal and social science reasons that these changes be studied, understood and where possible anticipated. This book aims to contribute to the literature shedding light on them but even more importantly, to provoke further research and debate.

Notes

1 Parts of this chapter draw on my article 'Enlargement, Institution Building and the EU's Administrative Capacity Requirement', *West European Politics*, 25:4 (October 2002), 171–190.

2 The post-communist states, which applied to join the EU in the early 1990s, were Bulgaria, the Czech Republic, Estonia, Hungary, Poland, Latvia, Lithuania, Slovakia, Slovenia and Romania. Since this book explores post-communist change in relation to enlargement driven change, it will not deal with Malta, Cyprus or Turkey, which have also been part of the enlargement.

3 This is not to say that enlargement has not had its opponents, but, so far, those openly opposing it have been voices from the far right such as Austria's Joerg Heider,

and have remained isolated. It must be noted, however, that many mainstream politicians in the west have taken a cautious stance towards enlargement, reflecting widespread popular prejudices and fear of diversity. See Amato, G. and J. Batt, 1999, *Final Report of the Reflection Group on the Long Term Implications of EU Enlargement: The Nature of the New Border*, RSC/EUI Working Papers, 12 (Florence, EUI, 1999).

4 V. I. Ganev, 'Dysfunctional Sinews of Power: Problems of Bureaucracy Building in Post-communist Balkans', conference paper presented at the conference Civil Society, Political Society and the State: A Fresh Look at the Problems of Governance in the Balkan Region (Split, 21–23 November 2001).

5 C. Offe, 'Capitalism by Democratic Design? Democratic Theory Facing the Triple Transition in East Central Europe', *Social Research*, 58:4 (1991), 865–892.

6 Ibid. See also P. C. Schmitter and T. L. Karl, 'The Conceptual Travels of Transitologists and Consolidologists: How Far East Should They Attempt to Go?', *Slavic Review*, 53:1 (1994), 173–185; J. Elster, C. Offe and U. Preuss (with F. Boenker, U. Goetting and F. W. Rueb), *Institutional Design in Post-communist Societies: Rebuilding the Ship at Sea* (Cambridge, Cambridge University Press, 1998); and J. J. Linz, and A. Stepan, *Problems of Democratic Transition and Consolidation: Southern Europe, South America, and Post-communist Europe* (Baltimore and London, Johns Hopkins University Press, 1996).

7 Offe, 'Capitalism by Democratic Design', p. 889.

8 This is not to say that there are no challenges to the newly established democracies in Central and Eastern Europe, but, as Tismaneanu points out, a decline into ethno-regional anarchy remains doubtful (V. Tismaneanu, 'Discomforts of Victory: Democracy, Liberal Values and Nationalism in Post-communist Europe', *West European Politics*, 25:2 (2002), 81. Ivan Krastev similarly argues that the most important threat to the democratic process does not stem from violent nationalism ('The Inflexibility Trap: Frustrated Societies, Weak States and Democracy', report on the State of Democracy in the Balkans, Sofia, Center for Liberal Strategies, February 2002). Instead both authors identify voter apathy, the erosion of participation and xenophobia as symptoms of the Europe-wide populist attack on democratic institutions.

9 Elster, Offe and Preuss, *Institutional Design*.

10 S. E. Hanson, 'Defining Democratic Consolidation', in R. D. Anderson, M. Steven Fish, S. E. Hanson and P. G. Roeder, *Post-communism and the Theory of Democracy* (Princeton and Oxford, Princeton University Press, 2001), p. 145.

11 G. Pridham, *Encouraging Democracy: The International Context of Regime Transition in Southern Europe* (Leicester, Leicester University Press, 1991); V. Tismaneanu, 'Discomforts of Victory', pp. 81–101.

12 M. Kucia, 'Public Opinion in Central Europe on EU Accession: The Czech Republic and Poland', *Journal of Common Market Studies*, 37:1 (1999), 146.

13 Tismaneanu, 'Discomforts of Victory', pp. 82–83.

14 K. Henderson (ed.), *Back to Europe: Central and Eastern Europe and the European Union* (London, UCL Press, 1999). The return to Europe and the enlargement project are clearly embraced by market oriented, international minded elites more than by the general populations, who are susceptible to the 'resurrection of historical phantoms', myths and 'fantasies of salvation' (Tismaneanu, 'Discomforts of Victory', p. 89). It is interesting to note that nowadays such fantasies of salvation are not limited to the east, but find expression in xenophobic populism among parts of the public in countries as diverse as Austria, Switzerland and the Netherlands.

15 The EU's reaction to the perceived diversity of the candidates is discussed for example by Zielonka and Mair in the special issue of *West European Politics* on the enlarged European Union which also presents a number of insightful studies of diversity and adaptation in the candidates. See J. Zielonka and P. Mair, 'Introduction: Diversity and Adaptation in the Enlarged European Union', *West European Politics*, 25:2 (2002), 1–19.

16 Such as L Friis, 'Approaching the "Third Half" of EU Grand Bargaining: The Post Negotiation Phase of the "Europe Agreement game",' *Journal of European Public Policy*, 5:2 (1998), 322–338; and F. Schimmelfennig, 'The Community Trap: Liberal Norms, Rhetorical Action, and the Eastern Enlargement of the European Union', *International Organization*, 55:1 (2001).

17 C. Preston, *Enlargement and Integration in the European Union* (London and New York, Routledge, 1997).

18 H. Grabbe, 'A Partnership for Accession? The Implications of EU Conditionality for the Central and Eastern European Applicants' EUI/RSC Working Papers, 12 (Florence, EUI, 1999).

19 A vast and varied literature on democratisations has developed since the 1970s which was given a remarkable impetus by the shift in analytical perspective introduced by Dankwart A. Rustow's 1970s article 'Transitions to Democracy: Towards a Dynamic Model', *Comparative Politics*, 2:2, 337–363. Regime changes in Latin America, Southern Europe and Central and Eastern Europe have generated a tremendous amount of studies and explanations inspired by the 'transitology' paradigm such as the article by T. L. Karl, and P. C. Schmitter, 'Models of Transition in Latin America, Southern and Eastern Europe', *International Social Science Journal*, 128 (1991), 269–284. Introducing a perspective which emphasised the unique challenges for post-communist Central and Eastern Europe, Claus Offe suggested that post-communist transformations towards a market economy, democracy and independent states would be so complex that they would need an external guiding power to succeed in his article 'Capitalism by Democratic Design? Democratic Theory Facing the Triple Transition in East Central Europe', *Social Research*, 58:4 (1991), 865–892. The difficulties in establishing stable institutions are discussed by him in Offe, 'Designing Institutions in East European Transitions', in R. Goodin (ed.), *The Theory of Institutional Design* (Cambridge, Cambridge University Press, 1998). Di Palma provides a more optimistic view in *To Craft Democracies: An Essay on Democratic Transitions* (Berkeley, University of California Press, 1990). A comprehensive overview of transitions to democracy can be found in the widely used book by J. J. Linz and A. Stepan, *Problems of Democratic Transition and Consolidation: Southern Europe, South America, and Post-communist Europe* (Baltimore and London, Johns Hopkins University Press, 1996).

20 There are some exceptions. Geoffrey Pridham has explored the role of the European Union and other international organisations as important external factors for democratisation. P. C. Schmitter, in, among other works, 'The Influence of the International Context Upon the Choice of National Institutions and Policies in Neo-Democracies' and Laurence Whitehead in the same volume stress the importance of external factors and the EU in particular in the post-communist transitions. See L. Whitehead (ed.), *The International Dimensions of Democratization: Europe and the Americas* (Oxford, Oxford University Press, 1998), pp. 26–55.

21 D. Stark, and L. Bruszt, *Postsocialist Pathways: Transforming Politics and Property in East Central Europe* (Cambridge, Cambridge University Press, 1998).

22 Such as V. I. Ganev, 'Dysfunctional Sinews of Power', 2001.

23 A. L. Dimitrova, 'The Role of the European Union in the Process of Democratization in Central and Eastern Europe: Lessons from Bulgaria and Slovakia' (Doctoral thesis, University of Limerick, 1998).

24 Dimitrova, 'The Role of the European Union'; and L. Whitehead, 'The Enlargement of the European Union: A "Risky" Form of Democracy Promotion', *Central European Political Science Review*, 1:1 (2000), 16–42.

25 For example adjustments associated with the transposition of the acquis of the Union currently comprising about eighty thousand pages.

26 Offe, 'Capitalism by Democratic Design', Elster, Offe and Preuss, *Institutional Design*.

27 F. W. Scharpf, 'European Governance: Common Concerns versus the Challenge of Diversity', Jean Monnet Working Paper, 6/01, Symposium: Response to the European Commission's White Paper on Governance at www.jeanmonnetprogram.org/papers/01/010701.html (Harvard, 2001).

28 D. C. North, *Institutions, Institutional Change and Economic Performance* (Cambridge: Cambridge, University Press, 1990).

29 K. Thelen, 'Historical Institutionalism in Comparative Politics', *Annual Review of Political Science*, 2 (1999), 390.

30 T. Risse, M. Green Cowles and J. Caporaso, 'Europeanisation and Domestic Change: Introduction', in M. Green Cowles, J. Caporaso and T. Risse (eds.), *Transforming Europe: Europeanisation and Domestic Change* (Ithaca and London, Cornell University Press, 2001), p. 1.

31 Risse, Green Cowles and Caporaso, 'Europeanisation'. See also, A. Héritier 'The Accommodation of Diversity in European Policy Making and Its Outcomes: Regulatory Policy as a Patchwork', *Journal of European Public Policy*, 3:2 (1996), 149–167; and A. Héritier, 'Differential Europe: The European Union Impact on National Policy Making', in A. Héritier, D. Kerwer, C. Knill, D. Lehmkuhl, M. Teutsch and A. C. Douillet (eds.), *Differential Europe: The European Union Impact on National Policy Making* (Lanham, Rowman and Littlefield, 2001), pp. 1–13.

32 F. Schimmelfennig, 'The Enlargement of European Regional Organizations: Questions, Theories, Hypotheses and the State of Research' (paper presented at the workshop on 'Governance by Enlargement' Darmstadt University of Technology, 23–25 June 2000). For a discussion of some of the characteristics of enlargement governance see H. Grabbe, 'How Does Europeanisation Affect CEE Governance? Conditionality, Diffusion and Diversity', *Journal of European Public Policy*, 8:6 (2001), 1013–1031.

33 Grabbe, 'How Does Europeanisation Affect CEE Governance?'

34 See M. Jachtenfuchs, 'The Governance Approach to European Integration', *Journal of Common Market Studies*, 39:2 (2001), 249–264; and B. Kohler-Koch, 'The Evolution and Transformation of European Governance', in R. Eising and B. Kohler-Koch (eds.), *The Transformation of Governance in the European Union* (London and New York, Routledge/ECPR Studies in European Political Science, 1999).

35 Eising and Kohler-Koch, *The Transformation*; L. Hooghe and G. Marks, *Multi Level Governance and European Integration* (Lanham, Rowman and Littlefield, 2001).

36 G. Avery and F. Cameron, *The Enlargement of the European Union* (Sheffield:

Sheffield Academic Press, 1998); A. Mayhew, 'Enlargement of the European Union: An Analysis of the Negotiations with the Central and Eastern European Candidate Countries', Sussex European Institute Working Paper 39 (Sussex, December 2000).

37 H. Grabbe, 'Europeanisation Goes East: Power and Uncertainty in EU Accession Politics', paper presented at the ECPR workshop 'Enlargement and European Governance' ECPR Joint Sessions of Workshops, Turin, 22–27 March 2002.

38 C. Preston, *Enlargement and Integration in the European Union* (London and New York, Routledge, 1997); M. J. Baun, *A Wider Europe: The Process and Politics of European Union Enlargement* (Maryland, Rowman and Littlefield, 2000).

39 A. Mayhew, *Recreating Europe: The European Union's Policy towards Central and Eastern Europe* (Cambridge, Cambridge University Press, 1998), p. 167.

40 A. Plesu, 'Towards a European Patriotism: Obstacles as Seen from the East', *East European Constitutional Review* (Budapest, Central European University, spring/summer 1997), 53–56.

41 European Council in Copenhagen, Conclusions of the Presidency Doc/93/3 of 22 June 1993. An added criterion was the ability of the Union to absorb new members, or the Union's own institutional reform – a fascinating topic in its own right, but one covered by a number of recent volumes on enlargement and therefore one which we will not deal with in this book.

42 For more on the administrative criterion, see A. L. Dimitrova, 'Enlargement, Institution Building and the EU's Administrative Capacity Requirement', *West European Politics*, 25:4 (October 2002), 171–190.

43 Ibid.

44 The book does not explore the impact of the third Copenhagen criterion as this is mainly about the Union's *acquis* than post-communist transformations.

45 R. E. Goodin, 'Institutions and Their Design', in R. E. Goodin (ed.), *The Theory of Institutional Design* (Cambridge, New York and Melbourne, Cambridge University Press, 1998), p. 23.

2

The method of the European Union's enlargement to the east: a critical appraisal

Klaudijus Maniokas[1]

The aim of this chapter is to provide an analysis of the new methodological features of the process of recent enlargement of the European Union. The outcome of the enlargement process is still not certain with regard to the changes enlargement will bring about in the Union and the candidate countries. However, certain new features of the process as compared to previous enlargements are evident. The uniqueness of the challenge of this enlargement for the countries involved, the difference in the level of their economic, social and political development compared to the Union's level, and the profoundness of their transformation required a qualitatively new response from the Union. These factors should have been reflected in the new philosophy or method of enlargement, meaning a certain set of principles or approaches governing the modalities of enlargement. Therefore in this chapter I will try to assess whether a new kind of enlargement method has actually been developed and, if so, what its main principles are. I will then try to assess the implications of this supposedly new method for the candidate countries in terms of benefits and possible risks.

The chapter is divided into two sections. The first is devoted to the new principles of the recent EU enlargement. This section shows that there are substantial differences in the logic of enlargement as compared to previous enlargements and draws certain conclusions about the rationale and implications of these new principles. Four new principles, conditionality, increasing asymmetry, complexity and differentiation, are identified. It is argued that they form a consistent logic of control aimed at, on the one hand, providing a template for the transition target for the candidate countries and, on the other, delaying enlargement and responding to the fear of dilution of the Union's *acquis*. Furthermore, the chapter will show that within the parameters defined by the member states' aim of postponing enlargement, the European Commission has been able to monopolise the relationship with the candidate countries and to increase its power considerably. The second section provides an assessment of the implications of the new enlargement method for the candidate countries, in particular concerning their national political consensus and, consequently, social and political stability in those countries. This section concludes that there is a risk of dilution of the national political consensus in the candidate countries because the new tools of enlargement are asymmetrical and aim only at the preservation of national political consensus concerning enlargement in the member countries of the EU.

The chapter draws on a range of interdisciplinary tools, ranging from comparative analysis and international relations theory to theories of economic and political integration, as well as insights from economic history. The arguments are supported and illustrated by empirical evidence derived mainly from the experience of, first, Lithuania and, to a lesser extent, other Baltic countries in dealing with the EU. This is important, given that most studies on EU enlargement draw heavily on the experience of the so-called Visegrad countries, mainly Poland, Hungary and the Czech Republic. However, since the Union applies standard instruments and principles of enlargement to all candidate countries and given that there are basic similarities of transition problems faced by all candidate countries, there is sufficient reason to believe that the main conclusions apply to all candidates.

New principles or the method of enlargement

It would be quite obvious to say that this enlargement process in many respects differs from the previous ones. The process is not complete and this prevents us from drawing any final conclusions about its outcome and implications, as well as about how this enlargement is different from previous ones. It is clearly much more difficult since so many very different countries have embarked on it. The difference in the development of the candidate countries in comparison to that of most EU countries is also a particular feature of the current enlargement process. However, the purpose of this chapter is not to analyse the differences in the initial situation in the candidate states and EU member states, but rather the difference in the approach adopted by the EU towards this enlargement.

As a basis of our investigation into the method and instruments of the current EU enlargement we will rely on the notion of the classical method of enlargement elaborated by Christopher Preston.[2] Preston defines the classical method as 'a constant pattern both to the formal accession procedures adopted, and to the implicit assumptions and principles which have shaped the expectations of the participants and the progress of negotiations'.[3] Preston identifies six principles of the classical enlargement method: (1) applicants must accept the *acquis communautaire* in full; no permanent opt-outs are available; (2) accession negotiations focus exclusively on the practicalities of the applicants taking on the acquis; (3) the problems arising from the increased diversity of an enlarged Community are addressed by creating new policy instruments to overlay existing ones, rather by fundamental reform of the existing instruments' inadequacies; (4) new members are integrated into the EC`s institutional structures

on the basis of limited adaptation, facilitated by the promise of a more fundamental review after enlargement; (5) the Community prefers to negotiate with
groups of states that have close relations with each other; (6) existing member
states use the enlargement process to pursue their own interest and collectively
to externalise internal problems.

The author himself tends toward the conclusion that developments in EU
policy towards the associated CEE countries until 1995, including development
of the Copenhagen criteria as well as of the pre-accession strategy and the White
Paper, suggest that the basic principles of the classical method were retained. In
this chapter I will try to analyse the development of EU policy further to see
whether this conclusion is still valid.

New method: four principles

First, I argue that a specific feature of the new method of enlargement is its
complexity. While previous enlargements, except the first one, were basically
devised as a two-stage process starting with a kind of association with the EU
and ending with negotiations, in this particular case there has been an intermediate stage between association and negotiations, in which a number of specific
instruments were used. The aim of this intermediate stage was to construct an
additional gate to negotiations and to allow better control of the process by the
EU. The role of a gatekeeper was naturally assigned to the Commission.
Generalising the argument further, I would say that the enlargement process
tends to become more complex, having more and more stages with more and
more possibilities to control the access to each stage.

One of the implications of this tendency to make enlargement more complicated and sophisticated and, to a certain extent, an implicit rationale for this
development, is the possibility of differentiating between the countries involved.
As the fifth principle of the classical method of enlargement states, the EC
prefers to negotiate with groups of countries. The experience of this enlargement allows us to amend this principle by stressing the importance of
differentiation. In order to ensure the possibility of differentiation, the process
was expanded into more stages and, what is even more important, a whole set of
conditions for entry was developed and kept flexible in order to respond to the
configuration of political preferences and the overall political situation in the
EU.

Conditionality therefore could be regarded as a third specific feature of the
process and the backbone of its new method. While conditionality had been, to
a certain extent, present in previous enlargements, three new features of the
conditionality principle can be identified. First, the conditions, which, in the
case of previous enlargements, were limited to the principle of the inviolability
of the *acquis*, were extended further. The famous Copenhagen criteria are the
best example of this extension. Second, conditions were not fixed. There was a
tendency to create new and more detailed conditions as for example happened

in the case of the accession partnerships (APs) which set out priorities for the candidates at a fairly advanced stage of the enlargement process. Third, even initially set conditions were made so flexible that adjustments in their content were allowed in response to the changing needs of a particular situation. In other words, the initial conditions were developed both extensively and intensively. They were enlarged in scope and their content kept changing by extending them and making them more specific and concrete.

These three features contributed to the growing *asymmetry* in the relationship between the candidate countries and the EU, as instruments based on unilateral obligations gradually replaced instruments based on contractual and more or less mutual obligations. This tendency is clearly demonstrated by the shift from the Europe agreements to the White Paper on law approximation and finally to the accession partnerships.

Let us then consider these four features and new principles of enlargement in more detail.

Conditionality: from guidance to differentiation

Conditionality is the core element of the method of this enlargement. While it is hardly a new phenomenon in the Union's external relations and foreign policy in general,[4] the application of the conditionality principle towards the CEE candidate countries requires particular attention here.

Its development can be traced to the Europe agreements signed with the first Central European countries in 1991. Following these, conditionality was reinforced and made explicit by the establishment of the Copenhagen criteria. Looking at the content of these criteria, it is striking how vague and flexible they are.[5] Take, for example, the second condition concerning the functioning of the market economy. It is at best an ideal type stemming from the basic idea about the method by which welfare is created by economic agents free to react to the demands of consumers. Only five years after its formulation, in the 1998 Progress Reports, did the Commission develop six sub-criteria making its content[6] more concrete, but these raise more questions than answers, mostly because the diversity of the market economies in the Union itself makes it difficult to know what model of a market economy the EU had in mind. Therefore it is surprising that this criterion was made a decisive one in determining the 1997 and 1998 recommendations of the Commission.

The second observation with respect to the content of the Copenhagen criteria is that they are stricter than the requirements for applicant countries in previous enlargements. While the first two criteria could well be attributed to particular features of new applicant countries, namely, to the political, economic and social transformation they were undergoing, the fourth criterion, related to the adoption of the *acquis*[7] is especially puzzling. This criterion formally requires the ability to <u>accept</u> the obligations of the *acquis* but not the obligation to <u>take over</u> the whole *acquis* before accession. However, the Progress

Reports of the Commission tend to interpret the criterion in the latter sense. Therefore, as some observers rightly noted, 'for the first time in the case of Central Europe, the Union is requiring countries to take over acquis before the negotiation starts'.[8]

The principal aim of these conditions was not only to provide much needed guidance for the efforts of the candidate countries, but also to construct an additional barrier for their entry. This aim played a crucial role in 1997 when the Commission recommended that the Union start negotiations only with five countries, as well as in 1998 when the decision not to enlarge the first group was justified by using the Copenhagen criteria. The 1999 Commission Report recommending to start negotiations with all candidate countries satisfying the political criterion once more demonstrated the limitations of the Copenhagen conditions.[9] However, it was still useful to differentiate Turkey from the other candidates.

It should be admitted that the application of the principle of conditionality changed after the start of negotiations and especially in their final stage. While the European Commission retained certain powers to control the opening and the closure of different chapters, the road map for negotiations proposed by the same Commission in 2000 and the political stimulus given to the negotiations in the first half of 2001, changed the situation in a quite radical way. An increase in the speed of negotiations considerably limited the possibility of further differentiating between negotiating countries. This was recognised at the end of 2001 when the so-called Laeken countries were named by the European Council as a group of candidates which were expected to finish negotiations and enter the Union at the same time.

Extensive growth of conditionality

The role of the Copenhagen criteria was somehow limited in the Commission's recommendations of 1999, largely because a number of other conditions were developed to replace them. First, the Commission proposed the introduction of the 'differentiation' principle in the negotiations phase. This gave the Commission the right to use conditionality before opening different chapters of negotiation and even to propose different chapters for different countries depending of their so-called 'preparedness'. Second, a new set of conditions based on the conclusions of the Commission's evaluation of the progress in each country was established through a new instrument, the accession partnerships. The accession partnerships contain priorities for candidate countries grouped according to the short and medium term perspective. These documents, it should be stressed, are unilateral documents of the Union adopted by the Council as Regulations based on a proposal from the Commission. The candidate countries were only consulted before their adoption and then expected to transfer these priorities into their national programs for the adoption of the *acquis*. The national programmes are meant to specify the measures planned to implement the priorities of the accession partnership for a particular country. The AP is the basis for distributing EU assistance to the candidate countries.

Since the principal aim of the conditions established is not so much to guide the candidates but rather to control the process, the conditions were not only extended but were also made very flexible. It is impossible to say, as noted above, whether flexibility was a result of a conscious attempt to have extensive room for interpretation, but it is at least clear that the flexibility of interpretation of the Union's conditions was used by the Commission and by the Union in general as an additional instrument of differentiation.

In the course of the negotiations the field of application of the principle of conditionality was further widened by applying certain conditions for the opening and closing of the negotiations' chapters. In the majority of cases the European Commission shaped those conditions on an *ad hoc* basis. The only guidance used in this process was provided by the above mentioned road map for negotiations. It stipulated the conditions for granting transitional periods. However, in practice the EU itself violated these conditions requesting the transitional period for the free movement of labour and the payment of direct subsidies for farmers. The candidates were also granted a number of limited transitional periods in the area of internal market.

The European Commission used to submit for the approval of the Council a special document specifying the conditions for the closure in the negotiations of sensitive matters. This included regional policy and structural instruments, justice and home affairs and agriculture as well as other areas. The conditions usually acquired their horizontal nature after negotiating them with one or two candidate countries used as a test case. The deals made were later presented to other candidates as conditions for the closure of the chapter.

The conditions have been very wide in scope. They encompassed not only the adoption of the relevant *acquis* under the chapter in question, but also elaborated the so-called administrative capacities necessary, according to the Commission, for the implementation of the adopted *acquis*. In certain cases financial implementation plans have been required in order to close the most complex chapters such as the environment. It should be noted that in the majority of cases the additional administrative and financial conditions were quite logical and did not raise much objection from the candidate countries. However, in the majority of cases those administrative and financial prescriptions <u>were not</u> part of the relevant *acquis* and, subsequently went far beyond the formal conditions for the EU membership applied in previous enlargements. In some cases, like in the negotiations in the chapter on financial control, the Commission went as far as to prescribe the rules of functioning of the whole national system of internal and external audit and financial control, which was and remains a national competence. The elaboration and application of the conditions extending far beyond the current acquis was a particular feature of the negotiations of all chapters requiring a high degree of mutual trust in the functioning of national institutions. Such sensitive areas included financial control, customs union, competition and other areas.

The development of conditions was driven by rather different forces within the Union. Sectoral interests or interest groups played a major role in determining the content of the conditions in the case of the association agreements. Further conditions, reflected in the Copenhagen criteria and their subsequent interpretation by the Commission have been a result of a mix of state foreign policy and EU foreign policy preferences.[10]

Qualitative changes of conditions: a case study of the Commission's Progress Reports on Lithuania

The changing nature of the conditions established by the European Council in Copenhagen can be demonstrated by analysing the three Commission reports released in 1997, 1998 and 1999. Since it is impossible to carry out a careful comparative evaluation of all reports concerning all candidate countries, I use the reports on Lithuania's progress towards accession as a case study. Lithuania is a suitable case, since the country was denied access to negotiations in 1997 and 1998.

The decision to exclude certain countries from the group of countries invited to negotiate in 1997 provoked much controversy. In response to this, the Helsinki European Council meeting in December 1999 decided to launch an accession process with all candidate countries – a decision that softened the negative reaction of all those who were initially excluded. However, the controversy surrounding the decision to differentiate resulted in a number of attempts to analyse the Agenda 2000 Commission Opinions and subsequent Regular Reports in order to assess whether there were serious arguments supporting the decisions made. The selection of Poland, Hungary and the Czech Republic was very obvious. These countries were well ahead of the others in a number of fields. They started to prepare for membership earlier and their efforts in economic reform were recognised by their admission to the OECD. Slovakia was excluded for clear political reasons. The choice of Estonia and Slovenia was less obvious. While Slovenia was well ahead of all other candidate countries in its relative economic development, its efforts aimed at the EU membership in terms of the adoption of the *acquis* were rather modest and comparable to the efforts of Latvia, Lithuania and some other countries that were excluded. The Commission recognised this fact later in its reports in 1998 and 1999. The difference in preparedness of Estonia with respect to other Baltic states was not obvious. At best, Estonia was ahead of the other Baltic countries in terms of economic development.[11]

The comparative analysis of the Commission Regular Reports does not provide very clear and convincing arguments in support of the choices made. There is no justification for the argument that only five countries passed the test. The reports themselves have been written using different standards for

evaluation and evaluation techniques.[12] Instead of clear methodology the
Commission used approaches that favoured certain countries and discriminated
against others. It seems that the conclusions were based on the general impression of a country, and the trust in a country, rather than based on the careful
examination of its internal preparation. The principle of 'the last ship in the
convoy', meaning that general progress of a candidate was judged by focusing
on failure to complete one or another reform which was not compensated by the
rapid progress made in other spheres, further distorted the general picture.[13]
Later, comments made by those who were involved in the decision-making
process suggest, for instance, that the decision to include Slovenia and Estonia
in the negotiations in 1997 was based mainly on geopolitical considerations.[14]
However, the decision was presented as an objective choice based on the
Copenhagen criteria.

Candidate countries excluded from negotiations in 1997 were looking
forward to the possibility of their positive re-evaluation in the new Progress
Report of 1998. However, the Report concluded that none of the excluded countries satisfied the criteria. In order to justify this decision the Commission used
formulations striking in their Byzantine complexity. While in 1997 with regard
to Lithuania the Commission simply stated that 'Lithuania has made considerable progress in the creation of a market economy', but it 'would face serious
difficulties in coping with competitive pressure and market forces within the
Union in the medium term', in its 1998 Regular Report the Commission found
that 'the sustained implementation of the remaining reform agenda would
complete the establishment of a functioning market economy, and enable
Lithuania to make the progress necessary to cope with competitive pressure and
market forces within the Union in the medium term'.[15] These formulations, as
well as the concrete analysis of the 1998 Report, suggest that the Commission
added a new criterion related to the sustainability of reforms. A similar formulation, although a little bit more positive, was used for Latvia. The 1998 Report
stated that 'Latvia had continued to make progress in establishing a market
economy and was well on the way to being able to cope with competitive pressure and market forces within the Union in the medium term'.[16] Afterwards,
unofficially, it was made clear that there was still not enough political will from
the EU side to enlarge the group of negotiating countries.

In 1999 the Commission finally recommended that all countries satisfying the
political criterion start negotiations. However, again, in the particular case of
Lithuania it was stated that 'Lithuania has continued to make progress in establishing a functioning market economy and is on the way to being able to cope
with competitive pressure and market forces within the Union in the medium
term provided it completes the remaining reform agenda'. The new argument
this time was a reaction to the Russian crisis. In addition, the level of analysis of
the Commission had shifted from a macro-economic to a micro-economic
level. Issues related to the productivity and profitability of companies become a
focus of the economic part of the Commission's report on Lithuania.[17]

While this overview of the Commission's arguments is not comprehensive, it is sufficient to demonstrate the changing content of the initial Copenhagen criteria. The criteria allow a very wide range of interpretation and adjustment as justified by the political situation in the Union. It should be acknowledged, however, that the Commission has gradually started to use more transparent procedures as well as clearer methodologies in assessing the progress made by the candidate countries.[18]

As noted earlier, the progress reports of Commission largely lost their initial significance after the start of the membership negotiations with all candidate countries. However, the Commission used them to justify the conditions for concluding negotiations in different chapters.

From the association to the accession partnerships: growing asymmetry

An extensive and intensive development of conditionality related to EU membership has been accompanied by the growth of the asymmetry of the process. This was evident in the development of the Union's instruments used in the pre-accession phase. The first main instrument devised to prepare the CEE countries for accession was the Europe (Association) agreements signed with ten candidate countries from CEE in the period from 1991 to 1996. While at the beginning of the process these agreements were conceived as an alternative to membership, starting from the Copenhagen decisions they assumed the role of the main instrument driving all pre-accession activities. These agreements implied commitments from both sides. The associated countries agreed to gradually open their markets for EU industrial goods, to speed up the approximation of their law to the *acquis* of the Union and to pursue their democracy and market oriented reforms. The Union, in turn, recognised their ultimate wish to become members of the EU, immediately opened its market to their industrial goods and undertook to provide assistance to these countries in pursuit of their reforms aimed at democracy, prosperity and EU membership. The agreements were criticised for a lack of commitment from the EU side to open its markets in textiles, steel, coal, and agricultural products. However, they still marked a stage of contractual relationships between the EU and the candidate countries.

The pre-accession strategy adopted in Essen marked an attempt by the Union to provide clearer and more concrete guidance for the associated countries. The main new element of this guidance was the White Paper on the approximation of law adopted in 1995. Its status was different and somehow unclear. It was presented to candidate countries as a set of non-mandatory recommendations, and as a guide to the harmonisation of law going on in the candidate countries. However, it was made clear that associated countries were supposed to respond with their national programmes for law approximation. In the White Paper itself and in further documents of the Union it was repeatedly stated that the associated countries were free to decide on their own national priorities.

The White Paper was then followed by the accession partnerships proposed within the package of Agenda 2000. The idea behind them was to further tighten up and target the preparation process in the candidate countries. This time there has neither been a demonstration of mutual obligations like the Europe agreements, nor a choice of instruments and priorities as was provided in the White Paper. The accession partnerships contain priorities for the candidate countries established on the basis of the Commission's evaluation. While originally the partnerships were supposed to be the Commission's guidance documents, it was later decided that the Council should adopt them instead, thus leaving the door open for the preferences of the member countries to play a role. The first accession partnerships were adopted in spring 1998.[19] The candidate countries then had to follow with their national programs for the adoption of the *acquis*. In this case the only room for manoeuvre was in the definition of additional priorities and measures. Otherwise the candidate countries were supposed to follow the AP priorities. Assistance from the Union, previously formally distributed according the national priorities of the candidate countries, was now clearly tied to the priorities. Another instrument aimed at ensuring the 'compliance' of candidates with the priorities of the AP was the Regular Report of the Commission. The Regular Reports provide an assessment of national programmes of the adoption of the *acquis*. Starting from the 1999 Regular Report, the Commission also provided an assessment of whether these priorities have been fulfilled and to what extent.

The accession partnerships radically altered the nature of the relationship between the Union and the candidate countries. Unilateral instruments placing all obligations and the entire burden of adjustment on the applicants replaced the contractual relations in the Europe agreements. It can still be argued that the Union assumed an obligation to provide aid to the applicants on the basis of the AP. However, first, the amount of this aid and its destination was decided unilaterally by the Union. Second, the amount of this aid was far lower than financial resources required from the candidate countries.[20] Evidence undermining the argument about the unilateral nature of the APs could be found in the procedure of consultation with the candidate countries used in 1998 and 1999. However, as the case of Lithuania shows, the Commission tends to take over proposals on the introduction of new priorities but refuses to remove priorities or correct them. In addition, there was a tendency to formulate the priorities in a more strict and demanding form.[21]

Another aspect of the evolution of the accession instruments has been an increase in their number. Since 1998 the technical EU assistance in the form of the PHARE programme has been gradually replaced by so-called twinning instruments, and the start of negotiations was followed by a new peer review mechanism.

The idea of twinning was formulated as early as in 1997 in the Commission's document Agenda 2000. However, it was formally inaugurated only in 1998 and its practical implementation started even later. The essential difference with regard to previous technical assistance under PHARE was that officials of the member states replaced consultants. The officials, or 'twinners' as they have been called, had the task of helping to prepare the administrative structures of the candidate countries for EU membership. However, the 'twinners' were confronted by the same problem, as the European Commission previously had been, namely that they did not have a definition of sufficient administrative capacities. The 'twinners' were supposed to transmit the best administrative practice in the application of the *acquis*. However, this practice substantially differs across the EU. Neither the EU nor the European Commission had a mandate to define it and, subsequently, to formulate a clear mandate for the 'twinners'. Not surprisingly, the 'twinners' have promoted different practices for the implementation of the *acquis*.[22]

A new monitoring mechanism of the so-called peer review was introduced in 2001 and became increasingly important at the end of negotiations. It was based on the inspections carried out jointly by the Commission and the member states in the sensitive areas of veterinary and phytosanitary control, customs, borders and other domains. Some of these missions could and had been carried in secret even without informing the relevant authorities in the candidate countries. The use of this mechanism once more illustrated the atmosphere of distrust reigning in the negotiations. Alternatively, peer review inspections can be seen as an attempt to play dawn the arguments of sceptical member states and interest groups about the superficial character of the adjustment process in the candidates.

Understanding the new method: the role of the Commission and the rhetoric and practice of enlargement

Understanding the role of the Commission in the process of this enlargement as well as the reasons behind the development of this role is essential in grasping the causes of the new method of enlargement. Later on I will try to demonstrate that, first, the specificity of this enlargement could be explained by the specific role of Commission in the process, and, second, that the latter could be linked to the lack of interest in the enlargement among some EU member states.

The role of the Commission in this enlargement process developed parallel to the development of the method used. At the earliest stages of development the Commission acted as the main generator of ideas and as a promoter of enlargement given the unwillingness of some member states to undertake serious steps forward. Although in certain periods the most active states, like Germany or the Nordic countries, led the process, the Commission was always the main protagonist in this exercise. Over time, the Commission almost monopolised this relationship. I argue that this is the most important development related to this enlargement within the institutional system of the EU with respect to the overall institutional balance of power. I further claim that the desire of the Commission to monopolise the relationship was motivated by the wish to increase its competencies and power within the institutional system. Additionally, I will try to demonstrate that this was only possible in the context of lack of a strong common will and difficulties in reaching consensus on enlargement between the EU member states.

The increasing role of the Commission in the enlargement process could be seen from the development of the method and the process of enlargement itself. While the periodisation of the short history of the relations between the Union and the candidate countries is based on the dates of important European Council meetings, the European Council and the member states played a leading role in designing the shape of the enlargement only at certain critical periods and more at the initial stages of the development. While it was the European Commission which designed the concept of the Europe Agreements and led to the historic decision made at Copenhagen, the role of the member states was crucial in determining the range of countries chosen as applicants as well as in pushing the Commission for more concrete steps in terms of the pre-accession strategy. Member states were also important for giving the process more concrete targets in terms of negotiation dates as the Madrid European Council decisions demonstrate. While through the Agenda 2000 the Commission brought fresh ideas to the enlargement process, it does seem that the very idea of differentiation was stipulated by the member states, particularly Germany,[23] and that the decision of the Luxembourg Council to start the accession process with everybody was again designed and pushed through by two small member states of the Union, namely Denmark and Sweden.[24] It should be noted in this respect that Germany's interests always played a major role in the enlargement process. However, as far as the Baltic states and Lithuania in particular are concerned, it should be concluded that despite the numerous official statements of German politicians and other officials about Germany as an advocate of the Baltic states[25] Germany never played the role it claimed it was playing. Instead, it seems that Germany was in favour of a kind of 'intermediate' status for the Baltic states. The main preoccupation of Germany were the Visegrad countries and Poland in particular.

The situation, changed, however, after the Luxembourg summit. Calls for stricter conditionality and the tools designed to control it, namely, the Commission's regular reports on the progress of the candidate countries and the accession partnerships, provided the Commission with a principal role in the enlargement process. Through these two closely linked instruments and given its traditional role in the distribution of pre-accession aid, the Commission emerged as single most important actor in the process.

In the course of negotiations the Commission asserted its role by defining the conditions of opening and closing negotiations in different chapters. In the most sensitive sectors with the most important financial implications, its power was still limited by the interests of the member states. Therefore one should not overestimate its role. However, an increase in the Commission's competences and its power vis-à-vis the candidate countries is beyond doubt.

The increase in the Commission's power is particularly striking in the context of the general institutional development within the EU during recent years, which has been characterised by an overall shift in power towards the member states. Almost all major initiatives in the area of further European integration have come from the member states and were executed without much involvement of the Commission. This applies to almost all achievements of the ten years starting from Economic and Monetary Union, the development of foreign, security and defence policy, closer co-operation in the justice and home affairs and ending with the major initiatives aimed at better co-ordination of employment and economic policy.

It is possible to identify two closely linked reasons explaining both an increase of the Commission's powers in the process of enlargement and the specific method chosen in this enlargement. The reason for the choice of the rigid, asymmetrical and overly conditional method of enlargement institutionally dominated by the European Commission was the lack of political will to expand the EU and the different geopolitical interests of the EU member countries. Both can be linked to the divergent national preferences of the EU member states concerning enlargement. They were accommodated only by the use of a rigid enlargement methodology and by the constant references to the basic values of the European Union.[26]

The lack of interest in EU enlargement among several member states was already evident in the negotiations on the Europe Agreements.[27] It was particularly visible at those critical periods of time when commitments to enlarge the EU were taken in 1993 and 1997.[28] It was also present in the course of negotiations.[29] This reluctance was based on the uneven benefits gained by the EU member states from trade with the candidates as well as on the possible loss of financial EU assistance after the enlargement.[30] Therefore the EU, trying to balance the interests of the member states, entrusted considerable powers to the European Commission within a mandate to make the enlargement process slow and exclusively oriented towards the national preferences of the EU member states. The slow pace and the rigidity of the enlargement process promoted by the European Commission was a price paid by those member countries interested in enlargement, the European Commission, and the candidate countries.

A further general assessment of the institutional balance of power in the Union and its changes is beyond the aim and scope of this chapter. However, it seems that the development of the Union's policy towards the CEE candidate countries and the new features of the method of enlargement provide an interesting case study of the institutional development of the Union. It supports the thesis that member states remain the single most important actor and their basic interests determine the outcomes of European integration. However, in cases when (1) these interests are divergent (2) political will is unclear, and (3) there is a considerable gap between longer term and short term interests of the member countries, as well as (4) a gap between long-term EU foreign policy interests and short-term sectoral interests of influential interest groups, as in the case of this enlargement, supranational actors, and the Commission in particular, are able to exploit the situation by increasing their own competence.

National consensus, enlargement and institutional stability

As demonstrated by the analysis of the EU method, increasing complexity, stronger conditionality and asymmetry are the driving features of this enlargement. The EU and the European Commission in particular justify these changes by the necessity to guide the candidate countries and to provide important incentives for reform as well as a firm policy anchor. This is certainly true. Clearly the Union has succeeded in bringing more discipline and more coherence to the reforms undertaken by the applicants. However, it seems that the development of the process, which was more and more influenced and shaped by another logic of action aimed at postponing the enlargement further, substantially distorted the officially declared motives and official logic of action. This distortion results or may result in a number of intended and unintended consequences, which put the whole enlargement exercise at risk.

In order to understand these inherent risks we should return to the basic idea of enlargement itself and to the process of Europeanisation which have taken place in all member countries, and that is taking place in the candidate countries as a process of adjustment to a new organisational logic brought about by European integration.

The enlargement process is attempting to satisfy the interests of both the Union and the applicant countries. In order to be successful it should ensure that both sides reach consensus and therefore are satisfied with the outcome.

The key concept here is consensus. The history of European integration shows that integration was first and foremost motivated by the desire to maintain the broad political consensus achieved in the aftermath of the Second World War and endangered by the increasing incapacity of a national state to control the economic conditions created by growing economic interdependence. Since this broad national political consensus was based on growing responsibilities of a national state in the economic and social sphere, and economic growth became the main test against which the political capabilities of the governments have been evaluated, the national governments devised the original mechanism of the European Communities that allowed them to regain some control over their own fate.[31] There are still disagreements about the role of different political and interest groups that regarded European integration as a new stage in human development, and that signified the end of the nation state as an organisational form of a certain society. However, the role of national political consensus is important under both approaches.

European integration has developed into a complex web of institutionalised decision-making processes that helped nation states to cope with the growing complexity brought by increasing mutual dependency. European integration, in turn, helped to keep the originally homogeneous national consensus. It is still very difficult to say whether and to what extent a convergence in the modes of decision making, interest representation, in the relationship between the states and the markets has taken place, but it is almost certain that at least a certain degree of homogeneity has been ensured.[32]

The candidate countries differ very much from most EU states. In addition, they have embarked on a painful process of transformation that has been further complicated by the fact that it had at least three dimensions, economic, political and socio-cultural, as already discussed in the introductory chapter of this book. This transition has already been completed in some areas. Some countries obviously were able to complete it earlier than others. However, in all candidate countries new institutions and practices are less consolidated than in the EU and a national consensus resulting in political and institutional stability is consequently much more fragile. In the literature on transformation and Europeanisation in the candidate countries this problem has been at least partially identified as a source of social anomie and interpreted as something associated with the inflation of societal norms, their insufficient institutionalisation and functional dualism.[33] Therefore even more efforts are required from the governments of these states to maintain this stability while developing new policies or adjusting the old ones. Moreover, the constant changes of rules related to the transposition of the *acquis* and the 'external' origins of these rules make this exercise even more difficult. As Balcerowitcz's famous trajectory of public support to reforms shows, radical and painful reforms can be politically feasible only in a quite short period of time when expectations related to the longer term future outweigh sacrifices in the short term.[34]

Hopefully, transformation has already paid off in a form of the economic growth in most candidate countries making other reforms more feasible and sustainable. However, an analysis of costs associated with the accession to the Union reveals that they are unevenly distributed across time and emerge at various stages of the accession process.[35] The costs of compliance tend to be mostly short-term and the benefits will occur only in the long term.[36] They even suggest that in most cases the short-term interests of the candidate countries and the Union are not the same, even assuming that the long-term interests basically coincide.

On the other hand, the analysis of the new features of this enlargement has demonstrated the extent to which the governments of the candidate countries have lost control of their own agenda and priorities of action, which are now set in the Accession Partnerships and closely monitored and even enforced by different instruments, starting with the Regular Reports on progress and ending with the screening of the *acquis* exercise, as well as control of the assistance. Strategies of accession adopted in the candidate countries largely follow indications and priorities provided by the Union since the room for manoeuvre has been constantly decreasing in line with a tendency towards a more conditional and asymmetric method or philosophy of enlargement.[37]

The classic argument used to justify this situation is largely one about necessary guidance. This was explained earlier, but since not only the conclusion but also the reasoning behind it is important, I will provide one of the best examples of such reasoning:

> The importance of criteria [conditions in general] is perhaps less to differentiate between candidates, than to give various performance anchors to domestic policy in the associated countries. Governments can sell bad-tasting medicine to the voters if it is part of a strategy leading to the goal of membership of the European Union. If there are no objectives set by the Union, the selling of such policies is more difficult.[38]

Indeed, many governments in the candidate countries used this argument to promote reforms related to accession. However, this situation may result in two unintended consequences that can increase the risk of a failure of enlargement. The first obvious risk is that the EU is presented as a scapegoat for unpopular decisions. This may result and has already resulted in diminishing public support for EU membership in some countries.

The second risk is even greater. Given (1) the time pattern of the accession costs and benefits indicating that the costs of adjustment are very high in the short term (2) a certain divergence in the short-term interests between the candidate countries and the Union, combined with (3) still decreasing possibilities of governments to control their own agendas and national policy-making processes, the essential requirement for success, namely national political consensus, is endangered. Governments might no longer be able to fulfil their primary responsibility of assuring national consensus and, consequently, maintaining the political, economic and social stability of their respective countries.

In other words, while the development of EU policy towards the CEE countries and the method used in previous EU enlargements is based on a two-level game[39] and largely driven by domestic concerns, the currently used method of EU enlargement denies the possibility for playing a two-level game in the candidate countries. Therefore the domestic concerns of the candidate countries are not reflected in this process.

It could be argued that the EU has always been a regime-setter and that every enlargement of the Union has been asymmetrical.[40] However, in the case of the current enlargement process, the asymmetry and rigidity of the EU are far greater than in previous enlargements and 'reflect the distaste for eastern enlargement in some quarters within the EU'.[41] Also, there is an obvious need for greater flexibility given the differences between the EU and the candidate countries.

The scenario in which candidates lose the ability to maintain domestic consensus is obviously a pessimistic one and a number of factors could well reduce the likelihood that this will occur. However, under certain circumstances the risks are even higher. The first variable is the economic situation in the candidate countries. If the economies continue to grow, the possibilities of maintaining the national consensus on the fundamentals of reforms, are more certain. However, if economic recession occurs, which could be caused not by internal structural problems but by external shocks, the risk is higher that the national consensus will be diluted.

One observation is necessary there. The whole process of European integration has been heavily dependent on rates of economic growth. Since (1) economic growth and an associated increase in a material well-being have become a basis of a national consensus and the main source of legitimacy for national governments in post-war Western Europe and (2) it was consciously built in into the very fundamentals or *raison d'être* of European integration itself, the slow-down of economic growth was largely followed by a slow-down of European integration.[42]

The second variable is the size of a country including the relative size of its economy. First, the small countries are more vulnerable to pressure from the Union and from the European Commission in particular. Therefore, their freedom of action is more limited. Second, the relative adjustment costs with respect to the Union are higher for small states.

The third and most controversial factor concerns interests. Supposedly, the long-term interests of the Union and candidate countries coincide. A number of arguments have been made and a number of studies have been undertaken to demonstrate that EU enlargement into Central and Eastern Europe will be beneficial for both sides. Security and stability will be better ensured and the larger common market will foster economic growth throughout the enlarged Union. However, fewer attempts have been made to investigate the question of the possible divergence of short-term interests. It does seem that in certain cases the divergence of these interests is quite obvious. Take, for example, the case of nuclear energy in the candidate countries. While nuclear energy continues to be a very important factor in the economic growth of certain candidate countries, for example, Lithuania, Slovakia and Bulgaria, the EU has been applying extraordinary pressure on those countries to close nuclear power plants.

Conclusions and solutions: avoiding the dilution on both sides

The main conclusion of this chapter is that in response to the different nature of this enlargement the Union has developed a new method for this process. The new method is based on four new principles: complexity, differentiation, conditionality and asymmetry. It was then argued that all four principles form a single logic of control. This logic largely aimed at slowing down the process of enlargement. The reason for this was a justified fear of dilution of the Union. In the context of this fear and a general lack of political will among member states to enlarge, the European Commission managed to extend its own competences in this sphere and almost monopolised relations with the candidate countries. This opened the process to the preferences of the Commission in addition to those of the member states and thus reinforced the rigidity of the method of enlargement. The argument then went further by challenging this logic on the basis of the reasoning about the importance of national consensus. It was argued that the candidate countries were largely deprived of all means to incorporate their own preferences into the process. It implies the same danger of dilution the Union is trying to avoid in its own backyard. The risk of dilution or instability of institutions in the candidate countries, it was argued, is based on (1) the time pattern of the accession costs and benefits, indicating that costs of adjustment are very high in the short term (2) a certain divergence of the short-term interests between the candidate countries and the Union, and (3) decreasing possibilities of the governments to control their own agendas and national policy-making process. Certain variables contributing to the risk of dilution were then identified. It was argued that the smaller the country and the higher the uncertainties related to economic growth, the higher were the risks of a breach of national political consensus.

Notes

1 I am grateful to the European Integration Studies Centre of the University of Bonn (ZEI) for the chance to spend almost two months of 'splendid isolation' in Bonn at the end of 1999. This chapter is a revised version of the paper resulting from this stay. I would like to thank Dr. Marcus Wenig and Dr. Peter A. Zervakis (ZEI) for the encouragement and comments provided and Žygimantas Pavilionis from the Lithuanian Mission to the EU in Brussels who commented on some of the proposals contained in this paper. I am particularly grateful to Ramūnas Vilpišauskas from the Institute of International Relations and Political Science of the University of Vilnius who commented extensively on the text and with whom many arguments surrounding EU enlargement were debated. The paper was revised in 2002.
2 C. Preston, *Enlargement and Integration in the European Union* (London, Routledge, 1997).
3 Ibid., p. 9.
4 S. Weber, 'European Union Conditionality', in Barry Eichengreen, Jeffry Frieden and Jurgen von Hagen (eds.), *Politics and Institutions in an Integrated Europe* (Berlin, Heidelberg and New York, Springer, 1995).
5 This evaluation is shared by many experts. See, for example, Heather Grabbe, 'The EU's Enlargement Strategy', in Otto Grobel and Atis Lejins (eds.), *The Baltic Dimension of European Integration* (Riga, 1996), p. 50; or Alan Mayhew, *Recreating Europe: The European Union's Policy towards Central and Eastern Europe* (Cambridge, Cambridge University Press, 1998), p. 162.
6 They are provided in all Regular Reports of the Commission published to date.
7 In its 1999 Report the Commission tends to refer to it as a third criterion, the previous two being merged into one economic criterion.
8 Mayhew, *Recreating Europe*, p. 369.
9 However, they still provide a sufficient basis for a justification of refusal to take Turkey on board.
10 U. Sedelmeier, 'The EU's Association Policy towards Central and Eastern Europe:

political and Economic Rationales in Conflict', *Sussex European Institute Working Report*, 7 (1994); Weber, 'Conditionality'.

11 For similar conclusions see, for example, Sven Arnswald, 'The Politics of Integration of the Baltic States into the EU: Phases and Instruments', in Mathias Jopp and Sven Arnswald (eds.), *The European Union and the Baltic states* (Helsinki and Bonn, Institut für Europäische Politik and the Finnish Institute of International Affairs, 1998), p. 76.

12 For example, the data on a percentage of administrated prices in the consumer price index basket, in itself an important indicator of price liberalisation, were used selectively and can be found only in some reports. It is unclear how the level of privatisation has been assessed. In some cases the share of GDP generated by the private sector is used as the main indicator of the success or failure of privatisation. In other cases the ratio of enterprises earmarked for privatisation and those actually privatised is used as a basis for evaluation (see Jonas Čičinskas, 'Progress Report: Discussion in Lithuania?', *Lithuanian Foreign Policy Review*, 2 (1998), 125.

13 Čičinskas, 'Progress Report', p. 123.

14 Mayhew, *Recreating Europe*, p. 176; Arnswald, 'Politics of Integration', p. 76.

15 European Commission, *Agenda 2000: Summary and Conclusions of the Opinions of Commission concerning the Applications for Membership to the European Union by the Candidate Countries* (DOC/97/8, Brussels, 15 July 1997); and European Commission, *Regular Report from the Commission on Progress towards Accession, Lithuania, 1998*.

16 European Commission, *Regular Report from the Commission on Progress towards Accession, Latvia, 1998*.

17 Europos Komitetas prie LRV (European Committee under the Government of Lithuania), Europos Komisijos antrojo Reguliaraus pranešimo apie Lietuvos pažangą siekiant narystės ES analizė. Santrauka [Summary of the Analysis of the Second Regular Report of the European Commission on Lithuania's Progress towards Accession) (Vilnius, 1999/10/22), p. 7.

18 For example, in its 1999 Regular Report the administrative capacities of the candidate countries have been assessed using consistent and uniform set of criteria elaborated by OECD's unit SIGMA.

19 For example, *Council Decisions of 30 March 1998 on the Principles, Priorities, Intermediate Objectives and Conditions Contained in the Accession Partnership with the Republic of Lithuania* (98/265/EC, OJ L 121/31, 23 April 1998).

20 Mayhew, *Recreating Europe*, p. 361. Lithuania's example could well illustrate that point. According to the Lithuanian National Programme of the Adoption of the Acquis the financial resources required to implement measures contained in it amount to approximately 4 billion litas (1 billion euros) only in the short-term period. Even taking into account the fact that many of those measures should be implemented independently of the requirements of the EU, as for example the most costly reforms related to land reform and improvement of transport infrastructure, the EU support is far inferior even in its range. In 1998 the PHARE support amounted to around 40 million euros. In 1999, taking into account new instruments of SAPARD and ISPA, it reached some 100 million euros: Governmental Commission for European Integration, *Lithuania's EU Accession Programme (National Programme for the Adoption of the Acquis)* (Vilnius, May 1999).

21 *Uniting Europe*, 72 (25 October 1999).

22 A good example could be the area of financial control. Since the *acquis* in this sector

was very limited in scope and the national systems of internal and external audit and financial control substantially differ across the EU countries, the opinions of the advisers having worked in Lithuania on this issue even within the same team differed quite radically.

23 Arnswald, 'Politics of Integration', p. 81. The role of Germany and the position of the chancellor, H. Kohl, which were aimed at promoting the membership of Poland, Hungary and the Czech Republic and at the same time neglecting other candidate countries provoked quite harsh comments from some candidates countries. See, for example, the article by former Lithuanian minister for European Affairs, Laima Andrikiene, 'As jus myliu, bet niekam nesakykite' (I Love You, but Don't Tell Anyone about It), *Lietuvos Aidas* (29 October 1997).
24 See Lykke Friis, 'The End of the Beginning of Eastern Enlargement: Luxembourg Summit and Agenda-Setting', http\\eiop.or.at/texte/1998–007a.htm (1998).
25 Examples are provided in Hans-Dieter Lucas, 'United Germany, the Baltic States and the Baltic Sea Region', in Jopp and Arnswald, *The European Union*.
26 On the use of rhetorical strategy based on the references to the basic values of the EU to move the enlargement process forwards see F. Schimmelfennig, 'The Community Trap: Liberal Norms, Rhetorical Action, and the Eastern Enlargement of the European Union', *International Organisation*, 55 (1), 2001, 56.
27 As a result of it they were dominated by sectoral interest groups. Sedelemeier, 'The EU's Association Policy'.
28 F. Schimmelfennig, 'The Community Trap: Liberal Norms, Rhetorical Action, and the Eastern Enlargement of the European Union', *International Organisation*, 55:1 (2001).
29 Mayhew, *Recreating Europe*.
30 It should be noted that in the negotiations on the financial implications of enlargement the EU has consistently tried to limit the possible negative impact of redirecting financial flows. The EU denied the candidate full access to direct subsidies under the CAP and refused to grant transitional periods for the payment of their contributions to the EU budget. For an extensive demonstration of a discriminatory character of the initial Commission's proposal on the financial package in the enlargement negotiations, see Alan Mayhew, 'Enlargement of the European Union: An Analysis of the Negotiations with the Central and Eastern European Candidate Countries', Sussex, *SEI Working Paper*, 39 (2001).
31 See A. S. Milward, *The European Rescue of the Nation State* (London, Routledge, 1994), pp. 2–21.
32 See Yves Meny, Pierre Muller and Jean-Louis Quermonne, 'Introduction', in Yves Meny, Pierre Muller and Jean-Louis Quermonne (eds.), *Adjusting to Europe: The Impact of the European Union on National Institutionsand Policies* (London, Routledge, 1996).
33 Heather Grabbe, 'European Integration and Corporate Governance in Central Europe: Trajectories of Institutional Change', in M. Federowicz and S. Vitols (eds), *Corporate Governance in a Changing Economic and Political Environment: Trajectories of Institutional Change on the European Continent* (Berlin: SIGMA/Wissenchaftszentrum Berlin, 2001).
34 Balcerowitcz, L., *Socialism, Capitalism, Transformation* (Budapest, CEU Press, 1995).
35 Gacs, J. and M. Wyzan, *The Time Pattern of Costs and Benefits of EU Accession* (Luxembourg, IIASA, Interim Report, May 1999), p. ii, quoted in Ramunas

Vilpisauskas and Guoda Steponaviciene, *Winners and Losers of EU Integration in Central Eastern Europe: The Case of the Baltic States. Economic Part* (Vilnius, Lithuanian Free Market Institute, October 1999), p. 3.

36 Vilpisauskas and Steponaviciene, *Winners and Losers.*

37 See, for example, Republic of Poland, *National Strategy for Integration* (Warsaw, Government of Poland, January 1997); *Lithuania's EU Accession Programme.*

38 Mayhew, *Recreating Europe*, p. 376.

39 Robert D. Putnam, 'Diplomacy and Domestic Policy: The Logic of Two-Level Games', *International Organization*, 42 (1988), 427–460.

40 Alasdair R.Young and Helen Wallace, *Regulatory Politics in the Enlarging European Union: Weighing Civic and Producer Interests* (Manchester, Manchester University Press, 1999), p. 124.

41 Ibid., p. 156.

42 For similar arguments see Milward, *European Rescue.*

3

Exerting influence on a contentious polity: the European Union's democratic conditionality and political change in Slovakia

Marek Rybář and Darina Malová

The central feature of Slovakian politics in the 1990s was the struggle over the rules of the democratic game. In the days after the breakdown of the communist regime in November 1989, free and fair general elections became the most important goal for the democratic opposition. Shortly after the peaceful division of the Czechoslovak federation in 1993, there were some concerns about the democratic nature of the political regime in newly independent Slovakia. These concerns contributed to the change of government in early 1994, when the parliamentary opposition was joined by several Members of Parliament who had previously supported the government in passing a vote of no confidence in the cabinet led by Prime Minister Vladimír Mečiar. However, it was only the early elections held later that year that started an era of serious political backsliding in democratic institutionalisation and practices. The period of 1994–98 also witnessed the most intensive diplomatic engagement in, and criticism of, the political situation in Slovakia by the representatives of West European and transatlantic international organizations. The situation changed after the elections of 1998, with the electoral victory of the reform-minded democratic opposition. This development was confirmed in February 2001 after a far-reaching constitutional amendment was passed in the Slovak parliament. That was an important step, for, as we argued elsewhere,[1] the unclear provisions of the 1992 Slovak Constitution generated many of the struggles that had shaken the stability of the institutional order in Slovakia. Moreover, as the opposition did not support the amendment, the agreement of all parties of the broad coalition government was necessary.

The aim of this chapter is to examine the European Union's political conditionality and to demonstrate the role it has played in political development in Slovakia. We argue that EU political conditionality does not work formally, i.e. the stability of institutions cannot be achieved only by establishing legal changes in a political system, it also requires a corresponding set of political actors, who comply with democratic rules and procedures. In other words, although the EU's political conditions include only procedural aspects of democracy, those cannot be fully established without credible political partners. In Slovakia the EU's political conditionality has facilitated political cooperation between non-nationalist political parties and shaped the nature of party competition. In turn, the political changes after the 1998 elections stimulated institutional improvements by refining the constitutional framework. First, we describe the nature and scope of EU political conditionality with regard to the candidate countries from Central and Eastern Europe (CEE). Second, we analyse the major political controversies in independent Slovakia prior to the 1998 elections and show the ways that EU political conditionality influenced Slovakia's internal political development. In the third section we describe the turn in the political processes after 1998 as well as recent changes to the Constitution that were aimed at clarifying the rules of the political game and were in part motivated by Slovakia's aspiration to full membership of the EU.

Defining EU political conditionality

How are we to understand the meaning of conditionality? Pridham defines it as a process that 'requires specifying conditions or even pre-conditions for support, involving either promise of material aid or political opportunities, and it usually includes political monitoring of domestic developments in the countries under discussion'.[2] Thus, concrete *conditions* to be fulfilled, *rewards* for complying with them, and a mechanism for monitoring and *evaluation* are the three constitutive elements of any conditionality process.

As we focus on political conditionality, we analyse the EU's basic political conditions on the applicant countries, the rewards being the prospect of eventual membership in the EU and the monitoring system embodied primarily in the political dialogue set up in the association agreements and in the European Commission's annual evaluations of the candidates' progress. Besides the incentives, we have to point out the limits of political conditionality, as this policy is based primarily on influencing and persuading the countries in question. Bilateral EU–candidate country meetings, expressing concerns, resolutions, diplomatic notes, demarches and other opinions are traditional methods of diplomatic influence and in principle do not have coercive character. As such, their impact may be rather limited, depending on the depth of commitment of the candidate's political representatives. Thus, in order to assess the independent impact of EU conditionality, we have to take into account the internal dynamics of the political situation in a candidate country. Hence, the European Council's strategic decisions on general policies towards the candidate countries, together with the threat of suspending the association agreements with the candidates, are the only tools with direct policy impact used in EU political conditionality. These decisions are based on the Commission's annual reports on the candidates. It was the European Council meetings in Luxembourg and Helsinki that have been of primary importance, with the former dividing candidates into the fast track and the slow track groups and the latter changing the system and introducing the so-called regatta system. The regatta metaphor suggested that all associate members would proceed with integration to the EU at their own pace. Thus, their performance and the date of entry to the EU would be assessed individually.

As the case of Slovakia illustrates, the policy of political conditionality was not successful with the uncommitted political representatives, who even started looking for an alternative foreign policy orientation. However, the consequences of EU conditionality played the role of a catalyst in uniting political opposition, increasing political awareness and mobilising the public. The Commission *avis* published in July 1997 coincided with the NATO decision not to invite Slovakia for the same reason: failure to meet political criteria. These two external decisions, with the former confirmed in Luxembourg in December 1997, were crucial factors whose implications eventually led to the victory of the opposition in the 1998 elections. Not only was a new government formed, but external pressure also led to changes in the overall political conduct and attitude towards political opposition. In a relatively short period of time Slovakia fulfilled all accession political conditions. Two major constitutional amendments passed in 1999 and 2001 were to provide more stable and effective framework for political competition and were in part motivated by the EU member states' experience and driven by the need to adjust the national constitutional framework to the obligations of future EU membership. Thus, political conditionality can probably work in countries whose overall institutional structure remains democratic even though some features of substantive democracy are violated. At the same time, consequences of EU political conditionality in the form of democratisation can materialise only if there is a viable democratic opposition that can mobilise the public and use foreign policy failure as a weapon against the incumbents.

Developing and adjusting political conditions for Slovakia

EU political criteria for membership were formally set up only when the question of admitting post-communist countries was opened. This decision differs from the response of the EU towards the Southern European countries, since they became members of the EU without political conditions. At that time one of the goals of EU enlargement was to support the consolidation of democracy in these countries. Now, applicants are expected to meet all the political conditions before accession.

The re-negotiated association agreement concluded with Slovakia in 1993 (following the break-up of Czechoslovakia) set up five conditions for the EU accession: the rule of law, human rights, a multi-party system, free and fair elections, and a market economy. The Copenhagen European Council in 1993 further elaborated political, economic, and administrative conditions for the EU accession. It stipulated that membership requires that the candidate country has achieved stabile institutions guaranteeing democracy, the rule of law, human rights and respect for and protection of minorities. These conditions were followed by a 'pre-accession strategy' that was launched at the Essen European Council in December 1994. The decision incorporated the Europe Agreements and the PHARE aid program as a special EU policy toward the CEE applicants. Copenhagen political requirements do not substantially differ from those that are stipulated by the Council of Europe or by the OSCE. They are based on the minimalist, electoral conception of democracy and the idea of protection of human and minority rights, therefore allowing individual countries to opt for different institutional solutions. Since launching the pre-accession strategy the European Commission had been screening the process of the implementation of all Copenhagen conditions. In July 1997 the Commission published its first views on the applicant countries to assess how individual countries had been fulfilling the Copenhagen conditions. All applicant countries with the exception of Slovakia were judged to meet the political criteria. Their fulfilment was considered to be necessary, though not sufficient, for beginning negotiations about the eventual accession to the EU as the example of Bulgaria, Latvia, Lithuania and Romania illustrated. These countries did not meet economic conditions. Thus, from among the post-communist candidates, the Commission proposed to start negotiations with the Czech Republic, Estonia, Hungary, Poland and Slovenia, i.e. countries that met political as well as economic conditions. The Commission's document Agenda 2000 set up also the accession partnerships by merging all EU demands and assistance within a single framework. Since the Europe Agreements (EAs) were signed, political criteria have not substantially changed in general, but they were elaborated in individual discussions, reflecting the different conditions of each applicant country. Structured dialogue functioned as the main channel for mediating EU conditionality. CEE countries had already learned during the EAs negotiations that 'the Community understands political dialogue as a channel to transmit its common positions and interests to like-minded third countries, rather than to initiate a real two-way-dialogue on a jointly set agenda'.[3]

The Luxembourg European Council in December 1997 basically confirmed the Commission's view. Even though it decided *formal* accession talks would involve all candidates, individual negotiations would start only with the most advanced countries. The Luxembourg decision was the first application of EU political conditionality with direct policy impact. Slovakia, though judged relatively favourably in meeting economic criteria, was not considered for accession negotiations because of its failure to comply with EU political conditions. The 1998 Accession Partnership on Slovakia stressed political criteria, and it emphasised them as short-term priorities. These included free and fair elections (parliamentary, presidential and local), the need to involve the political opposition into decision-making and control procedures, and a necessity to enact legislation on the use of minority languages. Two groups of candidates were created as a result of the Luxembourg decision; while the countries in the first group started direct negotiations on the EU accession in March 1998, the second group of countries were to get prepared within the framework of accession partnership and the reinforced pre-accession strategy. It was also decided that the Commission would prepare annual reports on candidate countries' progress. The Commission's opinions published in November 1998 highlighted some progress in Latvia, Lithuania and Slovakia. Consequently, the Commission proposed to change the overall strategy towards candidates in October 1999. The Helsinki European Council in December acknowledged the progress of the second group candidates and direct negotiations with them started in February 2000. The EU political conditions were considered to be met by all CEE candidates, even Slovakia, after a change in the 1998 elections.

The institutional framework for monitoring Slovakia

The Europe Agreement, concluded in October 1993 between the European Community and its member states on the one hand and the Slovak Republic (SR) on the other, established a framework for economic and political relations between the SR and EU. It also set up a political dialogue, which embraced regular bilateral consultations and meetings at the highest political as well as ministerial levels involving all topics of common interest. At ministerial level, political dialogue takes place within the Association Council, whereas at parliamentary level it takes place within the framework of the Association Parliamentary Committee.

The Association Council meets at least once a year at ministerial level and supervises the implementation of the Europe Agreement. It is composed by the members appointed by the Slovak government as well as by the members of the Commission and the Council of the European Union. The Association Council is assisted by the Association Committee (composed according to the same criteria as the Council itself) in preparing the meetings technically. The Association Parliamentary Committee is a joint parliamentary body composed of equal number of the Members of the European parliament and the Slovak parliament. The APC meets twice a year, once in the associated country and once in Brussels. The joint parliamentary committee's role is *formally* rather limited (it is 'informed' of the decision of the Association Council and may only 'make recommendations' to the Association Council), however, its activities were more resonant in the Slovak media and public. The main reason is the fact that the Association Council is mostly an expert body engaged predominantly in solving technical economic problems, whereas the Association Parliamentary Committee has been very open and critical about the EU political conditions and Slovakia's difficulties in meeting them. Prior to the 1998 elections it provided the opposition parties with a forum where they could have voiced their concerns to an international audience.

However, it was the Commission's official evaluations of the candidates that had the major impact on the internal political situation. The Commission's evaluations serve as the basis for the European Council's conclusions about the enlargement process. The first *avis*, especially, formally included into the

Agenda 2000, played an important role in Slovak political development. These documents were based on a whole range of information sources. In part they drew from the questionnaire each applicant had to submit, but attention was also given to the results of the bilateral consultations between the EU and the candidates (including, but not limited to, the institutions of the EA political dialogue). Reports from the Delegations of the European Commission as well as of other international (e.g. the Council of Europe) and non-governmental organisations were also taken into account. Beginning in February 2000, all CEE candidate countries have directly negotiated their membership in separate intergovernmental conferences. At this stage, however, their democratic character and stability are generally acknowledged and attention is given to substantive policy areas.

Losing democratic credibility: Slovakia in 1994–98

In the period prior to the general election of 1998, the EU criticism of Slovakia centred around three broad political issues: respect for the rights of the parliamentary opposition, protection of minority rights, and institutional stability. On several occasions the EU representatives criticised the practices not in line with democratic principles.

Distorted parliamentary democracy

Before the 1994 elections, due to the lack of party discipline and cohesion, the government in Slovakia operated mainly as an *assembly government.* This was evident from frequently occurring events: parliament opposing cabinet-proposed legislation, deputies voting against ministers from their own parties, quickly disintegrating coalition cabinets, and unclear accountability. At that time the fragmented political elite tried to resolve political conflicts by building procedural consensus, consisting of formal and informal rules. The key informal principle was proportional representation and the participation of the opposition in governing the parliament.[4]

After the 1994 elections the three-party coalition (the Movement for a Democratic Slovakia – HZDS; the Workers' Association of Slovakia – ZRS; and the Slovak National Party – SNS) managed to impose strong party discipline over their deputies. This influenced the performance of parliamentary democracy and functioning of separation of powers. The point when this process began was 3 November 1994 with the first opening session of parliament and continued in the immediate second session. During that night session the freshly formed parliamentary majority, controlling 83 seats out of 150, managed to change the institutional set-up of Slovakia's parliamentary democracy by changing statute laws and not following previous informal customs securing some parliamentary posts for the opposition. In one night, the parliamentary majority constituted absolute majority rule, with very few checks on executive and constitutional constrains on the cabinet. In one night, the majority succeeded in complete marginalisation of the opposition. Contrary to previous practice, the majority voted against opposition candidates for the vice-chair of Parliament, and opposition MPs were denied the chair of any parliamentary committees. The opposition lost their seats in the supervisory bodies overseeing the public mass media and intelligence service. Opposition representatives were also removed from the Supreme Auditing Office and National Property Fund (FNM) and the attorney general was replaced. The majority also amended the Large Privatisation Act and transferred decision-making competency from the cabinet to the FNM controlled by HZDS. National political discourse had changed in favour of a majoritarian interpretation of democracy, which differed from the original expectations that emerged immediately after the collapse of the communist regime.

After the session of the newly elected parliament, the ambassadors of the EU troika delivered a diplomatic demarche to the president, the prime minister and the speaker of the parliament. The EU pointed out that the ongoing process of Slovakia's integration in the EU brought about not only advantages but commitments as well. The EU presidency presented its concern about some facts of political life after the elections of 1994 and expressed its hopes that Slovakia, carefully considering its own interests, would continue on the road to democratic reforms. Thus, the EU warned that Slovakia could be invited to accession talks only after it met and respected all general democratic norms and conditions. In its official reaction, the Slovak government did not respond to the concerns of the demarche and only expressed 'its appreciation to the EU for attention paid to the developments in the Slovak Republic'.[5]

More importantly, the government's general policy towards its opponents had not changed substantially. Due to growing tensions between the cabinet and the president, verbal attacks on the Constitutional Court (which overturned several controversial laws passed by the parliamentary majority), and a suspicion that the Slovak Intelligence Service organised the abduction of a Slovak citizen, the EU took additional formal diplomatic steps. A 'second wave' of diplomatic demarches followed in October 1995, when the EU and later the USA voiced their concern about the political situation in Slovakia. The EU again reminded Slovakia of its obligation to respect the political criteria set up by the Copenhagen summit and stated in the association agreement. The Mečiar administration continued to deny responsibility for the matters in question. It spoke about an unfair attitude by the EU toward Slovakia and the allegedly different standards applied to Slovakia in comparison with other applicants. The demarches in 1995 were followed by a resolution by the European parliament calling for respect for democratic procedures and minority rights in Slovakia. The resolution warned that if the Slovak government 'continues to follow policies which show insufficient respect for democracy, human and minority rights and the rule of law, it will be necessary for the European Union to reconsider its programs of assistance and co-operation under the Europe Agreement which might have to be suspended'.[6]

Restricting national minority rights

Since 1993, the issue of minority rights was one of the most criticised areas of political life in Slovakia. Approximately 14 per cent of Slovak citizens belong to a national minority, of which Hungarians constitute an overwhelming majority. The 1990 Law on the Official Language in the Slovak Republic guaranteed members of a national minority the right to use their language in those towns and villages where they constituted at least 20 per cent of the population. The Ministry of Culture announced in May 1995 that it was preparing a new Law on State Language that would regulate the use of the state (Slovak) language in all aspects of public life. In autumn 1995 both the government and the Hungarian coalition separately discussed the proposal with the experts of the Council of Europe. However, the Slovak government did not accept substantial comments from the organization.[7]

In November 1995 the National Council adopted the new law. First, it cancelled the law from 1990 enabling the members of minorities to use their language in official communications. Thus, despite the constitutional provision guaranteeing the use of minority languages in the official communication, there was no law regulating this area. (In some villages with a majority of Hungarian inhabitants, organisations of local administrations adopted regulations that allowed the use of Hungarian language for official communication.) Second, the new law in fact outlawed publishing all non-Slovak periodicals. This was legalised only at the beginning of 1996, when the parliament amended the Law on Periodicals. Another law touching upon the right to use minority languages was adopted in September 1996 and concerned the rules governing parliamentary sessions. The new legislation, contrary to the previous law, did not allow the deputies to use minority languages during sessions of parliament.[8] The president vetoed the bill and sent it back to the National Council; however, the parliament adopted it without any changes.

After the elections of 1994, the HZDS-led government attempted to introduce the so-called 'alternative education', i.e. the system of teaching several subjects in the Slovak language in Hungarian schools. The supporters of 'alternative education' emphasise the need to improve the ability of members of Hungarian minority to speak Slovak. The sensitivity of the issue was underpinned by the historical context; the communist regime unsuccessfully tried to introduce 'alternative education' in the 1970s and 1980s, as well as by the fact that the language is the most significant element of national identification for the Hungarian minority in Slovakia.[9]

In June 1995 the Ministry of Education undertook preparatory steps to introduce alternative education, however. The association of directors of Hungarian secondary schools rejected it. The state authorities, which gained powers to do so in the new legislation, dismissed several of the most critical directors from their positions. This led to a strike by teachers, students and their parents in several primary and secondary (Hungarian language) schools. Responding to these protests the ministry introduced alternative education only in one primary and three secondary schools, always with the consent of the students' parents.

Another problem emerged in January 1997 when, according to the new Law on the State Language, the certificates with final grades were to be issued only in the Slovak language, contrary to the bilingual practice introduced in 1921. Several directors issued bilingual certificates and the Ministry of Education accused them of not complying with the law. The Slovak Ministry of Culture had been gradually decreasing financial support to Csemadok (the main cultural organisation of Hungarians) and redirected finances to a newspaper controlled by the HZDS.

Insufficient financial support from the state had gradually led to the further reduction of cultural activities of the Hungarian minority. The Law on State Language limited the legal use of minority languages in the official communication. The Slovak government, despite many urgent requests from the European Union, the opposition, and Hungary, did not prepare the law on minority languages and, in 1997, contrary to its previous promises, the cabinet announced that it did not even intend to prepare the law. This clearly ran counter to the EU position on the matter. For example, at the second meeting of the Association Council the EU stated that it 'looks forward to the timely introduction of legislation on minority languages'.[10] Similarly at the following Association Council 'the Union also expressed the hope that additional legislation concerning the use of minority languages will be enacted.'[11] However, all these claims proved futile and thus the 1997 Commission Opinion identified the unsatisfactory state of minority affairs as one of the major deficiencies of democracy in Slovakia.

Controversies over political institutions

After the 1994 election institutional instability took several forms. First, it was illustrated by the tensions between the cabinet and the president, initially expressed by the conflict over presidential powers and later fuelled by the president's support for the rights of the parliamentary opposition. Second, the parliamentary majority violated the civic rights of an MP, who was stripped of his mandate; later it ignored the Constitutional Court's ruling calling for a remedy. Third, the cabinet disregarded the powers of the Constitutional Court as well as of the Central Referendum Committee and thwarted a referendum on the direct election of the president and NATO membership in 1997.

Presidential competencies have probably been the most controversial issue of the 1992 Constitution. The president was weak compared to parliament and could be made politically accountable to parliament. At the same time the president was defined as part of the executive branch of power, within which he might enjoy relatively strong influence, as he might preside over cabinet meetings and require reports from ministers. To increase the incongruence of presidential powers, provisions defining the right to appoint and recall the prime minister, members of cabinet and other administrative bodies were not clear.[12] Presidential veto power was submitted to the prime minister, because the president had to return laws at the prime minister's request. The design of this component of power was even more complicated by confusing provisions regulating presidential elections.[13] These prerogatives created the possibility of institutional competition within the different branches of political power.

Indeed, several conflicts between the president, cabinet and the parliament occurred in 1994–98, as President Kováč refused to follow Mečiar's policies. These controversies emerged already in 1993, when Mečiar began dismissing ministers who resisted him. As there were two controversial paragraphs in the Constitution, President Kováč petitioned the Constitutional Court. The Court ruled that only the president has the power to appoint or dismiss ministers, while the prime minister may propose dismissals and appointments to the President. This decision had started serious controversies between President Kováč and Prime Minister Mečiar. The conflict even increased in March 1994, when the president's report on the state of the Slovak Republic pushed hesitant MPs to dismiss the prime minister.

The Constitution of 1992 stated that the president might be dismissed by parliament by a three-fifths majority if he acts contrary to the sovereignty or territorial integrity of the country or its constitutional and democratic system. We know of no democratic parliamentary system with a similar provision. Moreover, it created the possibility for the emergence of so-called negative coalitions, which are able to reach a consensus if they want to dismiss the President, but are not able to elect a new one. The HZDS-led cabinet and parliamentary coalition tried to discredit the president and launched a negative campaign in the government-controlled mass media. However, the government did not have the support of the required three-fifths majority of parliament to dismiss Kováč. The parliamentary majority first circumscribed president's powers by changing ordinary (statutory) laws specifying the competencies of the head of state. Later, the same parliamentary majority made an extra-constitutional 'vote of no confidence' concerning the president, a procedure not specified in the Constitution and thus without any legal implications. Eventually, attacks against the president and his family displayed clear signs of the Slovak intelligence services' involvement. The organisation was at that time controlled exclusively by the deputies representing the aforementioned parliamentary majority, since after the second parliamentary session the opposition deputies were not allowed to sit in the parliamentary committees controlling the intelligence services.

The last conflict concerned the presidential elections. To elect the president, parliamentarians had to muster a three-fifths majority of all Members of Parliament, i.e. to find a candidate who would receive at least 90 of all 150 votes. If any of candidates did not receive such a majority in the first round, the two candidates who received the most votes were scheduled for the second round. However, the number of required votes was not decreased in the second round, and the third one was not foreseen at all. According to the constitution, candidates who did not receive enough votes were simply eliminated from the race, and subsequent rounds of the presidential elections should start with entirely new candidates. The procedure created the danger that a president would not be elected and thus, the institutional structure established by the Constitution was incomplete. The danger of a vacant presidency had indeed become a reality and Slovakia did not have a head of state from March 1998 until May 1999. In addition, in case the presidency was vacant, the Constitution did not transfer all of the president's powers to the prime minister and some of them were not allocated to any institution, including the power to dissolve parliament, promulgate laws, and appoint the prime minister, cabinet ministers, and other principal officers. The opposition feared that this situation could result in a constitutional crisis, because the Constitution did not provide rules for the cabinet's resignation after the general elections scheduled for September 1998. The constitution stipulated that the prime minister must submit his resignation to the president and it was unclear how a prime minister could be removed from office if there was no head of state to which a resignation could be submitted. This was solved only in July 1998, after long political controversies, when Mečiar-led political forces made concessions, and the parliament passed an amendment to the constitution which transferred all above-mentioned powers, including the rule that the resignation of the incumbent cabinet be submitted to the chairman of parliament when the president's seat was vacant.

The unclear provisions of the 1992 Constitution also contributed to the escalation of conflict over the free mandate of a deputy, known as the Gaulieder case. František Gaulieder, a HZDS deputy, decided to leave his parliamentary party and stay in the parliament as an 'independent' MP. However, before the elections of 1994 he and all of his colleagues from HZDS signed an undated letter in which he resigned from his parliamentary seat. This was to discipline future HZDS deputies and to forbid them to leave the party. After Gaulieder left the HZDS faction, the letter appeared in the parliament as if it were sent by the deputy. The parliamentary majority simply 'accepted his resignation,' even though Gaulieder several times proclaimed that he had not given up his mandate. This led to conflict between the parliament and the Constitutional Court, to which Gaulieder appealed. The Court later ruled that Gaulieder's constitutional rights were infringed. However, the 1992 Constitution did not provide the Court with the power to cancel the parliament's decision. The Court only appealed to the legislature to reconsider its decision. Even though there was no demarche issued after Gaulieder was deprived of his mandate, a reaction came from Herbert Boesch, an MEP and a co-chairman of the Joint Parliamentary Committee of the EU and Slovakia. In a letter to A. M. Huska, a HZDS deputy and his colleague from the JPC, he wrote:

> to me, it is more and more difficult to understand why the National Council of the Slovak Republic takes decisions that clearly contradict the idea of numerous

statements ... concerning the intentions of Slovakia to build in your country a permanent parliamentary democracy ... If this trend does not change clearly and unambiguously, it will have serious consequences upon work of the Joint Parliamentary Committee and upon the chances of Slovakia joining the European Union in a near future.[14]

The MEP was joined by his colleagues in the European parliament who passed a resolution about the Gaulieder case in December 1996. The parliament stressed that, 'respect for fundamental democratic principles, including the free exercise of parliamentary mandates, is a condition for entering into and developing cooperation with the EU'.[15]

The government had tried to limit the influence of the Constitutional Court, since the Court was the last institutional barrier against the government's unconstitutional decisions. The ruling parties often criticised the Court as the institution that was not impartial and that backed the opposition. As a reaction, for example, in 1995 the cabinet withdrew some financial support to the Court chair, trying to punish him for the Court's independence. Moreover, a HZDS Member of Parliament proposed to amend the Court's decision-making procedure, which would replace simple majority voting by qualified majority voting. However, only after *Gaulieder* did the parliamentary majority openly refuse to comply with a ruling of the Constitutional Court. This constituted a qualitatively new dimension in Slovak politics, because before the Gaulieder affair the parliamentary majority had observed the basic constitutional rules of the political game.

Bearing in mind the possibility of a deadlock situation (following the inability of the parliament to elect the president after the term of President Kováč expired in March 1998) the opposition deputies in late 1996 presented a proposal for constitutional amendment aiming at the direct election of the president. This proposal was rejected in parliament and the opposition started to collect signatures for a petition asking the president to call a referendum on this issue.[16] This proposal was widely supported by the public, and within a period of six weeks the opposition collected many more signatures than required by the Constitution.

At the same time the ruling coalition tried to counterbalance this move by the opposition by trying to manipulate public opinion on NATO accession. The ruling coalition indicated several times that it would organise a referendum about Slovakia's membership in NATO. Signals from NATO headquarters as well as from several NATO members indicated that Slovakia, because of its unfavourable democratic record, would not receive an invitation to join NATO at the Madrid summit in 1997. The coalition deputies in the National Council approved the referendum proposal with the following questions: (1) Are you in favour of Slovakia's membership in NATO? (2) Are you in favour of the deployment of nuclear weapons on Slovak soil? (3) Are you in favour of establishing military bases in Slovakia? The opposition suggested that questions had been phrased to elicit a vote against membership and to provide the government with political cover if it failed to win an invitation to join. President Kováč called a joint referendum with four questions (three questions about NATO and the fourth one about the popular election of the head of state in May 1997. As early as April 1997 the Slovak government asked the Constitutional Court whether it was possible to change the constitution in a referendum, as the fourth question suggested. At the same time the cabinet ordered the state administration to prepare the ballot papers with only three questions, leaving out the question on the popular election of the president.

The Central Referendum Commission, a body composed of an equal number of representatives of all parliamentary political parties, is the only body with the powers to decide about the course and results of a referendum. The Commission emphasised that the referendum had been called with four questions, since the president called it in a legal way. In spite of this decision the interior minister announced that until the Constitutional Court decided, his ministry would not distribute ballot papers with four questions. The Court ruled on the case just one day before the referendum was to be held. The Senate of the Constitutional Court ruled that the legislative powers in the Slovak Republic rested both within the parliament and the people. Thus, it was possible to hold a referendum about the question concerning the constitutional changes. At the same time the annex to the fourth question (proposal of the constitutional amendment) was formulated in a way that contradicted legislative norms. Nevertheless, the judges of the Court announced that the referendum was valid with four questions, even though 'yes' for the fourth question would not cause an automatic constitutional change. Despite this statement the interior minister ordered that ballot papers to be distributed with only three questions. Eight opposition parties recommended to the voters not to take part in the referendum with three questions. The Central Referendum Commission issued a final statement in which it stated that only 9.8 per cent of the voters took part in the vote with the ballot papers issued by the Ministry of Interior. Since the valid ballot papers were not provided by the Ministry, the Commission proclaimed the referendum invalid.[17] In an immediate reaction, President Kováč and the opposition accused the government of destroying the democratic regime in Slovakia. Moreover, the foreign minister resigned, claiming that given the circumstances, he was unable to carry out the foreign policy priorities of the state. During an official visit to Slovakia just two days after the referendum, EU Commissioner Hans van den Broek again stressed the need to strengthen democratic institutions and procedures, and again reminded Slovak political representatives about EU political conditions. In response to the referendum affair, he labelled integration chances of Slovakia as 'politically controversial'. In June 1997 the meeting of the Joint Parliamentary Committee took place in the Slovak capital Bratislava. It was the last official meeting within the framework of EA political dialogue to take place before the Commission's *avis* were to be published. After three days of negotiations the committee adopted a 'last chance' resolution recommending the adoption of legislative norms and executive acts that would improve the functioning of the democratic system. In order to meet the political criteria no later than November that year (i.e. still before the Luxembourg summit), it recommended the re-creation of parliamentary committees on a proportional basis, increased chances for the opposition to control the intelligence services, and also urged a consensual preparation and adoption of a law on minority languages. It basically repeated what the JPC had stated in its conclusion a year before, when it specified thirteen problematic areas of Slovak politics and called for improvement. However, even these recommendations proved futile, as Slovakia's ruling majority basically ignored the JPC conclusions.

Political conditionality and the opposition

The results of the referendum, together with the ongoing EU concerns about the democratic character of the political regime in Slovakia, prompted five opposition political parties to create an alliance called the Slovak Democratic Coalition (SDK). The SDK also decided to deepen its cooperation with the three parties of the Hungarian minority. The 'EU factor' was strongly felt in the process, as the SDK many times emphasised the need to break Slovakia's growing international isolation and to improve relations with the EU in order to increase the chances of early accession. 'Appeals of opposition parties to voters have been increasingly typified by their stressing their "European compatibility", and their coming to power was presented as the only possibility of salvaging the country's weakened integration chances.'[18] Moreover, the cooperation of the SDK with the Hungarian parties was to indicate that the minority problems, a major weakness of the Mečiar administration, could be solved in a consensual way, i.e. by involving the minority representatives in decision-making processes. In addition, the parties of the opposition succeeded in attracting the attention of other actors in civil society in organising the so-called democratic roundtable discussions. At these meetings, the opposition parties conducted talks with the representatives of the trade unions, nongovernmental organisations and with the association of local self-governments. The meaning of these meetings was largely symbolic; they had to show that the opposition was able to talk and agree with the forces that were marginalised by the Mečiar administration.

The opposition's cooperation even increased after the Luxembourg European Council in December 1997 did not invite Slovakia to the first group of countries directly negotiating on accession. The opposition blamed the government for violating the democratic norms and criteria that led the EU to exclude Slovakia. After the Luxembourg summit, the Slovak Democratic Coalition pledged to fulfil all political criteria required by the EU of applicant states within one hundred days of coming to power. The opposition's cooperation was also prompted by the fact that parts of the ruling coalition started looking for an alternative foreign policy orientation. This was demonstrated by Mečiar's well-known statement to the foreign press in autumn 1995 when he indicated that if

Slovakia were not accepted in the West, it might well turn to the East. However, there were more substantial grounds for this kind of speculation. Mečiar's administration concluded a whole range of bilateral Slovak–Russian treaties with respect to energy resources that effectively rendered Slovakia dependent on Russia. Moreover, in 1996 the government even seriously considered concluding a treaty on a free trade area with Russia, even though such a treaty clearly contradicted the Europe Agreement. The opposition parties feared that Slovakia's isolation from the mainstream integration processes could lead to a closer alliance with Russia and to further decay of the democratic regime. Thus, for them EU integration had to play a dual role, that of a means as well as of a goal. As a means it was to integrate the country into an organisation whose political environment would be favourable to democracy. In other words, EU membership was valuable because it contributed to the consolidation of democracy. As a goal, the economic, political and cultural benefits of EU membership were most often stressed.

In February 1998 the Constitutional Court ruled that the Interior Ministry infringed the constitutional rights of citizens, since they could not take part in a legal referendum with four questions. In response the president called a new referendum with the original questions. However, before it was to take place, the five-year term of President Michal Kováč expired and the government (the prime minister) assumed some of the presidential prerogatives. The government immediately cancelled the referendum called by the former president. Moreover, the prime minister used his temporary presidential powers to declare an amnesty for the persons associated with the thwarted referendum in 1997. The measures were clearly politically motivated and aimed at protecting the interior minister. In addition, the prime minister also declared an amnesty for the persons who were involved in kidnapping a Slovak citizen and taking him to neighbouring Austria. There was strong evidence that the kidnapping was initiated, if not carried out, by the Slovak intelligence service. An official reaction from the EU followed a week later. The EU presidency issued a statement in which it clearly expressed that the Mečiar administration was not perceived to be a reliable and committed partner: 'The decision by Prime Minister Mečiar to exercise the presidential powers to grant amnesties ... brings into questions his commitment to commonly accepted principles of good governance and the rule of law.'[19] With the Slovak general elections scheduled for September in mind, the EU further stated: 'The EU regrets that such steps might represent a set-back to the legitimate aspirations of the Slovak people to international respect and progressive integration into European structures. [The EU] will continue to support these aspirations and to follow developments related to their fulfillment closely.'[20] By carefully distinguishing between the Slovak population and its government, the EU representatives tried to support the opposition forces that would be able to carry out a domestic political change.

Four months before the September 1998 general election, the Slovak parliament passed a number of amendments to the electoral law initiated by the

HZDS and the SNS. These changes were designed to reduce the strength of the opposition parties. The electoral alliances which these parties had formed were in effect rendered useless, as the new provisions of the law stated that each party in any alliance would have to pass the 5 per cent threshold in order to be allocated seats. This was directed against the Slovak Democratic Coalition, itself an alliance of five small parties, of which two were not expected to receive 5 per cent of the votes; it was also directed against three small Hungarian parties brought together under the name the Hungarian Coalition (the SMK). These two alliances had therefore to merge into two parties, which required difficult and lengthy negotiations during the election campaign. In addition to the newly founded SDK and the Hungarian party (SMK), a new catch-all populist party was formed under the name of Party of Civic Understanding (SOP), which looked for support among left-inclined voters of Eastern Slovakia as well as among disillusioned HZDS voters. Rudolf Schuster, the charismatic and populist mayor, a moderate nationalist in favour of EU membership, became the leader of that party. Together with the Party of the Democratic Left (SDL), these new opposition parties met prior to the election to discuss their campaign strategies as well as possible post-election coalition arrangements.

Closing the gap: political and constitutional changes after the 1998 election

The second general election since independence was scheduled for September 1998. They were held under the supervision of the delegations from the OSCE, and the Council of Europe. Several observers from the European parliament also took part in the supervisory teams. The four opposition parties emerged victorious, together gaining 58 per cent of the votes and obtaining 93 of the 150 seats in parliament. Mikuláš Dzurinda, the leader of the Slovak Democratic Coalition, was chosen to form the government. With 62 per cent of the seats and 93 MPs, the four-party government had a comfortable majority in parliament, which even allowed for a change of the constitution. Even though the pre-election statements of the then-opposition parties indicated their willingness to form a coalition government if they won, the negotiations of the four parties were difficult. Since the two parties (SDK and SMK) were themselves alliances composed of five and three factions, respectively, the divergence of their policy goals and strategies was considerable.

The first controversy emerged over participation of the SMK in the cabinet, when some of the SDL representatives suggested that the SMK could be excluded. However, that attitude met with strong disagreement from the other three parties. It was argued that the SMK's participation would increase the overall political stability in the country, give the cabinet the support of a three-fifth parliamentary majority and strengthen Slovakia's chances for EU accession. The creation of an oversized cabinet was also justified by the need to carry out important political reforms stabilising the democratic regime. Third, and most importantly, all parties of the new government shared the priorities of the foreign policy orientation towards the EU and NATO. Thus, they all agreed that in order to improve Slovakia' s chances for EU accession, unequivocal foreign policies as well as complying with the political conditions of the EU were essential prerequisites.

The newly formed ruling coalition tried to take a conciliatory stance towards the HZDS and SNS, the opposition parties, and offered them a roughly proportional share of the posts in the parliament as well as in other important semi-governmental control bodies. The opposition HZDS and SNS were invited to nominate a deputy speaker of parliament and were offered the chair of six out of 18 parliamentary committees, including the sensitive position of the chair of the committee overseeing the functioning of the SIS. Candidates from the opposition were elected into controlling bodies supervising the broadcasting of the mass media and privatisation. While the HZDS declined to nominate its candidates for the parliamentary committees' chair, the SNS accepted these offers and submitted its nominees. Only in the EU–Slovak Joint Parliamentary Committee did the HZDS make an exception and nominate a vice-chair of the committee.

The representatives of the EU welcomed the fair character of the elections as well as their results. The European parliament issued a resolution appealing to the Commission to take the new situation in Slovakia into account in preparing its further strategy towards the candidate countries. However, the European Commission was more cautious. In its second Report on Slovakia in 1998 it noted that 'a different political climate is emerging and a window of opportunity exists for a new government majority to address the ... [previously existing] ... shortcomings ... The new government now has an opportunity to demonstrate Slovakia's commitment to democratic principles, respect for human rights and the rule of law'.[21] Even though the expectations of the new administration for Slovakia's early inclusion into the first group proved too optimistic, EU–Slovak cooperation regained momentum. For example, in November it was agreed that a high level working group composed of experts from the EC and Slovakia would be created to help Slovakia to enter the accession negotiations.[22]

The new government set out to resolve the problems inherited from the previous years. Most importantly, Slovakia had been without a president since 2 March 1998. In January 1999, after several months of debating various proposals, the parties supporting the government passed an amendment to the Constitution, which provided for the direct and popular election of the president and changed some of his/her powers.

The Prime Minister Dzurinda and his coalition partners supported Rudolf Schuster, the chair of the governing SOP, in his election bid. Former Prime Minister Vladimír Mečiar decided to run as well. In the first ballot, Schuster obtained 47 per cent of the vote and Mečiar 37 per cent, with none of the eight other candidates having scored even 10 per cent. Schuster was then elected president in the second ballot with 57 per cent of the votes: the governing coalition had retained strong popular support. Thus, Slovakia's institutional system found renewed stability. Dzurinda's cabinet focused on those reforms connected with the EU accession process. In January 1999 legislation was passed that permitted the minority schools to issue grade certificates in minority languages, a policy they were denied during the previous government. Long-awaited legislation on languages used in the state administration, enabling persons belonging to the ethnic minorities to use their own language, was approved by parliament in July 1999. In December 1999 parliament issued a declaration expressing regret that Gaulieder was stripped of his mandate by the previous parliament.

The representatives of the European Union carefully observed these steps. In its report on Slovakia issued in October 1999, the Commission concluded that Slovakia fulfilled basic political criteria for opening negotiations on EU accession. The Commission acknowledged that Slovakia was meeting political conditions, including institutional stability, the rule of law and respect for human and minority rights.[23] Based on favourable reports on other candidate countries as well, the European Council meeting in Helsinki in December decided to start the direct negotiation not only with Slovakia but also with other countries of the second group created in Luxembourg. In Slovakia the decision was welcomed as a clear signal that the country had broken with its controversial political past of the 1994–98 period. The Commission, assessing the situation in Slovakia in 2000, concluded 'Slovakia continues to meet the political criteria which the last report had recognised, for the first time, as having been fulfilled. Slovakia has further advanced in the consolidation of its democratic system and in the normal functioning of its institutions.'[24] After political difficulties had been overcome, the relations between the EU and Slovakia now focus on concrete technical problems connected with accession to the Union. Since the 1998 elections, all the Commission's Regular Reports state that Slovakia has been fulfilling all political criteria for EU membership.

The Programme Declaration of the government in 1998 also promised to prepare other changes to the Constitution. There were three major motivations behind the constitutional change. First, many of the controversial provisions of the original 1992 Constitution were unclear, ambiguous or did not contain mechanisms for enforcement of the basic provisions guaranteed therein, as some of the above mentioned cases illustrated. Second, some changes were prompted by the prospect of EU membership, as embodied by the provisions that allow Slovakia to enter into a union with other states and that allow the government to issue regulations implementing the obligations stemming from Slovakia's membership in international organisations. And third, new provisions and institutions were established to improve the overall institutional framework and strengthen democratic institutions. These include, but are not limited to, changes to the structure of the Constitutional Court, creation of the Ombudsman office and provisions on the reform of the public administration.[25]

Conclusion

Even though the political conditions of the EU were often criticised for being very broad and difficult to measure,[26] their application to Slovakia played a major role in turning the country's regime back on the road toward consolidated democracy after the 1998 elections. In the period between 1994 and 1998, the Slovak government and its parliamentary majority severely circumscribed the rights of the opposition, entered into sustained conflict with the president, violated the rights of a member of the parliament, and later thwarted a referendum and ignored the rulings of the Constitutional Court. The European Union reacted to these processes in diplomatic demarches, presidency statements, and resolutions from the European Parliament. Official channels, including the institutions of the Europe agreement, political dialogue, as well as personal letters and declarations, were used to voice the EU's concern. On numerous occasions the representatives of the EU warned that the political criteria, namely the rule of law, stability of the institutions and respect for human and minority rights, constituted an absolute requirement for entering into accession talks with a candidate country. Besides these diplomatic tools, the Commission's regular reports and the European Council's decisions constituted major leverage for influencing the political situation in Slovakia. However, the direct impact of the EU political conditionality approached its limits, as the Slovak government representatives were unwilling to make concessions to the domestic opposition and even accused the EU representatives of adopting unfair standards for Slovakia as compared to other CEE countries. Moreover, the official Slovak representatives downplayed the EU's concerns about the character of the emerging political regime, using the rhetoric of a different (majoritarian) understanding of democracy in Slovakia.

The impact of EU political conditionality increases, however, if we shift from its conventional understanding as a bilateral international issue (involving the EU and Slovakia) towards viewing it as trilateral dialogue taking place between the EU, the Slovak government, and the Slovak opposition. From this perspective we can better understand the careful distinction between Slovakia's political representation and the population made by the EU (e.g. EU presidency statement in 1998 after the Mečiar's amnesties). The EU's involvement, especially in 1997 (the thwarted referendum, EU reactions, the Commission's *avis*) and its Luxembourg European Council decision, functioned as catalysts prompting the co-operation of the opposition and increasing the general public's awareness of the danger of Slovakia's international isolation. The representatives of the fragmented opposition decided to co-ordinate their activities and later created broad political alliances that were to break the growing international isolation and return the country to the path of democratic consolidation. At the core of the opposition's statements was the commitment to comply with the EU's democratic conditions. The EU's political criteria even played a guiding role for the acts of the new parliamentary majority after the 1998 elections. The inclusion of the SMK, a party of the Hungarian minority, was in part motivated by the intention to incorporate Slovakia's largest national minority into the decision-making process. This contrasted with the policies of the Mečiar 1994–98 government, whose minority policy was often criticised by the EU. The new government's attitude towards the opposition also contrasted with the previous oft-criticised practices. In addition, the success of the opposition parties in the 1998 elections endowed them with a parliamentary majority sufficient to amend the Constitution's most controversial provisions that were at the heart of many political controversies of the 1994–98 period. The constitutional amendments of 1999 and 2001 therefore increased the overall institutional stability of Slovakia and also included new provisions removing constitutional obstacles to entering into a lasting state union with other countries in Europe.

As the case of Slovakia illustrates, the EU's political conditionality can have a major impact on the internal political development of the country in question if there is a viable political alternative to the existing government and if the opposition can mobilise the population and use the government's foreign policy failure as a political weapon. The Slovak opposition, using the country's exclusion from the mainstream integration policies in Europe that were a consequence of not complying with political conditions, succeeded in winning a constitutional majority in parliament, formed a coalition government and later clarified the ambiguous rules of the political game.

Notes

1 D. Malová and M. Rybář, 'The Troubled Institutionalization of Parliamentary Democracy in Slovakia', *Politicka misao. Croatian Political Science Review*, 37:2 (2000), 99–115.

2 G. Pridham, 'Complying with the European Union's Democratic Conditionality: Transnational Party Linkages and Regime Change in Slovakia, 1993–1998', *Europe–Asia Studies*, 51:7 (1999), 1222.

3 B. Lippert, 'Shaping and Evaluating the Europe Agreements: The Community side', in B. Lippert and H. Schneider (eds.), *Monitoring Association and Beyond: The European Union and the Visegrád States* (Bonn, Europa Union Verlag, 1995), p. 29.

4 For example, when Prime Minister Mečiar had been dismissed in March 1994 and his party lost the majority in parliament, his fellow party member Ivan Gašparovič maintained his position as speaker of parliament. Similarly, many HZDS members had continued to chair parliamentary committees.

5 A. Duleba, 'Democratic Consolidation and the Conflict over Slovak International Alignment', in S. Szomolányi and J. A. Gould (eds.), *Slovakia: Problems of Democratic Consolidation* (Bratislava, Slovak Political Science Association, 1997), p. 215.

6 European Parliament, 'Resolution of the European Parliament on the Need to Respect Human and Democratic Rights in the Slovak Republic', *Official Journal of the EU*, C 323, 1995.

7 O. Dostál, 'Menšiny' (Minorities) in M. Bútora and P. Hunčík (eds.), *Slovensko 1995: Súhrnná správa o stave spoločnosti* (Slovakia 1995: Global Report on the State of Society) (Bratislava, Nadácia Sándora Máraiho, 1996), p. 55.

8 This provision was primarily of a symbolic value to the deputies representing ethnic minorities, since they did not use the right when it was guaranteed.

9 Dostál, 'Menšiny', p. 53.

10 Council of Ministers, 'Common Position of the EU for the Second EU–Slovak Republic Association Council', Brussels, 1996.

11 Council of Ministers, 'Common Position of the EU for the Third EU–Slovak Republic Association Council', Brussels, 1997.

12 The Mečiar-led cabinet used these constitutional ambiguities and shifted some powers of president to the cabinet. In April 1995, the president lost the right to name and recall the director of the Slovak Intelligence Service (SIS). In July 1995, the president lost the power to approve the chief of the general's staff of the Slovak army in favour of the Cabinet.

13 D. Malová, 'Slovakia: From the Ambiguous Constitution to the Dominance of Informal Rules', in J. Zielonka (ed.), *Democratic Consolidation in Eastern Europe, Volume 1: Institutional Engineering* (Oxford, Oxford University Press, 2001), 347–377.

14 Duleba, 'Democratic Consolidation and the Conflict over Slovak International Alignment', p. 219.

15 European Parliament, 'Resolution of the European Parliament on the Case of Frantisek Gaulieder, Member of the Slovak Parliament', *Official Journal of the EU C 020*, 1997.

16 On the referendum in the Slovak context see E. Láštic, 'Inštitút referenda v ústavnom systéme Slovenskej republiky' (Referendum in the Constitutional System of the Slovak Republic) in D. Horná a L. Malíková (eds.), *Demokracia a právny štát* (Democracy and the Rule of Law) (Bratislava: Friedrich Ebbert Stiftung, 2001), pp. 77–94.

17 On the 1997 referendum see G. Mesežnikov and M. Bútora (eds.), *Slovenské referendum '97: Zrod, priebeh, dôsledky* (Slovak Referendum 1997: Origins, Cause and Consequences) (Bratislava: Inštitút pre verejné otázky, 1997).

18 P. Učeň, 'Implications of Party System Development for Slovakia's Performance in European Integration', unpublished manuscript, 1998, p. 43.

19 European Council, 'Presidency Statement on Behalf of the European Union', in *Bulletin of the EU*, 9 (1998).

20 Ibid.

21 European Commission, *Commission Report: Slovakia* (Brussels, European Commission, 1998).

22 V. Bilčík, M. Bruncko, A. Duleba, P. Lukáč and I. Samson, 'Foreign and Defence Policy of the Slovak Republic', in G. Mesežnikov, M. Kollár and T. Nicholson (eds.), *Slovakia 2000* (Bratislava, Institute for Public Affairs).

23 European Commission, *Regular Report on Slovakia's Progress Towards Accession* (Brussels, European Commission, 1999).

24 European Commission, *Regular Report on Slovakia's Progress Towards Accession* (Brussels, European Commission, 2000).

25 Malová, 'Slovakia: From the Ambiguous Constitution to the Dominance of Informal Rules'.

26 H. Grabbe and K. Hughes, *Enlarging the EU Eastwards* (London, Royal Institute of International Affairs, 1998).

4

Constitutional change in Poland: adjustment in anticipation – legal and democratic dilemmas

Ewa Popławska

Aspiration to membership of the Communities and then of the European Union was manifest in Polish politics since the departure from the communist system, not to mention the hopes fostered even before that time by the circles of democratic opposition. Naturally, these aspirations were not and still are not approved by the whole nation, and one of the reasons for that was the particular emotional attachment to the relatively freshly regained independence. Poland's possible adherence to supra-national structures and – in practice – irrevocable diminishing of the competence of the national authorities in the areas in which European Communities have exclusive competence provokes considerable public resistance.[1]

Since their creation, the European Communities have been evolving towards an organisation displaying some features of federal structures, whose scope of activity includes some spheres which traditionally belonged to the competence of national authorities. Adding to it the principle of supremacy of Community law to the legal order of the member states, we realise how much the legal orders of the Community and of the member states have become integrated, and how much the European structures have become 'constitutionalised'. Given this process of constitutionalisation, new and existing member states of the Union are facing considerable challenges in the field of political and legal preparation for the next enlargement.

Poles had no objections to meeting the initial, purely political criteria, taken into account when considering new candidates to the European Union because these criteria matched the expectations of the Polish society as to the democratisation of the political system and safeguards of rights and freedoms.[2] The first step towards international recognition of the observance of democratic principles by Poland and other countries of the region, now aspiring to EU membership, was their admission to the Council of Europe. Poland was accepted as a member of the Council of Europe immediately after the first completely free election (1993). Acceptance of the need to undergo control of the observance of the European Convention on the Protection of Human Rights and Fundamental Freedoms established an international guarantee of its uniform application.

As with all the other candidates, Poland also had to make a number of adjustments associated with the EU's democracy criterion from Copenhagen and various elements of the Union's political conditionality discussed in chapter 1 of this book. The adjustments required by the need to comply with the *acquis* of the Union and the economic requirements associated with them remain the most controversial. The process of legal preparation of the candidate countries, including Poland, for EU membership resembles the well-known logical paradox of a turtle chasing a hare.[3] The process of adjustment of law in candidate countries – however fast it might be, and its speed still leaves much to be desired – is accompanied by the parallel increase in *acquis communautaire*.

Constitution of the Republic of Poland of April 1997: a step on the road to the European Union

The Republic of Poland, the country whose process of departure from the communist system started further radical changes towards democracy in the rest of Central and Eastern Europe, was paradoxically one of the last countries in this region to adopt a complete 'post-totalitarian' constitution. Some of the reasons for that were: the fact that the old regulation in force, the so-called Small Constitution of 17 October 1992, was relatively satisfactory from the point of view of effective functioning of the state system, the existence of considerable differences in the ideological sphere of drafts of the new constitution between the political parties participating in its preparation and the necessity to reach a compromise, as the draft constitution required a majority in the National Assembly, i.e. the joint chambers of the Parliament. The resulting delay – the Constitution of the Republic of Poland was adopted as late as 2 April 1997 – made it possible to include some norms anticipating Poland's adherence to the European structures among the constitutional provisions. Work on the shape of the future constitution was conducted with an awareness of the importance and delicacy of European integration problems. The 'European clause', as it was finally adopted, and its content and place within the dynamics of the constitution were the result of balancing various political, systemic, historical and psychological arguments.

A very important stage of constitutional work was preparing the country for accession to the European Union under an accession treaty, which requires ratification upon consent previously granted in a statute (cf. Article 89, para. 1, subparas 2, 3, 4 and 5). The current wording of Article 90 of the constitution takes into account the historical importance of this decision and the experiences of those countries which have joined the European Communities so far. The first conclusion that was drawn from these experiences was that a country had to be prepared in advance for the political, systemic and legal consequences of a decision on accession to the Union. Therefore, such a country must foresee early enough the possibility of delegating to this organisation the competence of organs of state authority in relation to certain matters. If Poland is to ever become a member of the Union, then, sooner or later, such transfer of power will inevitably occur. So we should not postpone the approximation of constitutional provisions (and this is a matter of the fundamental law) till the moment when it becomes necessary. These forecasts proved only partially true, since the issue of the 'European clause' aroused heated discussions and was one of the arguments used by opponents of the new constitution in the campaign preceding the referendum in which it was adopted, in May 1997. The reason why the 'European clause' was, and still is, being contested – now with lesser intensity, although growing in times of election campaigns – is the fear of losing state sovereignty, or at least reducing it, which is unacceptable in the understanding of sovereignty as presented by anti-European parties (conservative, nationalist and fundamentalist Catholic ones).[4]

The arguments in favour of adopting the constitutional provisions anticipating Poland's accession to the Union were systemic and political rationality and prudence, which required the fundamental law, on the one hand, to define the procedure for ratifying the accession agreement and thereby define the behaviour of public authorities responsible for the success of negotiations, and, on the other, to 'socialise' the citizens into making a decision on Poland's membership of the European Union, be it in the form of a referendum or through the appropriate choice of representatives in both chambers of the parliament.[5]

Here, we should also remind ourselves that, while working on the consolidated draft of the constitution, the Constitutional Commission of the National Assembly was constantly considering the conformity of the systemic provisions with the laws of the member states of the European Union. In accordance with Article 6 of the Treaty on the European Union, the principles of liberty, democracy, respect for human rights and fundamental freedoms and the rule of law, common to all member states, are also the basis on which the Union is built. The assumption was that if the fundamental laws of such countries as France, Italy, the Federal Republic of Germany, Portugal or Spain 'fit into' the Union laws, then, once the basic principles underlying the Polish constitutional solutions are in line with the norms adopted in these countries, they will also 'fit into' the requirements of the Union. The Constitutional Commission regularly compared the norms that were included in the draft on which it was working with the regulations presented in the constitutions of member states of the Union.[6]

Furthermore, the norms known in the primary legislation, including the Maastricht Treaty, have had the role of setting standards. Following the European principle of subsidiarity, the same principle was included in the preamble to the constitution of 1997.[7] Article 216, para. 5, of the constitution was also directly influenced by these regulations ('It shall neither be permissible to contract loans nor to provide guarantees and financial sureties which would engender a national public debt exceeding three-fifths of the value of the annual gross domestic product'). The authors of the Polish constitution of 1997 were aware of the fact that the instrument they were working on would, in the future, function in the European normative environment and if it was not to be in conflict with this environment, it must share the same basic principles. To a considerable extent, this kind of compliance was achieved.

The fundamental argument to support the thesis on axiological convergence of Polish constitutional solutions with the European Union principles is the fact that both these legal orders are based on the principle of subsidiarity. It was given the importance of a constitutional principle in the Polish constitution whose preamble formulates it in the following way: 'we, the Polish Nation – all citizens of the Republic, ... hereby establish this Constitution of the Republic of Poland as the basic law for the State, based on respect for freedom and justice, co-operation between the public powers, social dialogue and on the principle of subsidiarity strengthening the powers of citizens and their communities'. This old doctrinal conception, developed in the social teaching of the Catholic church, became generally popular after it was adopted as the starting point in the debate on systemic changes in the European Communities, which was to produce the Treaty on European Union. If the principle of subsidiarity applies both to the constitutional order of a contemporary democratic state and to the European Union, it is thanks to its universal character as the operating principle of all organisations of human communities stating that the main function of authorities is to satisfy the needs of the communities or individuals subordinate to it, independently making decisions on their lives and taking responsibility for it. The aims and tasks of authorities should not go beyond those shared by the subordinate individuals and groups.

A comparison of the place and role of subsidiarity in the Polish and European legal orders raises a question: was the constitutionalisation in Poland influenced by the fact that it had been included in the Maastricht Treaty? An affirmative answer is possible to a limited degree: the precedent of making an express reference to this principle in a legal instrument – the Treaty on European Union (and in accordance with its provisions, in the Treaty establishing the European Community) – could have had some impact on the works on the Polish fundamental law, even if the characteristics of an instrument of international law are considerably different from the requirements pertaining to constitutional legislation. The promoter of the preamble, Deputy Tadeusz Mazowiecki, referred to the functioning of the principle of subsidiarity in the provisions of EC law, justifying thereby the inclusion in the Constitution of an axiological element which would correspond to the need for building the public life in recognition that 'we are not faced with an omnipotent state, that there are various communities, self-government and family, associations and foundations.'[8]

Contrary to the constitutions of Germany (Article 23, para. 1) or Portugal (Article 7, para. 6), after the amendments made just before ratification of the Treaty on European Union, the reference to subsidiarity in the Polish constitution does not apply to European law, but to the domestic order since it is a basis of the constitution as the basic law for the state. Thus, we have to exclude the hypothesis that the principle of subsidiarity was included in the 1997 constitution as a direct result of the requirements for Poland's future membership in the European Union. The treaties do not make the requirement or even request for observance of this principle in the domestic orders of member states, as this is not within their scope. The principle of subsidiarity, accepted in the Treaty of Maastricht as a principle of the functioning of the European Union and assigning competence to levels of decision making in the European Community, is not an independent source of validity of this principle in domestic orders of member states. In fact the closest link between subsidiarity in Polish constitutional law and in European Treaties is the common ideological inspiration, derived from the doctrine of Christian democracy, and particularly from the universal vision of the social structure.

'European clause' of the Constitution

The constitutional norm that I called 'European clause' is contained in the provision of Article 90. Paragraph 1 thereof states that 'The Republic of Poland may, by virtue of international agreements, delegate to an international organisation or international institution the competence of organs of State authority in relation to certain matters.' It is a specific provision in comparison to the general principle, contained in Article 89, para. 1, subpara. 3, on the Republic of Poland's membership of international organisations. The element which differentiates these situations is the effect of the accession agreement, which is to move the competence of organs of state authority outside of the state constitutional apparatus. So if the membership of an international organisation does not entail delegating such competence, it is sufficient to use the ordinary procedure, that is, to grant consent to ratification of the accession agreement by means of a statute. It was according to this procedure that the Act of 17 February 1999 granted consent to the ratification of the North Atlantic Treaty by the Polish president.

Whether or not adherence to an organisation involves delegation of state authority competence, is decided in the contents of the treaty constituting this organisation. It must be an 'integrative' organisation.[9] Although the founding treaties of the Communities do not make a clear distinction of competence between the Communities and the member states, it was as early as 1964 that the European Court of Justice interpreting the Treaty establishing the European Economic Community concluded that 'by creating a Community of unlimited duration, having its own institutions, its own personality, its own legal capacity and capacity of representation on the international plane and, more particularly, real powers stemming from a limitation of sovereignty or a transfer of powers from the States to the Community, the Member States have limited their sovereign rights, albeit within limited fields, and have thus created a body of law which binds both their nationals and themselves'.[10] Article 90 of the

constitution does not touch upon the second aspect, but the possibility of delegating competence is coherent with the above characteristics of the Union as an
organisation.[11]

Article 90 para. 1 of the Polish constitution mentions the possibility of delegating competences 'in relation to certain matters'. Although one can draw a
conclusion that it is not permissible to delegate all competences, we do not find
any clues as to in what matters they cannot be delegated. If such a clause were
included in the constitution, it would help identify a specific 'nucleus of sovereignty', inviolable both at the time of concluding the accession treaty and later,
except when appropriate amendments had already been made to the constitution. The lack of specification about what types of competence were subject to
delegation was one of the reasons why this norm was heavily criticised before
the constitutional referendum: this was perceived as risking the chance of losing
sovereignty by the Polish state. It must be noted, however, that the Constitution
sets higher requirements of democratic legitimacy for such a decision to be
taken (Article 90, paras 2 to 4), therefore there is no risk that it might be taken
against the will of society.

An important role in setting the boundaries of delegation of competences and
establishing the criteria for resolving possible disputes about competence
between member states and the European Union or Communities is played by
the national constitutional courts or other organs responsible for the protection
of constitutionality of laws.[12] With the lack of exclusion of certain matters from
the scope of affairs transferred outside, it is also possible to verify each time the
constitutionality of the accession treaty or amending treaties.[13] The open
formula of competence transfer, adopted in Article 90, para. 1, of the Polish
constitution, does not rule out the possibility of the Constitutional Tribunal
setting limits for this type of instrument when checking the compliance with the
constitution of the statute granting consent to the ratification of an accession
treaty. The Tribunal could do so on the grounds of Article 4 para. 1 of the
constitution: 'Supreme power in the Republic of Poland shall be vested in the
Nation'; or Article 5: 'The Republic of Poland shall safeguard the independence
and integrity of its territory and ensure the freedoms and rights of persons and
citizens, the security of citizens, safeguard the national heritage.' Accession to
the European Union in its current shape would not infringe these provisions,
but the Union will evolve and it is difficult to predict the direction in which the
founding treaties will be developed.[14]

Procedure for ratification of the international agreement on the delegation of competence of state authority organs

In line with the last sentence of Article 49 of the Treaty on European Union, an
accession treaty 'is submitted for ratification by all the contracting States in
accordance with their respective constitutional requirements'. The Polish
constitution of 1997 established the grounds not only for making the decision

on Poland joining the Union, but also for delegating to it 'the competence of organs of State authority in relation to certain matters' (Article 90, para. 1). On the other hand it set the particular requirements of democratic legitimacy for making such a decision (Article 90, paras 2 to 4). While, in accordance with Article 89 para. 1 subpara. 3 of the constitution, the ratification of an international agreement on 'the Republic of Poland's membership in an international organisation' requires 'prior consent granted by statute', once such agreement involves Poland delegating 'to an international organisation or international institution the competence of organs of State authority in relation to certain matters' (Article 90 para. 1), the Constitution defines a special procedure for granting consent to the ratification of this kind of international agreement. This very procedure will apply to the accession treaty.

In such a case – according to Article 90, para. 2, of the constitution – the statute granting consent for ratification will be passed by the Sejm and Senate by a two-thirds majority vote in the presence of at least half of the statutory number of deputies and senators respectively. Note that the requirements envisaged here are stricter than the ones that apply to amending the constitution: for this an absolute majority of votes in the Senate will suffice (Article 235, para. 4, of the constitution). Exposing this argument seems to be particularly useful for stressing the democratic legitimacy of the whole procedure in view of the criticism that is likely to accompany the last stages of the accession process. Because if the chosen mechanism of granting consent was by statute and not by referendum, then particular attention would have to be devoted to the characteristics of the strict requirements envisaged in Article 90, para. 2, of the constitution. We can assume that if a referendum was not chosen for this purpose, this fact would lead to numerous opportunities for controversies or disputes in which the meaning of democratic legitimacy would be subjected to various interpretations.[15]

Alternatively, consent for ratification of the accession treaty may be granted in a nationwide referendum 'in accordance with the provisions of Article 125' (Article 90, para. 3, of the constitution), should the Sejm so decide by a resolution taken 'by an absolute majority of votes in the presence of at least half of the statutory number of Deputies'. Reference to Article 125 of the constitution indicates that a referendum will be deemed to have granted the consent for ratification of the accession treaty if its results are binding, that is if more than half of those having the right to vote participated in it (Article 125, para. 2) and if the referendum is decisive, that is, if the majority of participants have voted in favour of the ratification of the accession treaty (Article 9, para. 1, of the Referendum Act of 29 June 1995).

However, if this method is used in Poland, interpretation problems may arise in a situation when the result of the referendum is not binding due to the fact that the turnout was less than half of those having the right to vote (Article 125, para. 3, of the constitution). If we think how low the turnout at universal voting has been since 1989, this scenario is quite likely to occur. The next question is whether ordering a referendum means closing the parliamentary road for good. It may well be the choice of procedure for ratification of the accession treaty that will arouse the basic controversies, which in turn may affect the success of the whole procedure.

The choice of ratification path gives rise to serious political dilemmas. The decision about applying one of the procedures laid down in the constitution is an independent one by the Republic of Poland. Having regard to the historical dimension of Poland's accession to the EU, and even the circumstances – expressed also in the fears of eurosceptics – connected with that key step in the process of European integration, from a political, social or psychological point of view, there is very little room for applying any other solution than a referendum. The point is not just to meet the formal requirements of democratic legitimacy, as this can be achieved equally well by applying the statutory procedure of granting consent for ratification, but also to produce an appropriate psychological effect: society should identify itself with the decision on accession. If the institution of a referendum is not chosen, there will always be room for speculation whether the parliament's decision reflected the will of the sovereign. It is particularly important in the situation when sociological research shows that support for the European integration process is greater among the political elite than in society as a whole.[16]

Even though the major political parties are in favour of European integration, the level of support among the general public hardly exceeds 50 per cent, and sometimes has fallen below that figure. In the period following the entry into force of the constitution, numerous influential politicians announced that the referendum would be ordered in due time, apparently paying no attention to the fact that, according to the provisions in force, it is merely facultative. As a result of such declarations, the public became accustomed to the idea that it is the nation, and not Sejm and senate that will decide on Poland's accession to the Union. In the future, it will be difficult to disregard such announcements and promises.

If the result of the referendum would not be binding, the Sejm would have to decide upon the further course of action. A return to the statutory method may be conditioned by an analysis of the results of the referendum. In the case of lack of quorum in the referendum with the majority of votes in favour of the ratification of the accession treaty, the parliament has stronger moral and political grounds to express consent for ratification. One may argue that parliament is acting in accordance with the views of society, the majority of which was in favour of the accession. It would be much more difficult to go back to the statutory procedure in a situation when – also lacking quorum – the majority of those casting votes were against the ratification. Parliament, deciding to grant consent for ratification in a statute in spite of the negative opinion resulting from the referendum, would risk a serious constitutional conflict and put itself in an area of dubious democratic legitimacy.

The problem of control of constitutionality of the accession treaty is a complex one. As we have said above, competence is delegated by virtue of an international agreement, which can be submitted to the procedure of constitutionality check. Pursuant to Article 133, para. 2, of the constitution, before ratifying an international agreement, the president may refer it to the constitutional tribunal with a request for adjudication on its conformity to the constitution. In such a case the conformity check will apply to the whole of EC law, with some possible exceptions. If the constitutional tribunal adjudicates that the accession treaty (which means in fact the law of the Union) is not in conformity with the provisions of the constitution, the ratification is not permissible unless the indicated provisions are amended according to the procedure laid down in Article 235. We cannot also exclude the possibility of an adjudication *ex post* on the constitutionality of the accession treaty, as the constitutional tribunal was clearly vested with the power to examine the conformity of international agreements to the constitution (Article 188, subpara. 1). This would, however, put Poland in the position of either amending the constitution or renegotiating the agreement.

The admissibility of checking the constitutionality of statutes granting consent to the ratification of an agreement, which will delegate competence under Article 90 of the constitution, must be discussed separately for both the procedures provided for in the constitution. If the consent is granted by a statute, adjudication on the issue of constitutionality of the authorising statute is within the scope of the tribunal's cognition. Even though there is a special procedure for passing it, with even stricter majorities required than for amending the constitution, it is still a statute within the meaning of Article 188. The president may, before signing the statute, apply the procedure of preventive check and request the constitutional tribunal to adjudicate on its conformity to the constitution. Article 191 of the constitution lists the other subjects, including 50 deputies or 30 senators, that may apply to the tribunal for examining the constitutionality of an already passed statute granting consent. If this statute is found to be not in conformity with the constitution, before ratification the constitution would have to be amended following the procedure set in Article 235, which was envisaged solely for this purpose. If, however, the consent for ratification of an accession agreement was granted in a referendum, then examination of the constitutionality of such consent would be outside the scope of competence of the constitutional tribunal.

The law of an 'international organisation' in the hierarchy of sources of law

To start with, we should make some comments about the binding character of secondary legislation of the European Union in the Polish legal order, especially in view of the fact that the constitution of 1997 provides quite a comprehensive regulation on the relations between international and domestic law. It states that ratified international agreements, after promulgation in the *State Gazette*, constitute part of the domestic legal order (Article 91, para. 1) and are sources of universally binding law of the Republic of Poland (Article 87, para. 1), that the agreements ratified upon prior consent granted by statute have precedence over statutes (Article 91, para. 2) and that international agreements may be referred for adjudication upon their constitutionality (Article 133, para. 2, and Article 188, subpara. 1). The accession treaty will belong to the category of special agreements, referred to in Article 90 of the constitution, which undergo special ratification procedure. This will ascribe to it, and thereby to all provisions of the agreements constituting primary Community legislation, the same characteristics that Article 91 ascribes to international agreements ratified by virtue of a statute: they become part of domestic legal order, are directly applicable and have precedence over ordinary statutes. Thus, it will be possible to question a statute before the constitutional tribunal as not being in conformity with the treaties included in primary Community legislation (Article 188, subpara. 2 of the constitution).

The direct effect of sources of secondary Community legislation in domestic legal order results from the provisions of the founding treaties, that is, primary Community legislation. As a result of ratification of these treaties, Poland will be bound by all their provisions, as they were formulated in these treaties and as they were developed in the jurisprudence of the European Court of Justice. Therefore ratification will be tantamount to Poland's submission to all norms and principles in force in the Community legal order and the relation between this order and national laws of the Member States. The principles set in the 1997 Constitution are not independent in nature, they are just a confirmation of the obligations which will result from Poland's membership in the European Union and allow us to place these obligations against the background of domestic legal order.[17]

The already quoted Article 91, para. 3, does not specify what laws of an international organisation (or its institutions) will be applicable in the domestic legal order, leaving it to the adequate international agreements – the founding treaties in the case of the European Union – to settle the matter. These treaties state in what forms Community legislation may be enacted and what degree of imperativeness they have, and Polish law has no influence whatsoever on these matters. Article 91, para. 3, confirms therefore that it is the treaty norms and not constitutional ones that are of fundamental importance here.

Article 91, para. 3, places secondary Community legislation in a very high position as compared to the norms of domestic law, granting it precedence even over statutes. It is in the same position as international agreements ratified by virtue of an authorising statute (Article 91, para. 2). Precedence over statutes implies also precedence over all norms below the statutory level, which are part of the domestic legal order. Constitutional provisions do not determine who is responsible for protection and enforcement of secondary Community legislation, but this issue has already been widely discussed in European jurisprudence.[18] As we know, this jurisprudence is consistent in stating that the domestic courts, having the duty to apply directly the norms of Community law, also have the right and duty to refuse to apply a domestic norm if it is in conflict with the Community law. In such a case, a domestic court does not decide on the abrogation of the norm of domestic law, but simply refuses to apply it to the extent to which it is bound to give precedence to the norm of Community law.

It is also problematic whether Community law may be subjected for check of its conformity to the Polish constitution. From the constitution of 2 April 1997 we cannot infer that secondary Community law takes precedence not only over statutes, but also the constitution itself. In particular, if Article 91, para. 3, mentions the precedence of secondary Community legislation over statutes, this is not enough to extend such precedence to include the constitution too. Additionally, once we decide that the constitution must have precedence over the treaties being primary sources of Community law, it naturally must have precedence over the norms of secondary legislation. From a procedural point of view, the question is who and with what effect is to declare this precedence of the constitution in case of conflict with norms of secondary Community legislation. No national organ can abrogate the norms of this law, it is only Community organs, and particularly ECJ, that have such power. Yet this court only controls the conformity of secondary legislation to primary legislation, it is not competent to evaluate the relation between the Community law and national laws. Consequently, only national courts can examine the compatibility of Community law and the constitution of a given state.[19]

In our reflections on the future position and weight of secondary Community legislation in relation to the Polish legal order, the focus should be shifted from problems of examining the constitutionality of such legislation to the practical issues of teaching Polish judges to apply this law. In particular, they need to learn about the methods of applying Community law, about refusal to apply national laws in case when they are in conflict with Community law and submitting to ECJ questions regarding the interpretation of Community law.[20]

Legal dilemma: a need for a constitutional amendment before the EU membership?

A turning point in the development of the Union will be its institutional reform. Although it is designed to enable effective functioning of the extended Union, it may change the 'rules of play' considerably, which will create a new situation also for the new members. Resolution of the dilemma whether and to what extent the Polish constitution needs adjusting to the requirements of European law depends largely on the institutional and legal structure of the European Union as of the day of admission of Poland to its members. One can hardly expect changes in the fundamental principles of the Union, such as direct application of Community law in member states or common commercial or monetary policy. However, it is hard to predict the development of the institution of European citizenship or the participation of national parliaments in the decision-making process of the Union, and these are matters regulated in the constitution.

We cannot blame the authors of the constitution for limiting themselves to include therein a 'European clause' and a provision in the direct applicability of the laws enacted by an international organisation to the Polish legal order, not taking account of the need to adjust other provisions to European law. We may of course agree with the point of view of Community institutions and declare amending the constitution superfluous once Community law has supremacy over the national laws, including constitutions. It seems, however, that the emotional attachment to the constitutional principle stating that the constitution is the supreme law of the Republic of Poland (Article 8) will make the Polish authorities amend the constitution rather than tolerate the application of Community law substantially different from its provisions.

Election law displays the most apparent discrepancies between the constitution and the future European obligations. Article 62, para. 1, of the constitution provides that Polish citizens have the right to vote, inter alia, for representatives to the organs of local self-government. Since the Maastricht Treaty, active, and sometimes even passive, electoral rights in local elections in the member states are granted not only to citizens of the state in which such organs operate, but also to nationals of other member states, provided that they reside on the territory where the election is taking place (Article 19 of the Treaty establishing the European Community). It seems that the provision of Article 62, para. 1, in its present tenor would make it impossible for citizens of EU member states to vote in local elections in Poland, because it defines the group of subjects having *exclusive* rights to participate in elections. Other persons are excluded from this group. Though this provision establishes a subjective right of the citizen, but at the same time limits the rights of other persons. This interpretation prevails among the Polish constitutionalists.[21] If we were to accept that constitutional provisions granting some rights to Polish citizens, grant them *eo ipso* to citizens of other states as well (or foreigns national in general), the constitutional division between human and civil rights would be meaningless.[22] But we probably should expect an amendment of Article 62, para. 1, in the part pertaining to local elections.

The Polish constitution does not provide the grounds for covering the citizens of the Union staying within the territory of a third country, where the member state of which he is a citizen does not have its mission, with consular or diplomatic protection, granted under Article 20 of the Treaty establishing the European Community. It states only that 'a Polish citizen, during a stay abroad, has the right to protection by the Polish State'. It seems that because of the marginal practical importance of this provision of Community law and the emphasis on the beneficiaries of the protection and not exclusive character of the right this provision of the constitution will remain unchanged.

We should also be aware of the potential conflict between the Community law on migration and foreign nationals and the constitutional provision stating that 'anyone whose Polish origin has been confirmed in accordance with statute, may settle permanently in Poland' (Article 52, para. 5). In practice, this right is exercised by citizens of the Community of Independent States, deported from Poland during the Second World War. Under the Treaty of Amsterdam, the competence in the field of migration policy, which traditionally belonged to the national authorities, has been transferred to the Community. It seems that candidate countries will have to implement the *acquis communautaire* as a whole and they may not expect that their national particularities, following from the duty of national solidarity, will be taken into account.

Another example, also from the field of constitutional regulations: the possibility of Poland joining the Economic and Monetary Union would require a change in Article 227, para. 1, of the constitution, which grants to the National Bank of Poland an exclusive right to issue money, and formulate and implement monetary policy. But as countries enter the monetary and currency union, they renounce their independence in money matters. From then on, it is no longer central banks that decide upon the amount of money on the market, but the European Central Bank (on the other hand, it functions in the European System of Central Banks).

Although the next issue does not concern any conflict between Community and constitutional provisions, it imposes a difficult obligation on the state authorities. In accordance with Article 2 of the constitution, the Republic of Poland is a democratic state of law. This should mean that upon joining the Union, all its legal provisions in force that Poland accepted in the accession agreement should be available in official translations into Polish. Otherwise, it is hard to imagine that a country can be considered a democratic state of law if the citizens are unable to familiarise themselves with the contents of law that binds him. In spite of the efforts undertaken so far by the Office of the Committee for European Integration, this task seems unimaginable.

Another postulate is to involve – upon accession to the Union – the Sejm and the senate to a greater extent in the internal decision-making process concerning integration matters. It is consistent with the tradition of development of European integration, expressed, inter alia, in Protocol No. 9 of the Treaty of Amsterdam on the role of national parliaments in the European Union. This postulate follows from the tendency to limit the deficit of democratic legitimacy in the Union – because the law-making functions in the Communities are still exercised mainly by the Council, an institution composed of representatives of the executive power of the member states – and from the need to compensate the national parliaments for the loss of competence that will occur upon Poland's accession to EU.[23] Similarly, we should consider creating the conditions for including the organs of local self-government in the decision-making process regarding integration matters. According to the principle of subsidiarity, applicable both in the European Union and the Polish constitutional order, there must be a mechanism for exerting comprehensive social influence on the decision-making processes in EU institutions to ensure adequate articulation of national interests, as perceived in various fields and on various planes of social life.

Conflicting constitutional values: stability of the constitution or completeness of regulations?

The conflict in the title may seem only superficial. The application of European provisions in the Polish legal system is ensured by their supremacy, established by the Union institutions, over national laws, thus the Community may exercise its power *praeter legem fundamentalem*. It does not infringe the constitution directly, but diminishes the authority of the constitutional legislator and the prestige of the constitution itself. The competing supra-national power might also diminish the political, doctrinal, ideological and philosophical weight of the basic constitutional principles (especially that of Article 8 stating that the constitution is the supreme law of the Republic).[24] The possible amendments of the constitution would aim at preserving the authority of the state and its fundamental law.

There are several arguments against amending the constitution. First, by definition it is an inflexible act, with a more difficult procedure of amendments. In order to amend the constitution of 1997, a bill must be submitted by at least one-fifth of the statutory number of deputies, the Senate or the president and adopted by the Sejm by a majority of two-thirds of the votes in the presence of at least half of the statutory number of deputies and by the senate by an absolute majority with the same quorum. Moreover, the bill to amend the provisions regarding the state system, rights and freedoms, or to amend the constitution may be submitted for a confirmatory referendum upon application of its promoters. But, as we have already mentioned, the statute authorising the president to ratify the accession treaty is subject to even stricter requirements (adoption by a majority of two-thirds of votes in the senate). Thus we may expect that the constitutional amendments resulting from accession to the Union would not meet obstacles in the parliament. This remark is only true of the parliamentary procedure for granting authorisation, but it is highly probable that this procedure will be applied, at least in the second instance because of lack of quorum. Taking into account the fact that so far there has been more support for Poland's membership in the Union among the political and parliamentary elite than among the general public, and if the ratification is the result of a referendum, we can expect positive results of voting on amending the constitution from both chambers.

The main problem is not in the legal sphere, but in the political and psychological ones. The Polish constitution of 1997 required long and intense conceptual work, and then painstaking and delicate parliamentary negotiations in order to be adopted. The relatively good effect, achieved with such great difficulty, should be – in the opinion of some political forces – protected against destruction. Any bill to amend the constitution would probably result in a flood of other amendments being made 'along the way'. The above threat to the constitution is smaller than another, even more likely one. During the campaign preceding the constitutional referendum in 1997, one of the main arguments the right-wing parties used against the constitution was the threat to state sovereignty posed by the 'European clause'. Even today, objections to 'selling our sovereignty' are still raised in relation to some parties responsible for the negotiations with the Union and other pro-European parties. It is conceivable that there will be opposition against the constitutional amendments resulting from the accession and also against some pro-European provisions that are already in force.[25] Taking into account the fact that the constitution was accepted in the referendum by a slim majority of votes, and that its opponents were opting for diametrically different systemic solutions (such as strong presidency, a classical *invocatio Dei*, absolute prohibition of abortion), we can imagine there would be a strong possibility of attempts to amend the constitution radically. Their success would of course depend on the distribution of forces in parliament. After the experiences preceding the adoption of the constitution in 1997, we can expect angry and heated arguments between the opponents and supporters of the European option, be it either in connection with the decision on ratifying the accession treaty or on the occasion of making appropriate amendments in the constitution.

Therefore, the usefulness of making constitutional amendments to include the Community norms will require careful attention. As we have already mentioned, the scope of the necessary amendments will only be known at the time of accession, due to the continuous development of an *acquis communautaire*. And only then will we be able to choose between the risk of possibly shaking the authority of the constitution and that of radically infringing the body of its provisions.

Conclusions

The process of democratic and market transformations in Poland since 1989 has been accompanied by an awareness of the political elite that their aim should be full integration with the European structures.[26] One of the expressions of this was the regulation, contained in the constitution of 1997, on delegating part of the competence of state authorities to an international organisation, as well as the procedure for such delegation and its consequences for the domestic legal order. As the membership negotiations with the European Union and the process of adjusting Polish law to the *acquis communautaire* are progressing, there is growing awareness of the necessity to make further constitutional amendments. This contradicts the assumption, made in 1997, of ensuring the greatest possible stability of the Polish constitution, since any attempt to amend it involves the threat of starting the debate on the state system anew.

Within the legal framework set by the constitution of 1997, Poland will be able to join the European Union and participate in the process of European integration. The fact that Poland adopted its fundamental law so late did not prevent political conflict from surrounding the constitution, to which its basically pro-integration character has contributed. However, it has had no negative impact on the process of democratic transformations and the Polish society has obtained legal instruments facilitating the implementation of strategic goals of state policy.

The high formal requirements for obtaining consent for ratification of the accession treaty mean that Poland's membership in the Union is dependent on very strong social or political – it seems that in this case they can be considered separately – support. It is a paradox of the constitution of 1997 that it provides better protection against delegation of competence of state authorities to an international organisation than for the constitutional rights and freedoms of an individual. This is a result of certain old and recent national experiences which are referred to in the constitution, and particularly in its preamble.

Notes

1 Although according to results of a poll conducted by Centrum Badania Opinii Społecznej in November 2002, there are still over twice as many supporters of accession as its opponents (60 per cent of the respondents were in favour of accession, 23 per cent were against, with 17 per cent being undecided), in comparison with a poll conducted in June 1994, the percentage of votes 'for' fell by 15 per cent, and the percentage of votes 'against' rose by 17 per cent.

2 What I am referring to here is particularly the condition, envisaged in the Treaty of Rome, that the countries acceding to the Union be democratic states and the so-called first Copenhagen criterion – see further in the chapter. Cf. E. W. Böckenförde, *Państwo prawa w jednoczącej się Europie* (The State of Law in Uniting Europe) (Warsaw, Instytut Studiów Politycznych Polskiej Akademii Nauk, 2000).

3 According to this paradox, the hare (or Achilles, in another version) can never catch up with the turtle because any time the hare covers half of the distance, the turtle also moves forward by a certain bit. This way, the difference between the fragments of the path covered by both of them is never absolute.

4 A. Szczerbiak, *Decline and Stabilisation: Changing Patterns of Support of European Union Membership in Poland. Report* (Warsaw, Instytut Spraw Publicznych, 2000); Polish version: 'Spadek i stabilizacja. Zmieniające się wzorce poparcia dla członkostwa Polski w Unii Europejskiej', in E. Popławska (ed.), *Konstytucja dla rozszerzającej się Europy* (Constitution for the Expanding Europe) (Warsaw, Instytut Spraw Publicznych, 2000).

5 M. Wyrzykowski, 'Klauzula europejska RP – zagrożenie dla suwerenności? Suwerenność a klauzula ratyfikacyjna członkostwa Polski w Unii Europejskiej' (Does the European Clause of the Constitution Undermine Polish Sovereignty? Sovereignty and the Ratification Procedure of Polish Membership of the EU), in W. Czapliński, I. Lipowicz, M. Wyrzykowski and T. Skoczny (eds.), *Suwerenność i integracja europejska. Materiały pokonferencyjne* (Sovereignty and European Integration: Conference Materials) (Warsaw, Centrum Europejskie Uniwersytetu Warszawskiego, 1999).

6 P. Winczorek, 'Kilka uwag w kwestii dostosowania Konstytucji Rzeczypospolitej

Polskiej z dn. 2.04.1997 r. do wymogów prawa europejskiego' (Some Remarks on the Issue of Harmonising the 2nd April 1997 Constitution of the Republic of Poland with the Requirements of European Law), in E. Popławska, *Konstytucja.*

7 It will be discussed in more detail later on.

8 Cf. the shorthand record of the session of editorial sub-commission for general matters and provisions introducing the constitution of the Constitutional Commission of the National Assembly of 23 October 1996, p. 150.

9 K. Działocha, 'Artykuł 90' and 'Artykuł 91' in: L. Garlicki (ed.), *Kostytucja Rzeczypospolitej Polskiej. Komentarz,* vol. I (Constitution of the Republic of Poland': Commentary, Vol. I) (Warsaw, Wydawnictwo Sejmowe, 1999).

10 ECJ judgement in case 6/64 *Costa v. ENEL.*

11 W. Czapliński, 'L'intégration européenne dans la Constitution polonaise de 1997', *Revue du Marché commun et de l'Union européenne,* 436 (2000); K. Wójtowicz, 'Konstytucja Rzeczypospolitej Polskiej a członkostwo w Unii Europejskiej' (Constitution of the Republic of Poland and Membership of the European Union) in E. Popławska (ed.), *Konstytucja.*

12 Such as the Italian Constitutional Tribunal, the Spanish Constitutional Tribunal and the German Federal Constitutional Tribunal.

13 Cf. the practices of the French Constitutional Council, which worked out a constitutionality test of international obligations of the state in the shape of a question about whether such obligations 'do not infringe the fundamental conditions for the exercise of national sovereignty': J.-L. Quermonne, 'L'adaptation de l'Etat à l'integration européenne', *Revue du droit public en France et a l'etranger,* 5–6 (1998), 1405–1420. R. Arnold, 'Koncepcje suwerenności w konstytucjach państw członkowskich Unii Europejskiej a integracja europejska' (Sovereignty Concepts in the EU Member States' Constitutions and European Integration), in W. Czapliński, I. Lipowicz, M. Wyrzykowski and T. Skoczny (eds.), *Suwerenność* (Sovereignty).

14 K. Wójtowicz, 'Konstytucja Rzeczypospolitej Polskiej a członkostwo w Unii Europejskiej' (The Constitution of the Republic of Poland), in: E. Popławska (ed.), *Konstytucja.*

15 J. Jaskiernia, 'Konstytucyjnoprawne aspekty i społeczno-polityczny kontekst przyszłego traktatu akcesyjnego Rzeczypospolitej Polskiej do Unii Europejskiej' (The Constitutional Law Aspects and the Social Political Context of the Future Accession Treaty of the Republic of Poland to the European Union), in E. Popławska (ed.), *Konstytucja.*

16 Cf. L. Kolarska-Bobińska (ed.), *Polska Eurodebata* (Warsaw, Instytut Spraw Publicznych, 1999); similar poll results are quoted by J. Jaskiernia, 'Być sobą' w dobie integracji europejskiej (Społeczno-polityczne uwarunkowania procesu samorealizacji w okresie radykalnych zmian otoczenia społecznego)', *The Pecularity of Man,* 4 (1999); and A. Szczerbiak, *Decline and Stabilisation.*

17 L. Garlicki, 'Członkostwo Polski w Unii Europejskiej a sądy' (Poland's membership in the EU and courts), in E. Popławska (ed.), *Konstytucja.*

18 Z. Brodecki, 'Acquis communautaire: pojęcie nieznane Konstytucji RP' (Acquis Communantaire: An Unknown Concept in the Polish Constitution), in C. Mik (ed.), *Konstytucja Rzeczypospolitej Polskiej z 1997 roku a członkostwo w Unii Europejskiej* (Toruń, TNOiK, 1999).

19 K. Wójtowicz, 'Konstytucja Rzeczypospolitej Polskiej a członkostwo' (The Constitution of the Republic of Poland).

20 E. Łętowska, 'Sędziowie wobec prawa europejskiego' (Judges in the Face of European Law) and A. Wyrozumska, 'Członkostwo w Unii Europejskiej a sądy polskie' (Membership of the EU and Polish Courts) both in: E. Popławska (ed.), *Konstytucja*.

21 J. Barcz, 'Struktura przyszłego traktatu akcesyjnego RP do UE wraz z wybranymi odniesieniami konstytucyjnoprawnym' (Structure of the Future Accession Treaty of the Republic of Poland to the EU with selected Constitutional Law References); J. Jaskiernia, 'Konstytucyjnoprawne aspekty i społeczno-polityczny kontekst przyszłego traktatu akcesyjnego Rzeczypospolitej Polskiej do Unii Europejskiej' (The Constitutional Law Aspects and the Social Political Context); M. Kruk, 'Konstytucja Rzeczypospolitej Polskiej a członkostwo w Unii Europejskiej: kilka uwag' (Constitution of the Republic of Poland and Membership of the EU: Some Remarks); R. Wieruszewski, 'Obywatele RP – przyszli obywatele Unii Europejskiej' (Polish Citizens as Future Citizens of the EU), all in E. Popławska (ed.), *Konstytucja*.

22 P. Winczorek, 'Kilka uwag w kwestii dostosowania Konstytucji' (Some Remarks on the Issue of Harmonising the 2nd April 1997 Constitution).

23 It is estimated that with the current state of *acquis communautaire* the parliament of a state accessing to the Union loses approximately 60 per cent of the legislative 'substance'. Cf. J. Barcz, 'Struktura przyszłego traktatu akcesyjnego' (Structure of the Future Accession Treaty).

24 J. Galster, 'Konstytucyjnoprawne bariery przystąpienia Polski do Unii Europejskiej' (Constitutional Law Barriers to Poland's Accession to the European Union), in C. Mik (ed.), *Polska w Unii Europejskiej. Perspektywy, warunki, szanse i zagrożenia* (Poland in the European Union: Perspectives, Conditions, Chances, Threats) (Toruń, TNOiK, 1997).

25 J. Menkes, 'Konstytucja, suwerenność, integracja – spóźniona (?) polemika' (Constitution, Sovereignty, Integration: Late (?) Polemics), in C. Mik (ed.), *Konstytucja Rzeczypospolitej Polskiej z 1997 roku*. (Constitution of the Republic of Poland of 1997).

26 Cf. E. Popławska (ed.), *The National Constitutions and European Integration* (Warsaw, Scholar, 1995).

5

Key socio-economic problems of the European Union's Eastern enlargement seen from an Estonian perspective

Janno Reiljan and Kristina Toming

The economic rationale of enlargement

In seeking membership in the European Union, Central and Eastern European countries (CEECs) have been motivated by the belief that such membership would almost automatically ensure further progress in their complicated transformation process and their further independent political and economic development. If they remained outside the EU, they feared they would be among the least economically developed countries. The history of the world economy shows us that income differentials between industrialised countries and the less developed world have actually increased since the 1980s. Looking at the developments in world trade, we see that, in practice, poor countries are unable to develop mutual trading relationships, as the goods they produce are similar. So they are competitors rather than partners in the world economy. Trade relations with developed countries are often inhibited by trade barriers that prevent developing countries from exporting their main production and thus reduce their opportunity of living on their own incomes. At the same time, the type of domestic competition pressures that would force firms and employees to re-adjust in the developed world are often absent in developing countries.

Integration with well-developed market economies will open to the CEECs a common and balanced economic space that they urgently need for their development. For developing countries the competitive pressures coming from developed states is compensated for by free access to their markets with great purchasing power. Trade relations between the EU and the transformation countries have developed asymmetrically: while production from the EU has free access to the CEECs, the increasingly intensifying competitive pressure has not been balanced by opening the EU markets to the CEECs' production (especially to their agricultural products) to a comparable extent. This is of great concern to the CEE economies because it leaves around 50 per cent of their export potential behind the EU's trade barriers.

On the other hand, the European Union's decision to enlarge to the East is based on the understanding that, in order to ensure the world's political and economic stability, the CEECs should be integrated into the world economy as quickly as possible. This would provide economic growth and prevent problems caused by declining political stability and decreasing social security. If the CEECs were left in the so-called 'grey zone' between the democratic Western world and unstable Russia, their political and economic instability would be a permanent threat to the CEECs and could jeopardise the development of the whole of Europe. The EU, as a next-door neighbour and main partner in economic co-operation, is especially interested in the stability of the CEECs' domestic and foreign policies as well as in their economic stability.

The second half of the twentieth century was marked by the the triumphal progress of globalisation. The deepening of economic integration and the tightening of political co-operation have been recognised as a substantial impulse for intensified economic development. With this in mind, Estonia should also find its way into the world economy through integration. Estonia has followed a policy of integration into the EU and has made considerable progress.

Estonia has quickly left behind several stages in the integration process with the EU (see the appendix to this chapter), wishing to complete the preparations and become a fully fledged member of the EU in 2004. This demands great efforts from Estonia but still depends mainly on the readiness of the EU for Eastern enlargement. In view of the situation that emerged by the middle of 2002, it can be predicted that the first new members will most certainly participate in the elections for the European Parliament in 2004.

The main argument of this chapter is that the EU's Eastern enlargement involves a set of complicated and controversial problems. That is why the associated CEECs are still, in the economic sense, as far from integration as most developing countries despite all the institutional ties, sophisticated political declarations and signed agreements. We are still searching for solutions to the key socio-economic problems in the transformation countries' integration into the EU.

First, we will examine the opportunities and dangers involved in integration with the European Union with an emphasis on the Estonian economy. Secondly, we will discuss the EU accession criteria and preconditions, as well as their role in the process of transforming Estonia's economy. Thirdly, we will analyse in greater detail the changes in foreign trade related to Estonian integration with the EU as this aspect of foreign trade is especially important for a small country with an open economy like Estonia. Finally, some conclusions will be drawn.

The opportunities and dangers of the European Union's Eastern enlargement

Integration with the EU will give the CEECs new economic perspectives and incentives for development. At the same time, we must not overlook the dangers caused by the radical changes in the economic and political environment in the course of preparations for joining the EU. A clear overview of both the opportunities and dangers is urgently needed, not only for assessing the usefulness of the integration process, but also for making use of the possibilities and finding ways to avoid the pitfalls. EU Eastern enlargement is a process with controversial effects on different social, economic and regional interest groups. As a result there are many different opinions held about enlargement.

Considering the impact of EU Eastern enlargement on the CEECs, one has to bear in mind that they are already involved in the EU's integration process through association agreements which provide a method of co-operation prior to becoming fully-fledged members. Full membership of the EU would enable the CEECs to substantially improve their economic position in comparison with the association agreement. The economic benefits resulting from the EU Eastern enlargement are comparable to those that accompanied the introduction of the single internal market of the EU.[1]

From the perspective of Estonia, the main enlargement-related benefits and dangers are linked to the removal of EU trade barriers, an increase in Estonia's attractiveness to foreign investors, financial support from EU regional development and other funds, and the free movement of persons/labour.

One of the most important benefits of EU accession for the CEECs is their access to the large EU market. The trade barriers of the EU (import tariffs and quota restrictions, anti-dumping measures etc.) established in order to protect the so-called sensitive sectors of the member states affect a large proportion of the CEECs' export potential. If the Union opened its internal market fully to the CEECs' agricultural production, employment and incomes in the new member states would rise. At the same time, however, such a change would entail a number of adaptation problems for many enterprises and regions in the current member states and thereby diminish the desire of relevant interest groups to involve new member states.

For Estonia, the creation and provision of equal competition conditions and development perspectives in agriculture and the food processing industry is potentially of the greatest importance. Problems related to agricultural production and markets have been the main source of disagreement in the negotiations between the EU and membership candidates; one has to admit that solutions are still missing despite the fact that the negotiations should have been concluded by the end of 2002. The candidate countries insist on getting conditions for their farmers that are identical to those in the current member states (i.e. direct support at the same level as received by the current member states). However, the EU offered the candidates initially only 25 per cent of the current level of direct support, intending to increase it gradually to 100 per cent by 2013. Furthermore, agricultural production quotas and reference levels that the EU offers to the candidates depend on the production levels of recent years and do not take into account the difficulties the candidates have been facing in their transformation process. For instance, Estonia's agricultural production has dropped by more than 50 per cent since the early 1990s, mainly due to changes in agricultural structures, the breakdown of the country's traditional export markets, and the inflow of heavily subsidised imports. As a result, the production quotas offered to Estonia are far below potential output.

Another aspect of the free movement of goods is the adoption of the EU common external policy of trade with third countries. As it means an increase in Estonia's domestic protection level, import prices are expected to rise. According to economic theory, this will lead to a trade diversion with its welfare-reducing effect. This mainly concerns trade with Russia, the Ukraine and the US. The integration-related trade issues will be discussed in greater detail in the last section of this chapter.

Another benefit expected from EU membership is an increase in the attractiveness of Estonia for foreign investors in connection with market enlargement. In several branches in Estonia (first of all in agriculture and the food processing industry), investors can count on small markets with a low purchasing power because these have not been opened by free trade agreements. If the EU markets were opened, Estonia's local factors of production (surplus of arable land and inland waters, a relatively unpolluted environment, a low tax level and low wages combined with highly skilled labour) would become increasingly more attractive to foreign investors.

Table 5.1 shows the annual foreign direct investment (FDI) inflows to Estonia between 1993 and 2001. The proportion of inward FDI to the gross domestic product (GDP) has been between 3.5 per cent (in 1996) and 11 per cent (in 1998). According to a survey by Estonian economic experts, the estimated annual FDI inflow to Estonia for the period 2002–4 is 6.8 per cent of the GDP. With accession to the EU, this figure is anticipated to rise to 7.7 per cent in 2005–10. In the case of non-accession, however, the share of inward FDI to the GDP would fall to 4.6 per cent.[2]

Table 5.1   *Annual FDI inflows to Estonia, 1993–2001*

Year	FDI inflow (million EEK)	FDI inflow/GDP (per cent)
1993	2153	9.9
1994	2819	9.4
1995	2313	5.7
1996	1814	3.5
1997	3694	5.8
1998	8071	11.0
1999	4448	5.8
2000	6645	7.6
2001	9430	9.8

Source: Bank of Estonia 2002.

It has been claimed by some interest groups in Estonia that the enormous inflow of foreign capital would lead to excessive growth of foreign influence in the country's politics as well as to the alienation of land. At the same time, foreign capital owners are not allowed to either participate in politics or work in civil service. This measure is meant to curb their power and normalise the system of political relations. Therefore, the inflow of foreign capital to Estonia in amounts that would make Estonia economically dependent is very unlikely.

As EU members, the CEECs will contribute to the EU budget proportionally to their GDPs. The relatively low levels of the candidate countries' GDPs indicate that they would benefit from support from the EU Structural Funds and Cohesion Fund. Considerable sums are allocated to less developed regions from the EU's central budget so that they could catch up with other regions. The new member states will most probably be net recipients from the EU budget.

In the period 1992–2001, Estonia received in total 11.6 billion EEK as foreign aid, 40 per cent of which came through EU development aid programmes (PHARE, ISPA, SAPARD). As the prospect of joining the EU approaches, the amount of foreign aid has been increasing in recent years. In 2001, Estonia received 1.73 billion EEK as foreign aid (about 2 per cent of the GDP), 75 per cent of which came from the EU programmes. The annual pre-accession aid of PHARE 2000+, ISPA and SAPARD programmes will also amount to 0.9–1.1 billion EEK in the next few years.[3]

With accession to the EU, this pre-accession aid will be replaced with transfers from the Structural Funds and Cohesion Fund. If the EU treated the candidates on a par with the present member states, the annual EU support to Estonia would constitute about 12 billion EEK, which is equivalent to 15 per cent of the GDP.[4] However, transfers from the EU Structural Funds for the CEECs are limited to a maximum of 4 per cent of the national GDP for the period 2000–6.[5] Hence in the case of Estonia the maximum amount received would be around 4 billion EEK per year.

The allocation of structural fund money is conditional on the existence of appropriate projects and co-funding by the recipient country. Therefore, as pointed out by Mayhew, it is probable that in the first years of accession the CEECs will absorb only very low amounts of funds.[6] Furthermore, the support is likely to be lower for poorer new member states with lower capacity of administering the support and assuring co-funding. Estonia expects to get about 10.5 billion EEK of structural funds money in 2004–6 (more than 3 per cent of GDP annually). However, this estimate is optimistic, considering the experience of the present member states.[7] Additionally, an IMF study estimates that the transfers from the EU budget (related to agricultural, structural, and internal policies, and to cover collection costs) to Estonia's budget will constitute about 2.7 per cent of GDP annually in 2004–6.[8] The study assumes that Estonia will join the EU in 2004 and that real GDP will grow by 5.5 per cent per year after accession. The same study also indicates that after accession, EU-related spending will more than double between 2003 and 2004 (from 2.2 per cent to 5.1 per cent of the GDP). This reflects transfers based on Gross National Product (GNP) and Value Added Tax (VAT) to the EU budget (1.1 per cent of GDP annually in 2004–6), the required co-financing of EU-supported projects, and spending on the environment and the transport sectors. The last two categories together are expected to amount to 4 per cent of GDP per year in 2004–6. Nevertheless, as can be seen from these projections, Estonia is expected to be a net recipient from the EU budget.

However, support transfers from the EU should also be used efficiently, otherwise development can be inhibited. Integration with the EU calls for new institutions (technical delivery, staff training, etc.) to be established within a short period of time. EU politicians and officials have often referred to Estonia's insufficient administrative capacity, which is also illustrated by the low quality of the projects applying for aid from the EU Structural Funds.

Large investments are needed in both the private and public sector in order to meet EU standards for environment, health, worker and consumer protection. The estimated amount of investments is 40 billion EEK in total, of which 26 billion is for the environment alone. In agriculture and the food processing industry, the estimated need in investments is around 8 billion EEK. In the public sector, transfers from the EU Structural Funds will help finance the necessary investments, although here too some problems arise. The local authorities are insufficiently funded to be capable of co-financing and have difficulties in finding properly qualified project managers. In the private sector (especially in agriculture), the huge investment requirements force many small enterprises to close down.

It is generally expected that the main economic benefit of EU integration will be an accelerated convergence to the EU's income level as increased FDI will sustain a higher real growth rate. The most obvious example here is Ireland, where the income gap was narrowed by 11 percentage points in 24 years; it was eliminated by 1998, and by 2000, Ireland's income level was already 16 per cent above the EU average. This process was supported by very large FDI inflows (more than 20 per cent of the GDP in 2000 alone).[9] Furthermore, many studies find empirical support for a direct correlation between EU aid and convergence of per capita income of poorer regions to the EU average.[10] However, it must be recognised that real convergence is not an automatic process, as suggested by the experience of Greece, and to a lesser extent, that of Spain and Portugal.

According to some Estonian economic experts, the annual real GDP growth rate is expected to be around 4.6 per cent in 2002–4. The experts believe that EU membership can accelerate the growth rate to 5.6 per cent in 2005–10, while the non-accession scenario would mean a mere 4 per cent annual GDP growth. Similar tendencies are anticipated for real wages in Estonia: with accession, the real wage would grow by 5.5 per cent per year in 2005–10, otherwise only 4 per cent.[11]

The issue of labour migration is also much discussed. Accession to the EU would open a large market for Estonian labour. A survey made among economic experts shows that the expected unemployment rate is expected to fall to 11.6 per cent in 2002–4. Accession to the EU is expected to lower the unemployment rate to 10.1 per cent in 2005–10. The non-accession scenario, on the contrary, would mean an increase in unemployment compared to the estimates for 2002–4 (to 11.7 per cent).[12] By way of comparison: according to the Estonian Statistical Office, the unemployment rate in Estonia was 12.2 per cent in 1999, 13.6 per cent in 2000, and 12.6 in 2001.

Export of surplus labour would bring knowhow and income transfers back to Estonia. The structure of the Estonian education system does not correspond to the needs of the Estonian economy, producing well-qualified specialists for whom the Estonian economy fails to offer commensurate jobs. Integration with the EU would offer them an opportunity to use their qualifications in a better way. However, only Ireland, Sweden, Denmark and the Netherlands are willing to grant free movement to labour from Estonia immediately after accession. The United Kingdom will be ready for that only two years after the CEECs' accession to the EU, and the other member states require a transition period of up to seven years before granting free movement to labour from the new member states.

The main argument of EU sceptics in Estonia has been that accession-induced migration will cause an outflow of qualified labour instead of unqualified labour who mainly suffer from unemployment. Estonia is not willing to spend money on educating specialists for Western countries, but at the same time, very large wage differences between Estonia and the EU (the average wage in Estonia constituting only 20 per cent of the EU average) and constrained possibilities motivate Estonian labour to move abroad. In many cases they accept jobs in the EU requiring considerably lower qualifications, which most probably will lead to a deterioration of skills. Yet, the mobility of labour is relatively low even within the EU itself (less than 2 per cent of the labour force). Furthermore, considering the situation with the Estonian labour market, standard of living, societal development, and Estonia's geographical location, the trade unions in Estonia believe that the massive outflow of Estonian labour to the current member states or a significant inflow of EU labour to Estonia are quite improbable. According to the Estonian Ministry of Social Affairs, in 2000 only about five thousand Estonian citizens worked in the EU member countries, and no larger emigration is foreseen in the future. Although the public opinion polls show that about 14 per cent of the population in Estonia are ready to accept jobs in the other member states after joining the EU, they often lack prerequisites for that.[13] Therefore they hold that applying restrictions on the free movement of labour would discriminate against Estonian labour. However, they also recognise the need for considerable efforts by the state to stabilise the Estonian labour market.[14]

Although most of the EU enlargement-related studies suggest that integration with the EU would bring about macroeconomic stabilisation in the transition countries, it is believed in Estonia that accession would lead to higher inflation, at least for a short term. On the one hand, in the case of joining the EU domestic producers in Estonia can ask for a higher price for their products since the average price level in the EU is higher than in Estonia. On the other hand, the increased expenditures on the environment, and health and worker protection force producers to raise their prices. Economic experts estimate that in 2002–4 the average consumer price index (CPI) will be 4.3 per cent per year (compared to 4 per cent in 2000), and Estonia's accession would stabilise it in 2005–10. In case of non-accession, they believe, the CPI would fall to 3.7 per cent.[15]

Hence, comparison of the opportunities and dangers makes it clear that integration with the EU does not mean that enlargement will automatically solve all the socio-economic problems of the transition countries. But in our opinion, the positive aspects far outweigh the negative ones. This fact is very well understood by the CEECs that have submitted their applications for EU membership. So the EU is facing a historical challenge that is very difficult to manage both politically and economically.

Criteria and conditions for EU accession and their role in the process of transforming Estonia's economy

The EU is a voluntary union of states that is kept together and enhanced by recognising the same goals. These socio-economic goals include stable economic growth, environmentally sustainable economic development, a low level of unemployment, high living standards, and a high level of social security.[16] However, we would argue here that the goals are so strict that even some economically well-developed current members of the EU are experiencing difficulties in meeting these targets. For example, in the EU, one-tenth of the working-age population is affected by long-term unemployment, and no efficient tools have been found yet to lower the unemployment rate.

The CEECs are far behind the average level of the current member states with regard to achieving the EU's socio-economic objectives, and this situation will persist in the near future. The nature of these objectives should receive public recognition in the candidate countries, which should be expressed by purposeful and efficient work towards achieving them. Thus a general precondition for the CEECs' accession to the EU is expressed in the claim 'first transformation, then integration' and embodied in the Copenhagen criteria discussed in chapters 1 and 2 of this book. The criteria require:

- building up a democratic rule of law;
- transition to market economy;
- ability to cope with the competitive pressure of the EU internal market.

The associated countries have indeed been quite successful in their transformation from a centrally controlled economy to a free market economy. At the same time, we believe that it is not sufficient to adopt laws similar to those in force in the EU and establish institutions in order to build up a democratic rule of law. The rule of law and efficient work of institutions guaranteeing legal protection should be assured. On the technical side (adopting the laws and institutions that meet the EU requirements), the process of establishing the rule of law is making quick progress in the CEECs. As a matter of fact, the adoption of a civilised society's code of laws may often produce negative results because the development of social relations and consciousness are lagging behind, and because of inertia. The drastic rise in crime that has taken place along with the process of democratisation in the CEECs vividly demonstrates the inefficiency of the legal protection systems and insufficient law-abiding by citizens. Unfortunately, no radical shift can be expected. Assessments about the extent to which the establishment of the democratic rule of law is in compliance with the criteria may turn out to be problematic and lead to long discussions.

The EU requires the liberalisation of both product and financial markets, the privatisation of most state-owned enterprises and the establishment of an institutional and legal framework that would ensure the security of a market economy. Estonia has actually met the target set for liberalisation and privatisation. The condition requiring a secure institutional and legal framework should explain to everyone that an advanced market economy (i.e., market economy in the EU context) could not be created without establishing the rule of law.

We would argue, however, that the requirement to cope with the competitive pressure of the EU's internal market is controversial. The competitiveness of the CEECs' enterprises substantially depends on the obligations imposed on them according to the main EU rules. The need for large investments to meet EU requirements for environment, worker, health and consumer protection has been already mentioned above. Additionally, the daily operating expenses of firms are expected to increase. If the CEECs followed the claim about social and wage dumping a bit more rigorously (i.e. the requirement to approximate their costs to the EU level), then the CEECs' production would inevitably become uncompetitive and the CEECs would not fulfil the criteria of integration. For example, Estonia spends around 7 per cent of its GDP on pensions, against the 12 per cent of the respective GDPs spent by the EU member states on average. Moreover, the wages and salaries paid to people in the EU are several times higher than those earned in Estonia by holders of similar jobs.

Even though the CEECs make maximum efforts, assessments of the extent to which the accession criteria have been met by the candidate countries depend more on the political position (sense of perspective) and willingness of the member states to bear the economic costs and political risks associated with eastern enlargement. Hence, considering the controversial nature of the EU accession conditions, we believe that the common political will of the member states to take the plunge should be pointed out as the first precondition for the EU's eastern enlargement.

The direct neighbours of the CEECs will benefit most from EU enlargement (at least in the early stages of integration) and so they are the catalysts in the enlargement process. But even they are reluctant to accept the migration of cheap labour from the CEECs. The member states far away in the south and west will benefit less and are therefore also less interested in eastern enlargement. So there exists a source of conflict, which makes decision making difficult. The

eastern enlargement of the EU also involves other contradictions. The net
contributors to the EU budget are afraid that enlargement may bring about an
increase in their tax burden, and try to initiate reforms aimed at reducing aid
programmes. The net recipients from the EU budget in turn fear possible real-
locations of aid transfers and try to keep their shares intact.

On Estonia's side, during the pre-accession period the country must overcome its own inward-looking attitude which:

- idealises the weakness of the state and the passiveness of state institutions in
  regulating and directing society;
- does not see the positive impact of social stability on economic development;
- denies the need to develop the feeling of solidarity while constructing a
  civilised democratic society;
- causes legal nihilism as the imperfect and controversial laws and inefficient
  work of law-enforcement bodies are exploited;
- underestimates the importance of ethical norms and reduces their effect on
  regulation in society.

This kind of society does not measure up to the EU's socio-economic objectives
even if the institutions are formally established as in the EU, and all laws are
adopted. Therefore, we argue that the second precondition of the EU eastern
enlargement for candidate countries is to reach a level of social maturity necessary for integration into the EU.

In Estonia's experience, it can be said that such social maturity is developing
slowly and controversially in the direction needed for integration with the EU.
Some very powerful economic groups in the transition countries would like to
maintain the business environment that used to be free of responsibility. This
would enable them to benefit economically in the short run at the expense of
exhausting the society's resources for long-term development. These groups
have managed to provoke a remarkable degree of distrust among the population
– people have doubts about whether it is rational to join the EU.

According to public opinion polls, only 30 per cent of the Estonian population were in favour of joining the EU in May 2001. In October 1999 this
percentage was slightly higher – 38 per cent. By May 2002, the share of EU
supporters had risen to 38 per cent again. At the same time, the share of
EU opponents also rose from 15 per cent in 2001 to 32 per cent.[17] As the
Estonian government has always supported and worked for EU accession, it is
commonly believed in Estonia that the popularity of joining the EU mainly
depends on the rating of the government.

If the preconditions are fulfilled, the CEECs have to meet the main requirement with respect to their accession to the EU – the capacity of the candidate
states to take over the accumulated obligations and commitments agreed under
the treaties and legislation of the EC – *acquis communautaire*.[18] The introduction of the *acquis communautaire* does not mean only enforcing the code of laws
and other norms of the EU. It also means that all the co-operation principles

that are requested in order to deepen monetary, economic and political union should be followed.[19]

However, the co-operation principles that have been worked out to integrate the developed countries are often not feasible for the much less prosperous CEECs. We would say that the CEECs are (economically) able to adopt the set of rules to ensure that the single market would function without disruption, but there are problems that are difficult to solve in this field – first of all with regard to the above-mentioned law-abidingness of citizens and managers of enterprises as well as in the area of ensuring the efficient operation of legal protection among governmental and communal (or regional) bodies.

Furthermore, even some current member states have difficulties with meeting the criteria of monetary union, not to mention the economically and socially unstable CEECs. It is most difficult to keep inflation and interest rates in the required boundaries if the will or skills (or even both like in Estonia) of economic regulation are absent or weak.

We argue that the toughest task for the CEECs is still to ensure that social security, health and environment protection would meet the required EU standards. Health, environment and consumer protection and a high level of security are formulated as some of the main principles of the EU. In order to avoid the difficulty of defining what is meant by 'high level', the White Paper specifies the nature of this claim: with the help of environmental and consumer protection and the equalisation of the standards of workers' social security – avoiding so-called social dumping – the member states' enterprises (products) should be ensured to have equal competition conditions. If they raised these costs to the level of rich states (it is not possible to lower these standards in a well-developed society like the EU) the enterprises in the CEECs would become uncompetitive.

A low level of economic development that does not enable the CEECs to fulfil several main principles of the functioning of the EU will create a more serious problem. The economic lag of the CEECs is still too big. Table 5.2 shows the data characterising the GDP per capita in 1998 in nominal terms and in purchasing power parity (PPP).

GDP (in PPP) per capita in the richest CEEC – Slovenia – makes up 69 per cent of the EU average, whereas in Bulgaria the same figure is only 22 per cent. The poorest state in the EU – Greece – is more than three times more affluent than Poland and Estonia and over twice as affluent as the Czech Republic, according to the nominal income level. With respect to PPP, the Czech Republic lags behind Greece by about 15 per cent and Estonia lags behind Greece by about 50 per cent. If the CEECs, which have much lower income levels than the current member states, are required to meet the EU's social and environmental standards (a demand of harmonisation), they are required to boost their economic development level noticeably nearer to the average level in the EU as a prerequisite of integration. Such a requirement would make accession to the EU impossible for most of the CEECs. At the same time, the member states have

Table 5.2   *The level of incomes in CEECs and selected EU countries, 1998*

Country (nominal USD)	GDP per capita (PPP USD)	GDP per capita (EU–15 =100)	Index
Finland	24,280	20,847	101.4
Ireland	18,710	21,482	105.7
Greece	11,740	13,943	66.7
Portugal	10,670	14,701	73.0
Slovenia	9,780	14,293	69
Czech Republic	5,150	12,362	60
Hungary	4,510	10,232	49
Slovakia	3,700	9,699	47
Poland	3,910	7,619	36
Estonia	3,360	7,682	37
Latvia	2,420	5,728	28
Lithuania	2,540	6,436	31
Bulgaria	1,220	4,809	22
Romania	1,360	5,648	28

Sources: World Bank, World Human Development Report 2000, pp. 157–158, 202–203; Eurostat database, 2001.

no desire to commit themselves to excessive obligations in the realm of development aid.

We would argue that in EU eastern enlargement, the EU should lay down compromise criteria for measuring the implementation of the EU's social principles. They would equalise competition pressures (share of social costs in the GDP) on the enterprises in different countries instead of the absolute level of competition conditions. We would suggest that instead of raising social security, health service, environment protection etc. to the same level as in the EU, it should be agreed that the share of respective expenditures (in GDP) should meet the EU average level.

Changes in Estonia's foreign trade due to integration with the EU

EU membership will become one of the key factors in the Estonian economy. Accession-related implementation of the *acquis* of the Union also includes the adoption of trade-related principles of the EU, such as external trade policy (defined by the EU as the Common Commercial Policy) and the free movement of goods, services, people and capital within the EU (i.e. the single market). Estonia also has to harmonise its policies with other EU policies such as competition policy, Common Agricultural Policy (CAP), coal and steel policy, etc. For Estonia, a small open economy, the changes in its foreign trade situation will have an important impact on the whole economy.

In order to ensure the economic development of the CEECs (including Estonia), the integration with the internal market of the EU is vitally important.

This implies a removal of the external economic barriers (customs tariffs, quotas) from trade between the EU and the CEECs. Western politicians and economic researchers have publicly admitted that the CEECs' free market access to the EU would mean an imminent collapse of the so-called sensitive (non-competitive) branches of the EU.[20] However, the influence of the interest groups representing these branches is so strong in the EU that a radical breakthrough is quite unlikely.

The EU is naturally keen to promote its own enterprises where they are more efficient than those of their competitors in the CEECs. In the association agreements with the CEECs, it was negotiated that trade barriers would be removed from these products in ten years. The EU's agriculture, foodstuffs, textile, steel and coal industries as well as some branches of the chemicals industry are not competitive on the world economy arena, and often even in relation to the CEECs. The output of such industries can penetrate the world market only thanks to the help of export or producer subsidies. It is the production of these industries that constitutes the main export potential of the CEECs to the EU, but the EU has not agreed to include the development of equal competition conditions (i.e. removal of trade restrictions) into the association agreement with the CEECs with regard to these products. At the same time, the CEECs have been directed to remove their import restrictions and governmental support in these fields. Estonia imposed this kind of imbalance by not applying tariffs on imports from the EU countries, thus destroying its competitive branches in favour of its competitors from the EU. As a result, in 1998, Estonia's trade deficit amounted to more than 27 per cent of GDP, which mainly stemmed from trade with the EU (the share of the EU in exports and imports were 66.7 per cent and 67 per cent, respectively, and the trade deficit with the EU constituted about 70 per cent of the total trade deficit). The trade deficit dropped to 17.9 per cent of the GDP in 2001, and this mainly resulted from trade with the CIS (the share of the CIS in Estonian exports and imports was 4.5 per cent and 11 per cent, respectively, in 2001). The respective shares of the EU were 69.4 per cent and 56.4 per cent, showing a relative increase in exports with respect to imports (trade with the EU still remained in deficit). However, competition conditions have remained unequal. If we compare the producer support level in Estonia with that of the EU, we can see a substantial gap in the competition conditions. The producer support estimate (PSE) in 2000 was 38 per cent of the production costs in the EU, and only 10 per cent in Estonia.[21]

As mentioned above, accession to the EU would mean free access to the EU-wide market for Estonian agricultural and food industry products. Other Estonian products have been free to enter the EU market, therefore the change in the trading system will not affect exports of non-agricultural and non-food products. So far exports to the EU market of agricultural products and processed food have been restricted by tariffs and quotas, although the EU imposed preferential quotas (i.e. within the quota, the tariffs are lower than most-favoured-nation-based (MFN) tariffs or no tariffs are imposed) on

Estonian products. The importance of removing EU trade barriers was vividly demonstrated after July 2001, when the EU relaxed restrictions on Estonian products. Then the share of Estonian agricultural exports to the EU increased from 27.5 per cent in 2001 to 29.8 per cent in the first half of 2002. However, although the new preferential trade conditions implied extended quotas and lower tariffs for many products, only the exports of milk powder and butter covered and exceeded the quotas.

In July 2002, the EU lifted all tariffs and extended quotas on Estonian agricultural goods. As a result, however, no significant immediate increase in exports to the EU actually followed. Many Estonian exporters claimed that this was due to the administrative incapability of the European Commission which kept the actual quotas smaller than promised.[22]

Another reason for the low responsiveness of exports was obviously the fact that in many cases Estonian products do not yet meet the strict product standards of the EU. In the EU, all firms in the food-processing industry have to ensure that the production process, rooms, equipment, etc. do not pose risks to the life and health of people, animals and plants. Only for small firms serving the domestic market are some concessions made (for example, as regards the availability of different rooms for separate stages of production), but these firms likewise have to ensure that people, animals and plants are not endangered. Such requirements are essential, and according to the Estonian Food Law, all firms in the food processing industry have to meet these criteria as of 1 January 2003 at the latest.

Meanwhile, Estonian firms are making sizeable investments in order to meet these requirements. At the end of 2001, only 11 Estonian milk-processing firms (from the total of 384) and 27 fish-processing firms (from the total of 109) had a certificate that allowed them to sell their products on EU markets. No meat-processing firms (from the total of 219) have so far been able to meet the EU requirements and obtain a certificate allowing them to export products to beneficial EU markets.[23] In the case of EU membership, again, not only the possibility of exporting to the EU but also the permission to sell in the domestic market will depend on how well EU health standards are met. Unfortunately, many Estonian firms are unable to do this with their own resources. One possibility (and this is economically quite reasonable) is to let less efficient and unsuccessful firms go bankrupt or exit the market and allow those that are more efficient to gain additional demand. This is also supported by the fact that, for example, in the dairy industry, all the milk produced by Estonian farmers could be processed by a mere three to five firms. However, we have to consider the possible social problems as the exit of many firms from the market can lead to growing unemployment, especially in the regions whose unemployment rate is already high.

According to the estimates of the Estonian Ministry of Agriculture, by 2003 there will only be 25 milk-processing firms and 96 meat-processing firms remaining in Estonia which meet the EU standards and requirements. This requires about 700 million EEK in further investments to be made in the milk-processing industry and 1.2 billion EEK in the meat-processing industry.[24]

There is another point we cannot overlook. If Estonia becomes a member of the EU, all its trading partners will have to treat Estonia in the same way that they treat the rest of the EU. At the moment, Russia imposes tariffs on Estonian imports that are two times higher than MFN tariffs. This is reflected in the low share of Russia in Estonian exports (only 2.7 per cent in 2001). When Estonia becomes a member of the EU and Russia has not lowered tariffs on Estonian goods by then, EU membership will ensure that Estonian exports to Russia will face tariffs twice as low as current tariffs. Although the Russian market is very unstable and insolvent, it will still remain an important export market for Estonian producers.

Additionally, joining the EU means that the EU can no longer subsidise its agricultural and processed food exports to Estonia. However, it was already in July 2002, long before the formal accession date, that the EU ended its export subsidies for trade with Estonia. This means that the artificially created compet-itive advantage that EU products had enjoyed so far on the Estonian market was lost. On the one hand, the abolition of subsidies makes imports from the EU more expensive. On the other hand, Estonian non-supported farmers and producers can exploit their comparative advantage and need not compete with cheap EU products. However, here it is important to mention that Estonian products will be granted EU subsidies when exported to third countries as long as they meet the EU product standards. The removal of subsidies to EU prod-ucts sold in Estonia and the application of the export subsidies used by the EU on external markets would certainly benefit Estonian agricultural producers. Hence the adoption of the EU principles would also improve Estonian produc-ers' competitive ability in foreign markets, making the competition conditions with the present EU members more balanced.

On the imports side, accession to the EU would also mean a significant change in the level of protectionism as Estonia would have to give up its highly liberal foreign trade policy and adopt the common external tariffs and non-tariff barriers of the EU (import quotas, technical standards, etc.). Furthermore, Estonia will have to harmonise its trade agreements with third countries within the system of EU trade agreements.

Estonia will have to impose 10,794 different EU tariffs on trade with third countries. Adoption of the EU tariffs implies a significant increase in tariffs on imports from third countries in Estonia: based on Estonia's import shares, the average tariff for agricultural products is expected to rise to more than 10 per cent, compared with the current average tariff level of 0.57 per cent. The highest EU tariffs are applied to agricultural products.[25] Although Estonia introduced low tariffs on agricultural imports in January 2000 from those countries with whom Estonia does not have trade agreements, most agricultural trade remained free of tariffs.[26] The reason for this is the significant trade diversion that occurred as a result. Imports from third countries decreased almost immediately, while imports from the EU and other free trade partners (mostly CEECs) increased considerably. In 2001, over 60 per cent of food imports came from the EU (compared to 58 per cent in 1998). The share of countries with no trade agreements was nearly zero in 2001 (18 per cent in 1998), the only exceptions being poultry and condensed milk and cream, in which the share of the US was relatively high. Hence, in the case of most agricultural products, the adoption of EU tariffs cannot affect a large share of imports.

However, as an EU member, Estonia will have to harmonise its trade agreements with those of the EU. Estonia has concluded free trade agreements with the EU, all the CEECs except Romania, the EFTA countries, the Faeroe Islands, Turkey, and the Ukraine. As the European Council decided in Seville that the European Union was determined to conclude the negotiations with all candidate countries, free trade with the CEECs will remain after Estonia has joined the EU. In addition, as the EU practises free trade with the EFTA and the Faeroe Islands as well, and the share of Turkey in Estonia's trade is very small, the only problematic issue here is the free trade agreement (FTA) between Estonia and the Ukraine. This agreement will have to be given up as the EU has no intention of granting preferential trade conditions to the Ukraine. For Estonia, the Ukraine is a very important trade partner in steel products: about 40 per cent of its imported steel products originate from the Ukraine. The EU imposes quotas on steel imports from the Ukraine, but these quotas are very small. If the steel quotas on imports from the Ukraine are still in place in the EU when Estonia becomes a member, integration will lead to the complete diversion of steel imports from the Ukraine to the EU producers. The price can be expected to rise more than two-fold.[27] Although the quality of EU steel products is usually higher than that of Ukrainian products, such a rise in prices may harm Estonian industry which uses steel products as an intermediate input.

As a result of change in the import regime, imports from third countries will become more expensive, leading to a shift in demand towards imports from the EU. However, as discussed above, food imports from the EU will also become more costly after the export subsidies are removed. This results, under normal conditions, in an overall increase in import prices and a shift from imported goods to domestic products that compete with imports. But the adoption of the EU administrative prices predetermined by the CAP will likewise bring about an increase in the price level of domestically produced goods. Thus, consumers will be discriminated against by two types of measures. The beneficiaries of this development will be Estonian producers, who will get higher prices for their products. The question is whether their gains will outweigh the losses suffered by Estonian consumers. Furthermore, the tariff revenue will be collected by the EU, and not by the individual member states.

There is quite a large number of studies exploring the impact of Estonia's accession to the EU on trade in agricultural products and processed food.[28] The studies concerning the price effects in the agricultural sector stemming from the adoption of the common external EU tariff and the abolition of subsidies on EU exports to Estonia indicate that the price effects will actually be smaller than initially feared. Even though the EU common external tariff for agricultural products is in most cases higher than Estonian tariffs, Estonia imports quite a few agricultural products from third countries. Additionally, the import share of other free trade agreement partners due to join the EU at the same time as Estonia (i.e. the CEECs) is high. Besides the common external tariff, the abolition of the EU export subsidies can have a considerable impact on Estonian imports. Especially acute is the problem in the case of sugar, 99 per cent of which is currently imported from the EU. Sugar prices will increase almost 2.5 times; but it will not be possible to substitute the imports with cheaper domestic sugar, because no domestic production exists. In the case of other agricultural products, the effect is rather insignificant both when implementing the common external tariff and when abolishing the EU export subsidies. Even though the price of imported goods can increase slightly, imports can be substituted with domestic products, which means that, with the exception of sugar, there will be no sudden price increases due to the change in the trade regime after the EU accession. However, as the need to invest in EU product standards increases, more significant increases are expected in the prices of domestic agricultural products and processed food.

Based on Toming's study of the joint impact of EU trade measures and administrative prices on the market for agricultural products and processed food using a partial equilibrium framework, price increases are expected to be considerable if the application of EU administrative prices is taken into account.[29] Toming's calculations indicate price increases of 40 per cent, 10 per cent and 30 per cent, respectively, for poultry, wheat and rye. However, the rise in the prices of beef, milk products, sugar and rice is expected to be much more considerable: 2-fold, 3-fold, 2.4-fold, and 2-fold, respectively. In the case of the first two product categories, this is mainly due to the adoption of EU administrative prices. As Estonia does not produce sugar or rice, the price increase stems from an increase in import prices. Only the price of pork is expected to go down after accession to the EU. As a result, a net fall in economic welfare is expected in Estonia, ranging from 0.7 per cent to 1.4 per cent of the GDP.

Yet, the positive effects on the exports side can compensate for the economic loss induced by import price increases. However, the EU does not intend to pay direct subsidies to CEEC farmers on a par with the current member states within the first ten years of membership, and the production quotas for the CEECs will also be smaller than required by the candidates. This means that the losses induced by the accession-related price increases in Estonia will be entirely borne by consumers.

Conclusions

Accession to the EU is not only beneficial to the CEECs but it is also the only possibility for substantially accelerating the socio-economic growth rates and preventing economic and social deterioration. The enlargement of the EU is not a zero-sum game. In the long term both partners would gain. The benefits of the CEECs are more apparent as they are fast and direct, while the benefits of the current member states will become apparent more slowly and indirectly. In the EU there are both 'winners and losers' who either gain or lose from eastward enlargement. Consequently, the EU's enlargement to the East depends in general on the political will of the member states, their ability to overcome the frictions among themselves and their willingness to render aid to the CEECs.

It is not an easy task for the CEE transition countries to meet the accession criteria (rule of law, a functioning market economy and sufficient competitive ability). A variety of different subjective approaches are possible for measuring the readiness for EU membership of the candidates; therefore the assessment will depend substantially more on the political will of the member states than objectively on the level achieved by the prospective candidate states.

The direct adoption of the *acquis* by the CEECs is not possible because their economy is not yet able to bear the costs of the tight social security, health services and environmental protection standards. At the same time, the EU will certainly not abandon the principle of providing equal competition conditions for all member states. The eastern enlargement of the EU would be possible if trade-off criteria could be elaborated that would equalise the competition pressure.

Until now, mainly political convergence of the EU and the CEECs has taken place. No vast differences of interests have appeared in this area and integration has deepened quickly. It is far more complicated to reach a breakthrough in economic integration that is so vitally important for the CEEC. In economic terms, the CEECs are better prepared for eastern enlargement than the EU. The schedule for eastern enlargement will mainly depend on the readiness of the EU to open its sensitive (non-competitive) sectors to market competition.

The rapid deepening of integration is the EU's priority but this is likely to complicate eastern enlargement. The CEECs are unable to fulfil all the requirements (e.g., those of monetary union) even in the long term. Accession to the EU will take place through many stages. Accession can be realised only if all the partners reach an agreement about the whole process from beginning to end and if it is assured that switching from one form of integration to another will continue in accordance with the conventional criteria.

To sum up, accession to the EU will involve radical changes in many social and economic areas. Considerable changes will also occur in Estonian foreign trade. Estonia will have to give up its highly liberal foreign trade policy and adopt the EU's external trade policy. It will also have to implement the principles of the single market. This will open the large and wealthy market of the EU to Estonian exports, but prior to that, Estonian products need to meet the strict EU product standards. It is feared that the implementation of external tariffs, non-tariff barriers and the trade agreements system of the EU may bring along rising prices in the Estonian market. However, in most cases, the estimated price increases are not as significant as initially expected. One has to admit that even though these developments will obviously benefit Estonian producers, consumers will definitely be worse-off.

Appendix: the most important dates in Estonia's integration with the EU

27 August 1991: diplomatic relations between the EU and Estonia are established.

11 May 1992: the Trade and Economic Co-operation Agreement between the EU and Estonia is concluded; it enters into force on 1 March 1993.

June 1993: the EU decides to conclude free trade agreements with the Baltic states at the Copenhagen summit.

7 December 1993: the Estonian government sets up a committee to deal with the problems concerning potential integration into the EU.

18 June 1994: Estonia and the EU sign a Free Trade Agreement in Brussels; it enters into force on 1 January 1995.

15 December 1994: the negotiations between the EU and the Baltic states are opened in order to prepare the association agreement (European agreement).

January 1995: the Free Trade Agreement between the EU and Estonia comes into force, enabling preparations for the association agreement (European agreement) between the EU and Estonia to be started.

12 June 1995: the association agreement (European agreement) between the EU and Estonia is signed in Luxembourg, it enters into force on 1 February 1998.

1 August 1995: the Estonian parliament ratifies the European agreement.

24 November 1995: the Estonian government presents its formal application for membership of the EU in Brussels.

April 1996: the Commission issues a questionnaire to the candidate states in order to assess the preparation of the CEEC for accession to the EU.

July 1996: Estonia submits its reply to the Commission (a 1,500-page document), that deals with 23 areas that are present in the EU's White Paper.

12–13 December 1997: at the European Council's summit in Luxembourg Estonia together with Slovenia, the Czech Republic, Hungary and Poland are asked to open accession negotiations with the EU.

30–31 March 1998: the comparative analysis (analytical examination of the *acquis*) of Estonian and EU laws (screening) that releases the accession negotiations is started.

10 November 1998: on the grounds of an intermediary report of the European Commission the decision is made to start accession negotiations with Estonia.

August 2002: the negotiations between Estonia and the EU are concluded in 28 chapters out of 31; the negotiations on the chapters on agriculture and the budget are still in progress.

12–13 December 2002: at the European Council's summit in Copenhagen, the negotiations on the final financial package for the applicant countries are concluded; the negotiations on all chapters are completed.

19 February 2003: the European Commission approves the accession of ten new members: the Czech Republic, Cyprus, Estonia, Hungary, Latvia, Lithuania, Malta, Poland, Slovak Republic and Slovenia.

16 April 2003: after ratification by the European Parliament and the European Council, the Accession Treaty is signed.

14 September 2003: on an accession referendum, Estonians say 'yes' to the EU with 66.8 per cent of voters in favour; now the Accession Treaty needs to be formally ratified by all existing and acceding member states.

1 May 2004: the Accession Treaty comes into effect, Estonia becomes a full member of the EU.

Notes

1 See P. Cecchini, M. Catinat and A. Jacquemin, *The European Challenge 1992: The Benefits of a Single Market* (Aldershot, Wildwood House, 1988) and H.-J. Wagener und H. Fritz, 'Die Erweiterung der Europäischen Union und die Transformation in Mittel- und Osteuropa', *Policy Paper* (Frankfurt/Oder, 1996), p. 7.
2 Riigikogu EL teabekeskuse küsitlus 2002 (European Union Information Secretariat to the State Chancellery of the Republic of Estonia. The Enquiry, 2002).
3 Estonian Ministry of Finance 2002, database.
4 P. Palk, *Euroopa ühendamise lugu* (*The Story of the Unification of Europe*) (Tallinn, Tuum, 1999).
5 Enlargement argumentaire. DG for Economic and Financial Affairs, European Commission, *Enlargement Paper* 5 (2001), p. 53.
6 A. Mayhew, 'The Negotiating Position of the European Union on Agriculture, the Structural Funds and the EU Budget', *SEI Working Paper*, 52 (2002), p. 15.
7 See Mayhew, 'The Negotiating Position of the European Union', p. 25.
8 'The Baltics: Medium-Term Fiscal Issues Related to EU and NATO Accession', *IMF Country Report*, 02/7 (January 2002), p. 39.
9 'The Baltics', pp. 31–32.
10 See 'The Baltics' and the studies cited there.
11 Riigikogu EL teabekeskuse küsitlus 2002.
12 Riigikogu EL teabekeskuse küsitlus 2002.
13 V. Made, 'Elu- ja töötingimused Euroopa Liidus' (Living and Working Conditions in the European Union), *ELIS Bulletin*, 13 (January 2002): www.elis.ee.
14 J. Angerjärv, 'Madal palk ajab ajud Eestist' (Low Salary Leads to Brain Drain from Estonia), *Äripäev* (20 June 2001).
15 Riigikogu EL teabekeskuse küsitlus 2002.
16 White Paper, 'Preparation of the Associated Countries of Central and Eastern Europe for integration into the Internal Market of the Union' COM(95)163 (May 1995).
17 Elanikkonna monitooringu aruanne (Population Monitoring Report) (2001, 2002): www.elis.ee/est/index.html.
18 H. Wallace and W. Wallace, *Policy-Making in the European Union* (3rd edn) (Oxford, Oxford University Press, 1996), p. 52.
19 White Paper, 'Preparation'.
20 E.g., J. Rollo, 'Economic Aspects of EU Enlargement to the East', in M. Maresceau (ed.), *Enlarging the European Union: Relations between the EU and Central and Eastern Europe* (London and New York, Longman, 1997).
21 OECD database, 2002: www.oecd.org.
22 K. Traks, 'Segadus ekspordikvootidega' (Confusion Over Export Quotas), *Äripäev* (7 August 2002).
23 Põllumajandussaadusi töötleva tööstuse ülevaade 2001 (Overview of the Food

Processing Industry in Estonia, 2001). Estonian Ministry of Agriculture, 2002: www.agri.ee.

24 T. Saron, 'The Impact of Technical Measures on Estonian Dairy and Meat Industry', MBA project, University of Tartu, 2002, Appendices 11–14 (in Estonian).

25 *Trade Policy Review: European Union*, WTO, WT/TRP/S/30, 1997.

26 On imports of other goods to Estonia no tariffs are applied. However, as the EU applies tariffs on non-agricultural products as well, the adoption of the EU common external tariff will certainly affect the import of goods not considered here.

27 K. Toming, 'Euroopa Liiduga liitumise väliskaubanduspoliitiline mõju Eesti majandusele' (The Trade Political Impact for the Estonian Economy on Joining the European Union), MA thesis, University of Tartu, 2002, p. 98 (in Estonian).

28 U. Varblane, K. Toming, H. Riik., R. Selliov and D. Tamm, 'Võimalikud majanduspoliitilised instrumendid Eesti põllumajandussaaduste ja – toodete hindade ühtlustamiseks Euroopa Liidu hindadega' (Possible Instruments of Economic Policy for Harmonisation of Prices of Estonian Agricultural Products with EU Prices) (Tallinn, Estonian Ministry of Agriculture, 2001) and U. Varblane, R. Selliov, H. Riik, D. Tamm, 'Eesti põllumajandustoodete hinnaerinevused Eestis ja Euroopa Liidus: prognoosid liitumiseelseks ja –järgnevaks perioodiks' (The Price Differences of Agricultural Products in Estonia and the EU: Estimates for the Periods before and after Accession) (Tallinn, Estonian Ministry of Foreign Affairs, 2002).

29 K. Toming, 'Estonia's Accession to the EU: What Effect on Agricultural Imports and Economic Welfare', *Kiel Institute of World Economics Advanced Studies Working Paper,* 382 (Kiel, 2002), 32 pp.

6

Challenges to Bulgarian monetary policy on its way to United Europe

Gallina Andronova Vincelette

The transformation of the financial sectors of Central and Eastern Europe (CEE) from systems with fairly rudimentary and fragile financial sectors to competitive and relatively stable ones is among the most fundamental reforms undertaken in the post-communist environment. The reforms are driven by the principle that well-functioning financial systems accelerate long-run economic growth by allocating funds to more productive investments.[1] This empirically and theoretically supported insight has intensified calls for financial sector reforms that improve the operational environment of the sector to promote economic development and growth in the region.[2] Fundamental changes such as bank privatisation, deregulation and liberalisation of the financial sector take place in these countries in order to facilitate the process.

Parallel to this systemic change in the financial sector, which is part of the larger processes of post-communist transformation described elsewhere in this book, runs one more trend of the development of these countries, i.e. their accession to the European Union (EU) structures. The Copenhagen criteria, discussed in chapter 1, do not require compliance with the Economic and Monetary Union (EMU) convergence criteria, but they require the candidates to have functioning market economies. The CEE countries have to adjust their monetary regimes and undertake different initiatives to harmonise their financial environment with that of the EU. They are also, arguably, expected to join the EMU soon after joining the EU, even though not all existing member states are members of the EMU. The need to join EMU flows from the need to take on board all the objectives of the Union, including the goal of economic and monetary union. Setting aside the larger discussion of the legality of such a requirement in the light of the opt-outs of Denmark, the UK and Sweden, this chapter will discuss how prospective membership of EMU affects the design of the currently developing institutional environment in the CEE financial sector.

At first glance, there is a duality of the financial sector development objective in CEE. On the one hand, an independent market-based system of financial intermediation is aimed at as part of the transformation process, and on the other, monetary unification with the rest of Europe seems the most likely direction for the CEE countries once they join the EU. In fact, as this chapter argues, the two might well be complementary objectives calling for the emergence of credible institutions and regulation to ensure the shift from the socialist financial order to a market-based one and allow successful integration with the EU financial structures.

Looking at recent financial reforms in the accession countries one must wonder how the changing financial environment in CEE adapts and develops towards European enlargement. In addition, what factors determine a successful accession to the EMU? What are the optimal monetary regimes in the concrete conditions for every accession country? Finally, is joining the EMU a suitable choice for fostering economic development in the transition countries? This chapter discusses these important questions with regard to one of the accession country cases, Bulgaria.

The main objective of the chapter is to evaluate the various options for the monetary sector development for Bulgaria responding to the changes caused by the European integration process of the country. Section two introduces the context of the current monetary policy arrangement and discusses how the country came to the introduction of a currency board. Various institutional options for the monetary regime towards future EMU accession are reviewed in section three. The position of the European Central Bank (ECB) and the requirements for joining the monetary union are outlined in the section to follow. The chapter concludes with lessons, which fall within the study of financial transformation and EU enlargement, giving specific insights for a successful monetary and financial integration.

Recent transition developments in Bulgarian monetary policy

In 1996, Bulgaria entered into an economic and financial crisis, which created an enormous setback for its bid to join the EU and seemed impossible to resolve for many years to come. In the absence of financial discipline and clear ownership rights, deficits multiplied, being transferred from firms to banks through bad debts and eventually to the government budget through bailouts or monetisation. In April 1996, the Bulgarian currency started a continuous free-fall and collapsed in February 1997. The year 1996 showed almost six-fold depreciation, as the currency dropped from some 70 leva per US dollar in January to almost 500 leva per dollar at year-end. Moreover, at the beginning of 1997 this depreciation accelerated and reached unprecedented levels of about 3,000 leva per dollar in February 1997, while foreign exchange reserves dried out (see Figure 6.1). Financial intermediation was stalled because of the instability of the macroeconomic conditions in the country. Credibility in the banking system was at stake, when depositors ran to withdraw their savings or convert them into hard currency in order to retain their value. The threat of a systemic crisis brought the financial collapse of 14 out of 35 registered commercial banks in 1996.

Figure 6.1 *Monthly exchange rate (leva per US$1) and foreign exchange reserves (billion US$)*

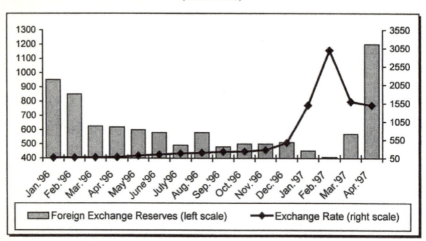

Source: Bulgarian National Bank Statistics: www.bnb.bg

The response of the Bulgarian political system to the economic instability in the country in January 1997 led to an unprecedented overthrow of the ruling socialist government. In July 1997, the caretaker government of Stefan Sofyanski supported by the international financial institutions introduced a currency board in order to produce rapid and credible anti-inflationary effects in Bulgaria. With the aim of restoring the credibility of the institution, the monetary authority committed to the principles of a currency board.[3] The adoption of a currency board in Bulgaria meant that the leva in circulation were strictly matched to the Bulgarian National Bank's (BNB) reserves, the local currency was effectively pegged to a foreign currency and the government's fiscal activity was severely restricted. The exchange rate became a nominal anchor of the stabilisation policy, while the Bulgarian central bank lost discretion over some monetary policy instruments.

With the introduction of the currency board arrangement a powerful message was extended to both the commercial banks and the government. The central bank was committed to stop pouring funds into politically driven lending and respect fiscal discipline. Moreover, the currency board arrangement restored public confidence and provided a new institutional environment for the functioning of the financial sector in the country.

The early results were positive. The currency board contributed to achieving a general macroeconomic balance by bringing both inflation and interest rate levels to single-digit numbers (see Table 6.1). The exchange rate fluctuations were terminated and the interest rate spread decreased after the introduction of the board. The commercial banks improved their capital-adequacy ratios, which improved from about 11 percent in 1996 to 26.86 percent at the end of 1997,

Table 6.1 *Selected economic and banking indicators, 1995–99*

Economic indicator	1994	1995	1996	1997	1998	1999	2000
GDP	1.8	2.9	-9.4	-5.6	4.0	2.3	5.4
Consumer prices (end-year)	121.9	32.9	310.8	578.6	0.9	6.2	11.4
Domestic credit (end-year)	37.1	18.0	216.5	93.6	-8.4	5.8	31.4
Broad money (M2, end-year)	78.0	65.4	71.0	32.8	28.5	30.3	30.3
Base interest rate[a]	72.0	34.0	180.0	6.7	5.1	4.5	4.6
Inter-bank interest rate (up to 1 month)	66.4	53.1	119.9	66.4	2.5	2.9	3.0
Deposit rate (1 month)	72.3	25.3	211.8	3.0	3.3	3.3	3.1
Lending rate (less than 1 year)	117.8	51.4	480.8	13.9	13.3	14.1	11.5
Exchange rate (annual average)[b]	0.054	0.067	0.178	1.674	1.760	1.836	2.127
Number of banks (foreign owned)	41 (0)	40 (1)	41 (3)	42 (3)	28 (7)	34 (17)	34 (22)
Asset share of state-owned banks (per cent)	na	na	na	82.2	66.0	56.4	50.5
Non-performing loans (per cent of total loans)	6.7	6.8	12.5	15.2	13.0	11.8	17.5
Domestic credit to private sector (per cent of GDP)	3.7	3.8	21.1	35.3	12.3	12.2	14.0

Source: European Bank for Reconstruction and Development, Transition Report (London, EBRD, 2000).
Notes: [a]Effective interest rate at end-month, based on the average annual yield attained at three-month government securities primary actions end of year.
[b]On 5 July 1999, the lev was re-denominated. The post-July rate is equal to 1,000 of the pre-July 1999 Leva. All data are expressed in terms of 1,000 of the pre-July 1999 leva. All data are expressed in terms of post-5 July 1999 lev.

about 23 percent in 1998, to reach levels of 41.8 at the end of 1999. Banking privatisation of the state-owned commercial banks gained momentum and foreign strategic investors started to acquire them rapidly.[4]

Several years after the introduction of the currency board in Bulgaria, it became obvious that the stabilisation measures taken in 1997 not only contributed to achieving a macroeconomic balance, but also gave impetus to the much needed market reforms. Their pace has been quick as macroeconomic stability was achieved, accompanied by low levels of inflation, stable currency, and a banking sector gradually freed from both private and state-owned loss-makers (see Table 6.1). By terminating the inflationary financing of the budget and the bailouts of commercial banks and firms, both financial discipline and fiscal responsibility were achieved.

Despite these accomplishments, an array of challenges for the development of financial intermediation in Bulgaria lie ahead in relation to its outward-looking European economic policy. Among the challenges is the board arrangement itself and its future suitability for the EMU accession. The absolute nominal exchange rate rigidity prevents the swift adjustment of prices and consequently hinders the adaptability of the real economy to monetary policy signals. In addition, the currency board presents incompatibility with the established orthodox path of EMU integration (see below).

By what means will the country phase out its currency board, given that once economic growth is restored the currency board may turn into a 'buffer' instead of an 'engine' of economic development? Searching for alternatives, this chapter investigates the question of the monetary regime strategy for Bulgaria in relation to its European integration process.

The challenge

One of the key chapters in the negotiations of Bulgaria with the EU is the economic and currency union, which translates into negotiations about the shape of the monetary and financial sector of the country. Given the EU's approach to negotiations, discussed in chapter 1, adherence to the *acquis* will determine to a great extent the institutional side of the financial environment in the country. The consequences are of an overall economic effect – from the currency, to the channels that exert influence on the real sector.

Negotiation talks and understanding are mechanism through which differences in the exchange rate regime could be overcome upon progression towards the monetary unification of Bulgaria with the rest of Europe. The existence of a currency board arrangement prevents the country from following the widely experienced in Europe three-stage path of EMU membership.[5] The problem is the incompatibility of the currency board arrangement with the second stage of monetary accession (ERM-II), where a floating exchange rate has the aim of demonstrating in a sustainable manner the convergence and stability of the accession countries towards the macroeconomic policy of the European Union. For countries with currency boards like Bulgaria, this implies a reversal to a flexible exchange rate and abrogation of the principles of the currency board. While the Bulgarian government must keep in mind a strategy, which comprises institutional viability and economic fit with the framework of the EMU, decision makers must also ensure that the overall economy operates in a self-sustainable manner. The challenge is in the potential conflict between the exchange rate based stabilisation efforts and European monetary integration, which is translated into a decision to keep the board or to abandon it and return to the float as a pre-accession monetary policy instrument.

The monetary target of the future membership of Bulgaria in the EU structures is the acceptance of the euro, as a currency unit of the country, as it has been explicitly expressed numerous times by Bulgarian policy makers.[6] Yet, such an intention does not necessarily need to be materialized even after the country becomes a full member of the EU. There is a possibility for the member states to keep their national currency and to execute domestic discretionary monetary policies by their own independent central banks or via their own currency, as in the cases of Denmark, Sweden and the UK. The EU provides flexible enough monetary framework, which raises the question about ambiguity of its criteria and the fact that existing strong currencies such as the British pound stay out of the EMU. Moreover, EU membership is not contingent upon a full EMU participation, and the member states decide independently whether to be a part of the common monetary policy or not.

Thus, the choice that Bulgaria has to make is based on two temporal decisions. On the one side, this is a choice about preserving the current monetary policy regime, and on the other, a decision about joining the EMU. In either case, however, establishing financial institutions that ensure market-based intermediation of resources need to support the development and growth of the local economy. This is the primary objective along the accession road for Bulgaria. What are the options for the country, in these talks, and what makes the decision difficult? The policy options for the monetary regime in Bulgaria are discussed in the subsections to follow.

Monetary regimes: options for Bulgaria

Keep the currency board: pros and cons

The first option, to keep the currency board arrangement, calls for no immediate policy changes. With respect to the outward looking European orientation of Bulgaria, the currency board arrangement might be considered not only an as a stabilisation measure, but also as an instrument that contributes to meeting the constraints imposed by the Maastricht Treaty. By ruling out inflationary financing of the deficit, strengthening the independence of the central bank and restricting the autonomy of monetary policy tools, the board in fact achieves what is the basis of the pre-accession requirements. Thus, in a way the currency board could be viewed as a 'transitional stage towards a monetary union', which fulfils the basic logic behind the irreversible anchoring of the European monetary policy to the exchange rate, and the introduction of a rigid exchange arrangement through the single currency.[7]

However, keeping the board after macroeconomic stability is achieved raises some legitimate concerns, spurred by the currency arrangement itself. This is, mainly, about the extent to which the economic development of the country is hurt if the board stays in place in its current shape. Currency boards are considered as one of the most expensive tools for economic stabilisation.[8] The primary reason is that the restrained monetary base holds back the potential for fast economic growth. The monetary authority is restricted to alter the exchange rate parity and respond to signals from the real sector. Instead, the currency boards allow for slow adjustment of wages and prices, which in turn harm the establishment of conditions for rapid growth of output. Conventional economic wisdom postulates that such an exposure to country-specific aggregate shocks tends to be costly precisely because of the absence of alternative monetary policy instruments.[9]

Macroeconomic data from Bulgaria somewhat support the concerns of hindered industry output by the existing exchange rate regime after achieving macroeconomic stabilisation. The main source of corporate finance in Bulgaria is the banking system, and given the improved macroeconomic environment the expectations would be for increased crediting and economic activity towards the local economy. However, the level of deposits in the banking system, for example, struggled to reach its pre-crisis levels for several years after the crisis (see Figure 6.2). In addition, the lending policy of the Bulgarian commercial banks has been quite passive after the crash of the system, regardless of the comparatively high liquidity positions in the banking sector. For instance, while the amount of reserves increased two-fold in just a year (from approximately 10 to 20 percent of total assets), credit activities have not come back to its pre-crisis point. The ratio of total loans to GDP in 1998 was at its lowest level at 20.7 percent, and in addition, loans to the private sector had severely declined (see Table 6.1). The obvious discrepancy between the relatively low levels of interest rates and inactive domestic crediting, attests to the above concerns for potentially restrained growth. Thus, even though the banking sector has been increasingly gaining credibility, public confidence and full-scale economic activity are yet to be restored in Bulgaria.

Figure 6.2   *Deposits as a per cent of GDP in Bulgaria, 1995–99*

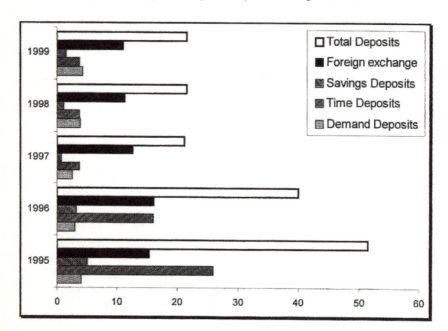

Source: E. Ulgenerk and L. Zlaoui, 'From Transition to Accession: Developing Stable and Competitive Financial Markets in Bulgaria', *World Bank Technical Paper*, 473 (2000), p. 41.

However, recent empirical work questions the rigidity of the currency boards in preventing economic development.[10] Observers have demonstrated that over the period between 1974 and 1996 countries with currency boards not only have had lower levels of inflation, but on average they also have had similar (if not higher) levels of output growth, compared to countries with other exchange rate regimes.[11] They attribute the reasons for the surprisingly high levels of economic growth in such institutional arrangements to the fact that boards were installed usually after economic and financial collapse in order to restore macroeconomic stability and trigger radical reforms. Such research results weaken one of the most frequently used arguments against the currency boards, i.e. their inability to use monetary policy through the adjustment of interest rates or the exchange rate to stimulate the growth of the real sector.

The second risk in keeping the currency board regime in place comes from the fact that the currency board arrangement is unable to fulfil the requirements for full membership in the monetary union. With a certain degree of flexibility in the monetary regimes, the countries joining the EMU may find it easier to meet simultaneously the inflation and the exchange rate criteria compared to the countries with currency boards.[12] Limiting the exchange rate flexibility with a currency board arrangement could be a possible solution for Bulgaria, however, even though it comes with a hanging condition regarding the capability of sustaining the nominally fixed exchange rate and adjusting without the discretionary power of other monetary policy regimes (see below).

The third threat to keeping the board until the potential acceptance of the country in the EMU comes from the peculiar arrangement of the operating currency board in Bulgaria, which itself is a deviation from the classical and more conservative board arrangements.[13] The Bulgarian government has a deposit at the issue department of the BNB, which can be used only for the financing of the budget deficit, or for covering the negative differences in net financing.[14] Considering that revenues from the privatisation of state-owned enterprises will be exacerbated soon, and funds from the international financial institutions are only on a conditional basis, the government might run short on revenue for its deposit account.[15] In cases of low levels of fiscal revenues, the regulation gives a certain leeway to the government to cover artificially its deficits precisely through the issue department deposits. However, using this deposit account for covering budget deficits will question the fiscal discipline, which the board implies, and create moral hazard behaviour on the part of the government, which will be damaging for the credibility of the monetary regime.

Keeping the currency board arrangement in place is related to some inevitable economic risks with an impact on the process of integration into the European structures. However, Bulgaria will need to phase out its currency board at some point in the future, and proponents of the case against the board regime claim that the sooner the better. They argue that discretionary monetary policy conducted by an independent central bank ensures a prompt response of the monetary policy to the changes in the real economy. Countries with flexible exchange rate regimes find it institutionally easier to adjust their monetary policy, precisely because they could make full use of the flexibility of the nominal exchange rate movements, interest rate management by the central banks, and full execution of intervention rules. Currency boards come with institutional restrictions because of the inflexibility of the exchange rate, pegged to the foreign exchange reserves of a country.

However, removing the board and reintroducing a floating exchange rate regime in Bulgaria brings uncertainties about the ability of the government to respect fiscal discipline without institutional regulation, i.e. the currency board. Abandoning the board will automatically abolish its main benefit, i.e. the financial stability in the country, and allow the government to find avenues for intervention. Moreover, the board was introduced a few years ago (1997), and the public still fears the potential for skyrocketing inflation and rapid exchange rate depreciation.

Another argument for having an independent central bank replace the board is regaining the lender of last resort function as well as the power of imposing minimum reserve requirements on commercial banks.[16] With the introduction of a currency board this ability of the central bank is largely limited to the extent that an orthodox currency board does not provide any help in the form of credit to commercial banks or other enterprises when they face insolvency problems. As already mentioned, however, the currency board arrangement in Bulgaria is not that of a classical board and takes care of both of these issues somewhat smoothly. The issue department of the BNB was formed to manage the excess coverage of the currency board arrangement, and in only limited occasions extend it to the commercial banks in case of severe liquidity problems. In such a way, the source of and decision to finance illiquid but sound banks is upon the discretion of the structures of the central bank. The law postulates maximum constraint on the possibility of refinancing the banking system to the extent of the value of the banking department deposits with the issue department.[17]

As per the minimum reserve requirements on commercial banks, the banking regulation does not exempt any operating commercial banks in the country from maintaining a certain level of minimum reserves. Thus, by law, the currency board in Bulgaria has retained these (even though limited) features of a classical central bank in order to prevent possibility of crisis and mitigate the fragility of the banking industry.

The euro as a legal tender

The third option for the monetary policy regime in Bulgaria is to introduce the currency of the union as a legal tender in Bulgaria at present. The advantages are centred around adopting a credible and stable (compared to the Bulgarian lev) currency, which might potentially ease the access of the country to the EMU. In addition, adopting the euro solves the inherited currency board problems of rigidity and inability to automatically adjust. The policy makers may well make the case that for the sake of having a strong and stable currency the best choice of the country would be to adopt the euro, especially given the possibility of a future acceptance in the Union. Introducing the euro as legal tender in Bulgaria diminishes the risks of currency devaluation and keeps the interest rates at low levels, providing for increased inflow of investments. That becomes beneficial in particular for the public and for investors in Bulgaria.

Criticism of this idea is twofold. By giving up the local currency, the government loses not only its monetary sovereignty, but also seigniorage.[18] Seigniorage is one of the main streams of revenue that goes to the financing of the deficit on the current account. Even the currency board arrangement earns seigniorage through the interest from its holdings of reserve-currency securities. In contrast, if a foreign currency is used as legal tender in the country, the foreign issuer collects the revenues from seigniorage.

In addition, a unilateral introduction of the euro at present as a currency in Bulgaria would not bring the intended benefits from the currency. In fact, the free movement of capital, goods, services or people comes only with membership, but not with a unilateral acceptance of the European currency.[19] Ultimately, it is a policy decision that may call for abandoning the short-run, but important, economic impact of the revenues from seigniorage versus the more medium-run access to capital markets. The trade-off on this aspect amounts to estimating the cost of lost seigniorage by the government and the benefits of euroisation.

The EU position and its accommodation

Considering the fact that the costs of abolishing the currency board regime are high, countries like Bulgaria, Estonia and Lithuania seek opportunities for monetary solutions in the process of European integration. Willingness to find an accommodating solution was expressed in the position of the European Central Bank governing body of 13 April 2000 for a flexible approach in the monetary accession process.[20] The ECB position implies that the possibility for accession to the monetary union for the countries with currency board arrangements exists. Nevertheless, before joining the EMU the candidate countries have to ensure that the following EU-defined conditions are fully met: facilitating nominal convergence, passing the market test for adequate exchange rate stability, ensuring that the counties enter with an appropriate exchange rate, and institutionally devising the central bank to operate in the eurozone.

Technically, the level of fulfilment of the conditions can be tested without switching to a central bank, even though exchange rate variability is a good indicator for testing the macro-economic fundamentals. The design of the monetary union allows for plus or minus 15 per cent standard fluctuation band around the central rate of participating currencies, but at the same time narrower bands are also possible. Whether this band could be close to zero is a matter of agreement within the union. In the context of the currency board in Bulgaria indication drawn from the current account, reserves in the system, monetary aggregates, and interest rates fluctuations could signal well the exchange rate level.[21] In addition, the interest rate convergence requirement could be assessed as soon as the capital mobility is full. Bulgaria restricts only short-term capital at present, and as soon as it sustains its stability in the financial sector, the restrictions would be lifted, as did Estonia for example.[22]

Furthermore, the key to the nominal convergence is in fact in the macroeconomic stability providing conditions for growth-enhancing structural transformation in the country. The best indicator for ensuring that the country enters with an appropriate exchange rate level in the Union, is its own institutional viability, a steady output growth, and a demonstrated flexibility of the prices, wages and resources to adjust in the conditions of the currency board.

Given the systemic transformation and macro-economic fluctuation in the accession countries, evidence to which exchange rate regime should be preferred is not found.[23] Rather, a stronger emphasis is placed on the consistency in the stability-oriented overall monetary policy than on its institutional form prior to accession. There is no uniform path to be followed and countries with both central banks and currency boards will be institutionally capable of entering the monetary union, as long as they meet the criteria for unification. Thus, the arguments that the Bulgarian currency board should be abandoned for the benefits of a discretionary monetary policy to facilitate the integration process do not appear sound. The board can facilitate the accession process, while preserving its hard-won credibility in the monetary policy of the country.

Thus, given the unorthodox shape of the currency board arrangement in Bulgaria and the current prospects for membership of the EU, phasing out the operating currency regime only to be replaced with a central bank may bring more instability than the expected facilitation of the integration process and sustainable economic development in the country.

A possible alternative

Considering the reviewed options for a monetary regime in Bulgaria, the best outcome might be a combination between the first and the third option, i.e. retaining the currency board at least until the acceptance of the country into the EU, and introducing the European currency only after the country is fully integrated in the European markets. This hybrid solution is based not only on the objectives of the accession process, but also on the importance of financial stability in the country prior to its acceptance in the EU structures. As long as the country continues to demonstrate sufficient growth under the restrictions of the board, the currency board should stay in place. Attempting institutional changes invokes more instability than keeping the current arrangement and its credibility.

Thus, the monetary arrangement in Bulgaria should focus on establishing an efficient monetary and financial sector, which can facilitate the intermediation of financial resources and direct them towards productive investments in order to stimulate the overall economic growth of the country. The design of the monetary policy stance to facilitate the full monetary integration of Bulgaria into the eurozone, while proving its institutional and economic soundness, is a challenging task. The policy choice, however, determines the prospects of the country in joining the Union. Abandoning one institutional arrangement for the sake of introducing another one entails costs and raises concerns about the credibility of the policy-makers' commitment to fiscal discipline.

Why, at the end, should Bulgaria join the EMU? The answer to this question lies in the stability of the European monetary institutions and the overall political orientation of Bulgaria towards European accession. Moreover, the public will most probably see accession to the EMU as evidence of increasing certainty in the macroeconomic environment and respectively in the monetary policy. The overall benefits from a monetary union accession for the country are multiple – starting with the credibility of the high-quality[24] single currency, more stable interest rates, lower transaction costs, and transparency. Joining the EMU might well be a net gain to Bulgaria, regardless of the challenges that a monetary union brings. The member states work together to assert their single currency and the trust they have invested in the European monetary policy institution.

Concluding remarks

In view of the advances in structural reforms, banking privatisation and regulation in Bulgaria, the country advances serious claims for European accession. However, the question of which monetary regime would best facilitate its integration into the European Monetary Union remains open.

The following propositions have been formulated in this chapter. First, on the institutional side, it claims that a working environment for a stable monetary sector is imperative for the accession of Bulgaria to the EU. In this regard, the operating currency board in the country is an unusual institutional mechanism for bringing the accession process to monetary unification. However, as long as the exchange rate regime provides monetary stability in the country for successful accession, it should be kept in place. Second, the accession to the EU precedes the accession to the European monetary structures for Bulgaria, implying that even after joining the Union the country would need to effectively manage its monetary and financial environment, in order to fulfil the eurozone requirements. The chapter claims that even at this stage the currency board can facilitate the successful transition to the euro as a legal tender if the country chooses to become a full member of the monetary union.

Thus, the current priority on the reformers' financial agenda should be to create an adequate economic, institutional and regulatory environment that completes the transformation to a free market economy necessary for accession to the EU and for the development of the country's economy. The existence of a stable financial system, prudent supervisory authorities, adequate regulatory framework, market infrastructure and fair competition in the process of financial intermediation are conditions to be met before achieving full EU membership. Whether the country will go a step ahead and opt for full membership in the monetary union is a policy choice yet to be made.

Notes

1 R. King and R. Levine, 'Finance, Entrepreneurship, and Growth: Theory and Evidence', *Journal of Monetary Economics*, 32:3 (1993), 513–542; R. Levine, 'Financial Development and Economic Growth: Views and Agenda', *World Bank Policy Research Working Paper*, 1678 (1996).

2 R. Levine, N. Loayza and T. Beck, 'Financial Intermediation and Growth: Causality and Causes', *World Bank Policy Research Working Paper*, 2059 (1999).

3 The underlying proposition of the board is 'the rule for money creation', i.e. the authority defines a narrow monetary aggregate and backs it fully with the foreign exchange reserves at a chosen fixed exchange rate. In many countries with similar monetary arrangements across the world, foreign reserves of 105 to 110 per cent are maintained in order to provide a margin of protection of the local currency. In addition, any fluctuation in the chosen monetary aggregate must originate from changes in the reserves, but not from the discretion of the monetary authority. Thus, the money supply of a country under a currency board arrangement becomes endogenous to the economy. For more on currency boards, see S. Hanke, L. Joung and K. Schuler, *Russian Currency and Finance* (London, Routledge, 1993); K. Schuler, *Should Developing Countries Have Central Banks?* (Baltimore, Institute of Economic Affairs, Johns Hopkins University, 1996); A. R. Ghosh, A. M. Gulde and H. C. Wolf, 'Currency Boards: The Ultimate Fix?', *IMF Working Paper*, 8 (1998); A. Schwartz, 'Currency Boards: Their Past, Present and Possible Future Role', *Carnegie-Rochester Conference Series on Public Policy*, 39 (1993), 147–187.

4 By 2002, all but the State Savings Bank were sold to strategic foreign investors.

5 Phase I – pre-accession to the EU structures; Phase II – EMU membership with a derogation; and Phase III – full EMU membership.

6 See for example speeches of the governor of the BNB; S. Gavriisky, 'Statement of the BNB's Governor', presentation at a press conference held at the Central Bank on 11 May 2000, accessed at www.bnb.bg; S. Gavriisky, 'Currency Boards and EMU: A Bulgarian Perspective', presentation at the seminar on the accession process organised by the ECB and the Bank of Finland, Helsinki, 10–12 November 1999, accessed at www.bnb.bg.

7 R. Avramov, 'The Introduction of the Euro: A Make-Believe Solution', *Capital Newspaper*, 20 (2000).

8 K. Osband and D. Villanueva, 'Independent Currency Authorities', *IMF Working Papers*, 50 (1992); Schwarts, 'Currency Boards'.

9 Ghosh *et al.*, 'Currency Boards'.

10 E. Ulgenerk and L. Zlaoui, 'From Transition to Accession: Developing Stable and Competitive Financial Markets in Bulgaria', *World Bank Technical Paper*, 473 (2000), p. 41.

11 A. M. Gulde, J. Kahkonen and P. M. Keller, 'Pros and Cons of Currency Board

Arrangements in the Lead-up to EU Accession and Participation in the Euro Zone', *IMF Policy Discussion Papers*, PDP/00/1(2000).

12 P. Backe, 'Exchange Rate Regimes in Central and Eastern Europe: A Brief Review of Recent Changes, Current Issues, and Future Challenges', *Focus on Transition* (Austrian National Bank) 2 (1999), pp. 46–67.

13 D. Dobrev, 'The Currency Board in Bulgaria: Design, Peculiarities and Management of Foreign Exchange Cover', *Bulgarian National Bank Discussion Paper*, 9 (1999).

14 Funds are generated through tranches from the international financial institutions to Bulgaria and privatisation revenues.

15 A. M. Gulde, 'The Role of the Currency Board in Bulgaria's Stabilization', *IMF Policy Discussion Papers*, PDP/99/3 (1999).

16 The lender of last resort is a special executive function of the central bank, which is performed in cases when illiquid but solvent commercial banks face liquidity problems. The lender of last resort aims to ensure an in-time response to incident banking panic and/or to reduce the chances of accelerating the panic. See G. Caprio Jr, M. Dooley, D. Leipziger, and C. Walsh, 'The Lender of Last Resort Function under a Currency Board: The Case of Argentina', *World Bank Policy Research Working Papers*, 1326 (1996).

17 Law on the Bulgarian National Bank, accessed at www.bnb.bg.

18 Seigniorage, in the case of a currency board, refers to the revenues from the foreign exchange reserves management and operations.

19 Avramov, 'The Introduction of the Euro'.

20 See European Central Bank Press Conference, 13 April 2000 and European Commission, 'Exchange Rate Strategies for EU Candidate Countries', Brussels, 22 August 2000, ECFIN/521 (2000).

21 Gulde *et al.*, 'Pros and Cons of Currency Board Arrangements'.

22 See the Bulgarian foreign exchange law on capital mobility and restrictions, accessed at www.bnb.bg.

23 Backe, 'Exchange Rate Regimes'.

24 High-quality currency is a currency that fulfils the textbook functions of money as a means of exchange, unit of account and store of value. Among the standard measures for high-quality money are low inflation and currency convertibility, in the long run. See Schuler, *Should Developing Countries Have Central Banks?*

7

Development of institutions supporting the agricultural land market in Slovenia and the EU accession process

Andrej Udovč and Richard A. Baldwin

In our times of expanding globalisation and computerisation of economies, one could easily assume that land, one of the four basic production factors, is losing its importance. But is that justified? We do need less area for producing more food, but more people need more space to live in, and increased consumption of goods needs more space for their production. So the performing of economic activities is still very much connected to the availability of land. Land still matters and is becoming an increasingly scarce commodity, for which the market is developing very rapidly.

Land has a number of characteristics as a marketing commodity that distinguish it from other goods and services that may be traded in the marketplace. There is an emotional element that enters into the ownership of land that constrains the land market and hence cannot be ignored. While the economist may view land as a commodity that is immovable and strictly limited in supply, the landowner may not view it from an economic perspective but rather as cultural heritage. In post-communist countries considering land ownership legislation, what may make short-term economic sense, drawing investment back into a country, may be totally unacceptable for political and social reasons. This development can be observed in all transition countries, but the case of Slovenia is probably best known, since Slovenia signed the so called 'Spanish compromise' with the European Union, regulating the access of foreigners to the land market on the principle of full reciprocity, already before the signing of its EU association agreement.[1]

Pressures from the European Union on the candidate states from Central and Eastern Europe to open up their land markets as part of the freedom of movement of goods, services and capital in the context of the internal market are only part of the story. Post-communist countries in transformation have been involved in complex reforms to change the system of property ownership and to establish the market for land in the first place. To analyse the problems of establishing the land market in Slovenia, we shall first consider what are the necessary conditions for the creation of a functioning land market. Then we shall discuss the land market and especially agricultural land in the context of enlargement. In the next section we will consider what is necessary to complete the institutions needed for the establishment of an agricultural land market and what recommendations can be made in the context of enlargement. Then we shall outline the development of the agricultural land market in Slovenia and analyse it according to the model created in the first section, identifying key problems. Next we shall evaluate these developments in the light of Slovenia's accession to the EU and draw some conclusions regarding the relationship between the establishing of the land market and the enlargement process.

Developing a model of functioning land markets in a market economy

There is a general consensus that in order for a land market to work, there must be

- a clear definition and sound administration of property rights;
- a minimum set of restrictions on property usage consistent with the common good;
- the transfer of property rights must be simple and inexpensive;
- there should be transparency in all matters; and
- there must be an availability of capital and credit.

These requirements are necessary but not sufficient to guarantee an efficient and effective land market. It is obvious that underpinning all land and property development there need to be clear and consistent land policies that operate within a stable institutional framework.[2]

The market operates through participants buying and selling goods and services. These market operations need to be supported by three regulated sectors – land registration and the cadastre, valuation services, and financial services. These supports may be regarded as the regulatory pillars that stand as the basis of land policy (see Figure 7.1). The three regulatory pillars are constructed upon the legal framework of a country and are strongly shaped by the land policies adopted by government. If government is able to adequately establish and support the pillars then the land market will provide a dynamic environment that includes the participants (land owners and tenants); the goods and services (the land and its use); and the financial instruments (mortgages, credit, capital financing, etc.).[3]

The three-pillar model

Regulatory pillar one (land registration) provides the connection between land and property on the one hand, and people and legal entities on the other. Regulatory pillar two (valuation) provides the connection between land and property and finance mechanisms, while the third regulatory pillar (financial services) establishes the connection between finance mechanisms and people and other legal entities. In the communist era, the first regulatory pillar (land

Figure 7.1   *The three-pillar model*

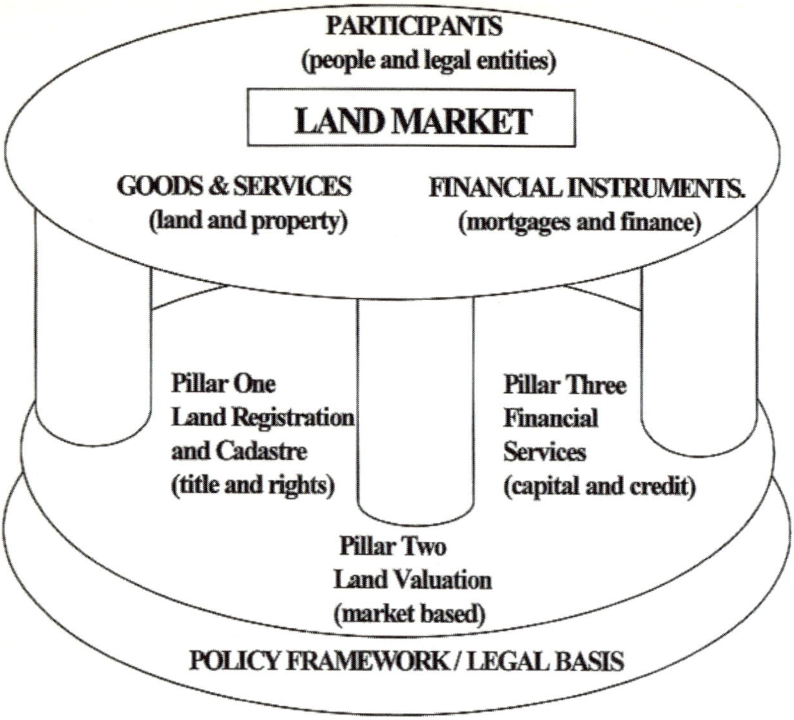

Source: P. Dale and R. Baldwin, 'Lesson Learnt from the Emerging Land Markets in Central and Eastern Europe', *Quo Vadis: International Conference Proceedings, FIG Working Week 2000*, 21–6 May (Prague, 2000).

registry and cadastre) was modified to focus on land use, the second regulatory pillar (valuation) reflected the potential use rather than market value of the land, while the third regulatory pillar (financial services) was almost non-existent.[4]

The elements of each component of the model can be used as indicators of the current status of the land market. Using the scoring methodology presented in Table 7.1, it is possible to assess the state of development of each of the regulatory pillars; the policy and regulatory framework and the state of the market in the country.

Agricultural land and the EU enlargement process

While in the Western world land is a common market commodity with well-defined property rights, that was not the case in the former CEE countries where land (urban and agricultural) usually had a certain status of state or common property. With the political changes in the late 1980s and the start of the

Table 7.1   *Scoring for the land market indicators* (LMI)

Score	Criteria
0	There is no evidence at all that this matter is being addressed.
1	There is minimal evidence that the stated feature is present, but it is not clear that the requested functionality is provided.
2	There are some major problems, the system cannot be said to work adequately, but the basic components are in place or being developed.
3	The functionality is basically provided. There are some known problems, but things basically work.
4	The system works smoothly and could be considered consistent with what one would find in another market economy.
5	The feature or functionality offers performance levels consistent with that required for EU membership and with what one would expect in an EU member state.

Source: P. Dale and R. Baldwin, 'Lessons learnt from the Emerging Land Markets in Central and Eastern Europe', *Quo Vadis: International Conference Proceedings, FIG Working Week 2000*, 21–26 May (Prague, 2000).

economic systems transformations in the early 1990s ownership relations concerning agricultural land were radically changed. The state or collective ownership over agricultural land was abolished and land was either restituted to former owners or privatised according to different models. In the majority of countries this changes happened both on a constitutional level (reintroduction of private property over land and establishing new institutions to support it) and also on a political level with the introduction of new rules.

In the legal system of the EU, there is no specific legislation, which regulates functioning of the land markets. Access to farm land is potentially affected by the provisions of the Treaty of Rome concerning the free movement of workers and the freedom of establishment. Article 48 of the treaty provides that the free movement of workers shall entail the abolition of any discrimination based on nationality between workers of the member states as regards employment, remuneration and other conditions of work or employment. Article 52 provides for the abolition of the restrictions on the freedom of establishment of nationals of member states. According to the second paragraph of this article, freedom of establishment includes the right to take up and pursue activities as self-employed persons and to set up and manage undertakings, in particular companies and firms, under the conditions laid down by the host member state for its own nationals. On the other hand, Article 222 states that the EU shall in no way prejudice the rules in Member states governing the system of property ownership. Furthermore in Article 54(3)(e), the EU provides that the Council and Commission shall carry out their duties to achieve the freedom of establishment, *inter alia* by enabling a national of one member state to acquire and use land and buildings situated in the territory of another member state, insofar as this does not conflict with the principles laid down in Article 39(2) concerning the common agricultural policy.[5]

So in the process of enlargement the EU generally has not placed any specific demands for organisation of land and property markets in the candidate countries, which go beyond the requirements in the Treaty of Rome regarding free movement of workers and free access to the land and property markets also in candidate countries. It should be emphasised that there is no such thing as a completely open land market since all countries have restrictions of one kind or another, especially in the agricultural sector. Many of these restrictions are concerned more with whom, and under what conditions, the land may be used, and with local social considerations, rather than with economics or law.

The development in enlargement negotiations in year 2001 have resulted in the acceptance of a transition period, which allows the new members to restrict the access for non-nationals to their agricultural land markets for seven years. This was then in the year 2003 extended to all real estate with the exception of Slovenia. Slovenia has, according to obligations accepted in the 'Spanish compromise', not requested a transition period. The 'Spanish compromise' allowed access to the Slovenian real estate market (including agricultural land) to all foreigners which had their residence in Slovenia for at least three years, provided that in their home country Slovenians can acquire the same kind of real property (principle of reciprocity). Since 1 February 2003, the restriction of three years residency in Slovenia expired for all EU nationals, and from the day of full membership (1 May 2004) reciprocity will not be a restriction any more. But this general rule has an exception regarding the accession countries, which decided to enforce up to seven years of transition periods. For these countries the reciprocity rule is going to stay in force as long as they restrict access for Slovenians to their real estate markets.

In 1996 a study[6] was made examining the situation in land markets in Central and Eastern Europe and to seek to identify policies that would be useful in overcoming transitional problems and in establishing a well regulated functioning land market, especially during the period leading up to EU accession[7]. This comparative study made some general recommendations which were valid for all developing countries that seek to achieve the level of land markets existing in the member states of the EU. The policy recommendations concentrate on those aspects that will bring real sustainable benefits in the development and nurture of land markets and in general apply to all transition countries. These are:

- *Recommendation 1: completion of the transition process.* It should be a policy objective of the government to complete the transition process in the land sector and establish the base conditions for market forces. This must include regularisation of all titles and ownership relations and the settlement of any likely future claims as a prerequisite for completing the process of economic transition.
- *Recommendation 2: the establishment of a coherent national land policy.* Governments should develop an integrated national land policy, including the identification and provision of the necessary supporting means and

instruments that will allow high level political debate and the obtaining of broad inter-ministerial support. The creation of a coherent integrated strategy for dealing in land and property should be a priority for both urban and rural land.

- *Recommendation 3: EU accession and land ownership.* It should be a policy objective of the applicant government to negotiate a transition period for the full liberalisation of the agricultural land market. Given the start of the accession negotiations in 1998 and the planned accession of first countries in 2004, these issues are of extreme importance at the present time.
- *Recommendation 4: land administration – institution building.* There needs to be institutional strengthening of the land administration sector, which includes the three pillars of the regulatory authorities (registration, valuation, real estate financing) and the underlying legal framework. There is also a need to establish the technical systems required to implement and provide a national level of service within a reasonable time and with a high level of security and confidence.
- *Recommendation 5: land market support measures.* There needs to be a declared policy objective of liberalising the agricultural and urban land markets through creating more open competition, providing support for information flows and removing entry barriers and disincentives. In addition it is necessary to provide incentives for voluntary land consolidation.

In the following sections we will discuss how these recommendations apply to Slovenia and which changes were introduced in the process of Slovenia's post-communist transformation and which ones were driven by the enlargement process.

The agricultural land market in Slovenia

The transition from the communist period seems to have had only a small effect on land mobility largely because the majority of the agricultural land was always in private ownership. Farm sizes are small. In the private sector, 82 per cent of all farms are below 10 hectares while the average size is below 6 hectares. Farm sizes have remained relatively stable over the period 1960 to 1991, with an increase in the number of farms under one hectare (from 26 per cent to 28 per cent of all holdings) and a decrease of the number of large holdings (from 21 per cent to 18 per cent).[8]

Currently the land markets are much more active in urban areas than in rural. This is in part because, as in many other transition countries, rural land values are so low that owners are unwilling to sell and in part because there are still major disincentives that arise owing to structural impediments in the market arising from the socialist legacy. One consequence is a growing informal leasehold market in rural land that enables noncontractual arrangements for the use of land while circumventing the need for the formal transfer of land ownership rights.[9]

Generally, the urban land markets are most buoyant in the capital cities, although progress is still hampered by incomplete reform of the administration (such as technical delays in the land registration process). Property investment is still perceived as high risk, especially while bankruptcy and mortgage laws are considered inadequate or non-existing to safeguard an investor's interest, and the valuation system is perceived as weak or inconsistent.

The biggest player in the agricultural land market is actually the state, acting through the land fund. Than there are private physical and legal entities which are buying agricultural land through speculations, that it will be converted into building land and as such become much more profitable. This is specially often the case around bigger settlements and cities. And very often they are buying the best agricultural land. All these activities are pushing agricultural land prices up (e.g. 1 square metre around Ljubljana costs on average 5 euros, in the rural areas the price is between 0.2 and 0.5 euros). The farmers are buying the least, because they cannot cover such high costs with their production.

The Slovenian land market is noticeably less active then that in other candidate countries. Until the present time, the market suffered from a lack of technical infrastructure within the land registry. There is no large restitution programme and there are no significant potential outstanding claims. Three-quarters of agricultural land remained private during the socialist period, and consequently the ownership fabric (small plots) has largely been preserved. The same families have been settled on land for generations in small plots and these are not often offered for sale. While people like to be associated with the land, they are not so interested in its active use. The second and third pillars of the model follow the same pattern as in the other candidate countries, though financial services have been even slower to develop in Slovenia, as the general economy has remained more closed to outside companies. The chief impediments are considered to be the lack of technical infrastructure and a lack of reliable information services from the land registry.[10]

The overall assessment shows that in general, the reforms and institution building within the land registration sector (pillar one) have been more effective than the reforms in the valuation and financial services sector. There is a recognised weakness in policy formulation and co-ordinated institutional activities and a weakness in the establishment of a sufficient number and variety of participants in the land market itself.

Regulatory pillar one: land registration and the cadastre
In all market economies the basic legal relationship between real property and its owner is officially documented in land registers that also record obligations or encumbrances that are charges upon the land. The official recording of this information is normally carried out by the state administration although professionals in the private sector may be empowered to carry out some of the processes. In many countries there is, in addition to the land title registers, a cadastre that was created to support land and property taxation. Unlike some

land registers, the cadastre is map based, the plans recording the precise extent of the property boundaries.

Slovenia, similarly to several other Central and Eastern European countries has followed the old Austrian practice of having the land register (the land book or *Grundbuch*) separate from the cadastral map, where the land register and cadastre are maintained by separate authorities.[11]

Regulatory pillar two: valuation

In the first stage of the reform process, emphasis has been placed on cadastral reform and on computerising the land records. Only when this began to gain momentum did the focus move towards property valuation, a process that aims to establish the connection between monetary value and the property itself by producing an estimate of the capital value of the asset. Generally, the valuation has suffered from a lack of expertise and a lack of data about market prices because of low market activities. So even today the existing methodology for valuation is based on values that are calculated from land parcel areas, soil types and other objective criteria rather than on estimates or recordings of market price. During the communist period, there was no need for an assessment of market value as the agricultural land value was connected to its potential productivity. Now that the restitution programmes are nearing completion, the infrastructure for providing a valuation service and for the mass appraisal of real property is being put in place with the help of international financial support and expertise.

Regulatory pillar three: financial services

The third regulatory pillar needed to support the land market is the delivery and regulation of financial services. A market economy requires that adequate financing mechanisms are in place to support the buying, selling, leasing and development of property assets, and it is essential that these financing mechanisms are regulated and supported by appropriate law. In Slovenia, as in other socialist economies, only some financial services for buying and selling land were developed. Totally absent were leasing and mortgage institutions.

The modernisation process in the land market sector has concentrated on the legal framework and technical infrastructure. The legal framework, including the enactment of laws for the ownership[12] and usage of land,[13] the definition of legal rights and their registration, restitution and compensation are now mostly in place. The technical infrastructure of the cadastre (strengthening of the control, new measurements, adoption of computer technology) is proceeding well. The modernisation of the technical infrastructure of the land register is beginning, and the information demands from the public and other government users are now expanding significantly.

Policy

The regulatory framework: government policy
In the period after 1990 Slovenia did not develop a separate land policy. Land policy is only weakly defined within the country's agricultural policy. Also the strongest player on the market – the Agricultural Land and Forests Fund is not showing a consistent land policy. There is no land policy forming group able to cut across ministerial briefs. The policies have not created a positive impression for the public.

Government policy uses both market intervention and market mechanisms to regulate the land market and its activity.

- *Non-market interventions of the state*: These are concerned with the planning process and administrative procedures. The regulating force is applied through land use controls, which are exercised at the community level, and oriented towards protecting the land fabric (especially agricultural land) and controlling building development. The land use controls themselves are defined as part of the regulatory framework supported by law. Agricultural land is closely regulated in terms of permitted usage, disposal and conversion (e.g. restrictions on the size of units that can be sold, approval of regulations for sales, change of use, priority for different purchasers, etc.).
- *Market mechanisms*: The government policy is to help provide the basic conditions necessary to allow a market to operate. These include the legal framework to define, own and transfer property rights; the provision of a regulatory environment in which these rights can be clearly defined and traded; mechanisms to support credit and security of loans; the provision of information; and the promotion of competition. The land fund acts as a market trader, albeit with certain state privileges.

In terms of market mechanisms, the market itself is young, and does not yet have adequate financial mechanisms to fuel expansion and development. There is a lack of corporate developers in the urban sector, domestic investment is at a low level, and the Slovene government has not encouraged foreign direct investment. Access to credit is still limited and most building development is financed by natural, rather than legal persons and is the self-financed construction of homes.

Land profitability and mobility in the agricultural sector
Agricultural land accounts for approximately 43 per cent of the 20,000 square km of the country. Forests cover 52 per cent and urban land 5 per cent. Thirty per cent of the agricultural lands are suitable for high-quality arable use, the rest being pasture or less productive hilly/mountainous areas. The land fund manages 300,000 hectares of forests and 140,000 hectares of agricultural land. The rest, which is approximately 700,000 hectares of agricultural land and 700,000 hectares of forests, is privately owned.

An efficient and effective land market can be characterised in terms of the effectiveness of the regulatory pillars; the land policy; the regulatory framework; and the dynamism of the market itself. Table 7.2 identifies those elements that are considered to have a significant impact. Where these elements are present, or are well supported, then this is a positive factor, while if the elements are clearly inadequate or weak, then land market development will be inhibited.

Fiscal and trade policy related to land matters

The ministry of finance is responsible for tax laws and for tax assessment and collection. The tax policy on land matters is shifting to a tool of land management, rather than as a revenue instrument. There is an awareness of the difficulty of making valuations and the current tax assessment is more oriented towards potential usage, rather than actual usage. The ministry of finance would like to support the following aims within its taxation policy:

* encourage preservation of large farming units;
* encourage accurate reporting of land usage;
* encourage registration of leases (place tax on user, not owner, in first instance);
* move the agricultural income tax base to farmers who have farming as main activity;
* remove exemptions for non use of agricultural land.

Trade in land and property has been liberalised. There are no restrictions except those imposed by planning and usage restrictions, plus certain preferences in terms of who may purchase agricultural land.

Financing

Agricultural land prices are high compared to land profitability figures. The land is very fragmented and there is a lack of good quality, well-formed agricultural holdings coming onto the market (people wish to retain land). Restituted land is the most commonly available land for sale, and this will often be in the form of a land unit that is not optimal (having poor access, located within another parcel, etc.). In these cases the result is quite often that the land will be leased, or purchased by the land fund, which is the largest single market player. The land fund finances purchases from its lease income. Mortgage markets are practically non-existent.

Legal matters

The basis of the legal system that secures the ownership is the classic Austrian model with separation of the land register (*Grundbuch*) that records the relationships between people, objects and rights, and the land cadastre that records the physical boundaries and land usage.[14] The cadastre is both juridical and fiscal, forming the basis of property descriptions and tax assessments.

The basis of tenure is registration of title in that it is the entry into the

Table 7.2 *Land policy framework matrix for Slovenia (the text in italic is applicable for Slovenia)*

	COMMAND ECONOMY	TRANSITION ECONOMY			MARKET ECONOMY		EU
LMI score	<1.5	1.5–1.90	2.0–2.4	2.5–2.9	3.0–3.4	3.5–3.9	>4.0
Policy level framework	Government does not support land market development or individual property rights.	Weak political support for objectives of land market. No broad political consensus.	Inconsistent or inadequate policies leading to fragmented land management.	*Individual policies sound. Some policy difficulties with coordination and information exchange.*	Policies are coherent and preparations have started for EU accession.	All reforms are complete and negotiations for accession are under way.	Clearly defined and integrated land policies that comply with EU regulations.
Market assessment: Participants	Relationship between land and people is weak with focus on use rights and occupancy, not ownership. Strong informal sector. Poor information.	Participation severely restricted with unclear ownership rights and outstanding legal claims. Identification of owners and parcels difficult.	*Participation starting but interest limited due to structural problems and lack of market confidence. Data flows are weak.*	Relationship between land and people becoming clear. Growing interest in land as a market commodity. Data flows improving.	Strong connection between land and people with a range of participants and types of land for sale. Information flows are working.	Institutional investors and investment funds are active in the market. Risks in real estate investment seen as low. Information is transparent.	Large range of participants, goods and services. Real estate seen as a good, safe long-term investment.
Pillar one: Land registration and cadastre	Registration not legally required. Insecure laws with respect to ownership, inheritance and disposal of rights. Weak regulating authorities.	Registration is legally required but there are inconsistent laws and confusion over administrative responsibility between agencies.	Compilation of registers and land reform under way. Institutional arrangements and land law need to be strengthened. Poor title information.	Requirements for land title registration are basically satisfactory but delays in transactions occur due to technical and organisation problems.	*Land Registration System is basically working. Problems with titling are mainly in large cities and in areas under land reform.*	Records near completion. System working efficiently (except in capital cities). Titles are secure. Land reform is complete.	System is efficient and supports secondary market services, significant private sector involvement and cost recovery.

Table 7.2 *Land policy framework matrix for Slovenia (continued)*

	COMMAND ECONOMY		TRANSITION ECONOMY		MARKET ECONOMY		EU
LMI score	<1.5	1.5–1.90	2.0–2.4	2.5–2.9	3.0–3.4	3.5–3.9	>4.0
Pillar two: Valuation	Absence of any accepted methodology for market based valuations. No body tasked with valuation.	There is a valuation methodology but little up to date or reliable data. Valuation may not be connected to market price.	*Valuations tied to market price but results are unreliable due to poor data, low level of transactions, and poor reporting.*	Systematic valuation records being compiled. Valuation seen as necessary to support the land market. Real estate prices volatile.	Valuation system able to support market based property tax. Regulatory procedures are in place to monitor data quality.	Secure, reliable system supporting land transactions and fair and efficient property tax collection.	Complete valuation data sets available that can link to other land administration records. Significant private sector involvement.
Pillar three: Financial services	Almost complete absence of financing mechanisms.	Cash sales take place but the market is volatile with few transactions and potential speculation.	*Mortgage support being introduced but foreign investment into real estate may be restricted.*	Mortgages have become more accepted, and development financing is emerging.	Mortgages more widely available, interest rates near to EU/G7 norm.	Macro-economic stability helps real estate investment, encouraging institutional investors.	Pension funds, investment funds, life assurance and major investors are in place and safe.
General assessment	Land market operates through informal sector outside government authority.	Severe strategic impediments to land market activity with reforms progressing very slowly.	Major impediments to a formal land market. Reforms in progress but there are major policy weaknesses.	*Reforms are being implemented but with unresolved difficulties that inhibit development.*	System is basically working and land rights are seen as secure and transferable.	A mature market is beginning to appear with transparent land dealings.	Stable and secure real estate market, secondary market services developed.

register that is the legal definition of ownership. A contract must exist before an entry can be made. The existence of a contract alone is not proof of ownership, but may count as strong evidence.[15]

The system has survived the socialist era, and was kept up to date in the rural areas. The situation is different in urban areas, where all building land was nationalised and inconsistently registered in the land register. It is known that the records of owners are incorrect, and the land registry is unable to keep to the official deadlines for dealing with cases, because of backlogs resulting from updating the land register after the change. This problem is being solved now with the financial help of EU support programmes.

The land register is totally manual. The law allows automation, which has just started. The manual approach increases the possibility of mistakes in the entries. Valuation methodology is supported by law but is considered to be unworkable. In particular, the cadastral culture is often incorrectly recorded, and the methodology is complex and confusing. There are no incentives for owners to correct entries, as often this will increase their tax assessments.

Institutions

The regulatory institutions (land register, cadastre) largely survived the socialist era. The following institutions regulate and assist the land market as part of their overall responsibilities:

- *Supreme Court*: is responsible through the 44 county courts for the operation and upkeep of the land registry offices that maintain the land registers.
- *Surveying and Mapping Authority of Slovenia (SMA)*: is responsible through its central office and 46 district offices for the maintenance of the cadastre. It also has responsibility for all geographic information matters (as part of Ministry of Environment and Spatial Planning).
- *Ministry of Environment and Spatial Planning*: is responsible for physical planning at the state level, and for supervision of municipal physical planning.
- *Ministry of Justice*: is responsible for legal matters concerning the land register.
- *Ministry of Agriculture*: is responsible for agricultural land policy, valuation, land consolidation, activities of the Land Fund, and monitoring and approval of agricultural land sales.
- *Ministry of Finance*: is responsible for taxation.
- *Municipality*: is responsible for the issuance and management of building and land use permits, and for local physical plans.
- *Valuation Commission*: is appointed by direct act of parliament to create valuation services for taxation purposes.
- *Restitution Commissions*: is locally appointed to make decisions concerning restitution claims.[16]

The responsibilities for the land management sector in Slovenia are heavily fragmented across the institutions and largely decentralised in that all decisions and entries (in the first instance) are undertaken locally.

Land registration officers within the land registry decide in the first instance on what should be entered in the land registers. In the event of difficulty, queries are referred to a judge for ruling. The land registry will ordinarily notify the cadastre and the tax authorities following a change of entry.

The institutional responsibility for land valuation is not clear. The basic cadastral culture and classification are contained in the cadastre, but there are no attempts at keeping this information accurate. In the event of a sale, then a valuation assessment will be made, but this will not be fed back to the cadastre. The technical procedures for the valuation are complex.

Procedures and information flows

The procedures for most activities in the land management sector are either prescribed by law, or by regulation issued by the authoritative ministry. While many of the procedures are perceived as clear, their operation, and their incorporation into workflow is seen as weak for two reasons.

First, most procedures appear to be open ended, in that little automatic checking is built into the process. Also, there is no final stage of validation that checks if all procedures have been carried out correctly. This contributes to the uncertainty of the updates in the land register, the inheritance problem, the incorrect owners, and the uncertainty as to the cadastre being informed of the completion of the process.

Second, the information flow itself is weak and slow. Procedures are rather bureaucratic, and do not currently take advantage of information technology. This is especially important where one transaction (e.g. a transfer) involves many separate institutions.

Valuation is an exception to the above. Current valuation procedures are considered to be inadequate and no information flow exists.

Land fund activities

The land fund has 22,000 hectares leased to small private farmers (the average area is 1.2 hectares), and 50 large enterprises with 5,000 to 20,000 hectares (former state farms and co-operatives). Where small units are held by the land fund, and the land ownership pattern is complex, then the small units will stay in the hands of the state unless a buyer comes forward. These land units may have values of the order of 1 euro per square metre (this is equivalent to 10,000 euros per hectare), and the land fund will typically charge 50–100 euros per hectare for rental (i.e. less than 1 per cent of the sale price). It is not normally in the interest of private farmers to buy at these prices as they can secure a lease without any capital outlay.[17]

Where the restitution process results in the fragmentation of a larger land unit (e.g. a small piece within a large unit is to be restituted), then the land fund will purchase the small piece from the new owner. The fund will then add it to its own stock, thus preserving a larger continuous unit. This means that the land fund is playing a role in the land market, as it is highly unlikely that the new owner could sell this land to any other person or entity.

The land fund also buys odd shaped parcels, difficult access parcels, and will even buy land adjacent to an existing farm, at the request of the farmer, and then lease the land to him or her. However, the amount of land sold is very small at the present time.

Key problems

Agricultural land in Slovenia does not suffer from the very strong user/owner separation that was part of the communist heritage in other countries, with the associated technical problems that this induced (such as a lack of physical evidence of boundaries that forced land to be leased to co-operatives). Slovenia has avoided these market distortions.

The government is using both interventionist and market mechanisms to participate in the land market. The land fund is playing a role as a land consol-idation broker allowing parcels that otherwise might have remained unused to be joined to adjacent units. There is also the possibility of linking the land fund to regional development. There are, however, poor information flows that inhibit transparency and competition in the land market. The scarcity of trad-able land resources emphasises the value (real and perceived) of the land.

The key problems identified in the 1997/98, immediately after signing associ-ation agreement, were:

- At a policy level, there has not appeared to be a lead agency or policy forum that was co-ordinating land administration.
- With the exception of certain technical activities of the SMA, there has been little attempt to involve the private sector.
- From the land market viewpoint, the mechanism to bring together buyers, sellers and financing tools were still not developed. The private sector had estate agency services, but knowledge of saleable plots was held locally and not widely disseminated.
- The provisions for mortgage financing were still developing. Capital financ-ing was weak owing to the lack of investment in general and FDI in particular.
- The land fund was the dominant player in the agricultural land market, and therefore in a unique position to influence development. It was acting as a kind of 'cleaner', buying up odd parcels and putting others together. It protected the land against fragmentation, and allowed the more efficient patterns of land use that were developed over the socialist era to be main-tained instead of enforcing a return to the previous pre-1948 fragmented use.
- The weakness of land valuation affected the transparency of land sales.
- Agricultural and urban land values were very high compared to income levels.
- There was a weakness in the information flows – information about land was not easily available.

- Tax policies was in development and oriented towards land management, but very dependent on the new valuation system.
- Transition seemed to have had relatively small impact on agricultural land.

Enlargement related development within the land market in Slovenia

The political changes and Slovenia's accession process were not a driving force to establish its agricultural land ownership as well as other property market, because it was existing even in socialism. The only exception was of course industrial property. Political changes have, especially for private investors, contributed to its easier accessibility and higher legal security including legal registers, but the process started already before the political decision was taken to join the European Union. The first push was given already within Yugoslavia in 1990 when the model of privatisation of social property was introduced. That this is an interesting market for Slovene investors we can observe by the increase of private real property agencies in the first half of the 1990s. Interest was and still is particularly high in dwellings and building land. Transactions with agricultural land are less frequent and are rarely closed through property brokers.

Although the agricultural land market, as with real property market in general, is not a separate section of issue of the Union *acquis* (it is integrated into legislation which regulates free movement of goods and capital), the enlargement process and preparation for accession have had a considerable influence on the Slovene land market in at least two major ways. The first major impact had to do with the opening of the market to foreigners at the time Slovenia negotiated its association agreement with the EU.

Even in the socialist period, the lack of high quality agricultural land forced Slovenia to protect valuable agricultural land resources (quality agricultural land is excluded from any other use within the national physical plan). The cultural connection of people to the land is strong (one-third of the population have some connection through ownership of agricultural land), and hence awareness of the population of land ownership is high. So in spite of the advocated free market for all commodities including land, a political consensus emerged in Slovenia to include into the constitution an article which restricts the transfer of land to foreigners. The reason for such an article being entered into the first Slovene constitution was not economic, land prices were already much higher than the EU level, but above all socio-political (i.e. fear that land would be intensively bought by neighbouring Italian and Austrian citizens). In its Opinion on Slovenia's application for membership of the EU, the Commission made an explicit reference to the difficulty of the entry of foreigners into the real estate market demanding that the Slovene government remove all restrictions on buying land for foreigners. Italy especially, because of its historical connections to the western part of Slovenia, was very uncompromising. This led to the signing of the so-called 'Spanish compromise', as a result of which there was a constitutional amendment in 1997.

Thus, as a direct result of Slovenia's EU accession negotiations, the Slovene land market was opened for foreigners according to the 'Spanish compromise'. This means that foreigners can buy land in Slovenia, if they can prove to have been resident for at least three years, and that their country is allowing Slovene citizens to purchase land there. But this had no effect on the market itself. Because of the high prices and expectations of their fall in the future, there is no economic incentive for foreigners to enter the Slovene land market at this moment. The result of this situation is that Slovenia has not, in its accession negotiations, raised questions regarding the land market or asked for any transition period. The Slovene government has only demanded the full reciprocity from those candidate countries which will enforce the transition periods.

The second influence is even more important and it has to do with the Union's requirements that Slovenia modernise and make more transparent its existing system of land and other real property registration as part of its preparation to implement the Union's *acquis*. The need to bring more order into real property and markets was evident already at the beginning of the 1990s when the processes of privatisation and restitution have started, but the real boost was given with the start of accession process. That the subject is acquiring priority on the political agenda was evident from the inclusion of an article into the coalition agreement of the Slovene governmental parties, which foresees the introduction of a real property tax in the year 2004. The European Union is providing funding for several aspects of this modernisation.

A new project, jointly financed from World Bank and European Union PHARE Funds, was started in 1999. This project is bringing a significant change into the system of real property evidence and property taxation in Slovenia. One of the main issues is, beside digitalisation and updating the existing real property databases, the modernisation of institutions which support functioning of the property market. The most important among them are the land registry, the land cadastre, real property valuation and the reform of mortgage banking.

Among those institutions the EU gives highest priority to the land cadastre and land register. Their modernisation is co-financed by the PHARE program, with 3,000,000 euros. The aim of this particular project is to support Slovenia by harmonisation of its real property market and legislation with conditions that are in force on the real property markets of the member states. The majority of financial funds are intended for hardware and software for modernisation of both institutions, and part is going to be used for expert-technical support (provided by the UK and Spain) for building up the necessary institutional environment. Institutional support is given specifically for analysing and improving: the organisational structure of SMA; the existing legislation dealing with land register and land cadastre; information technologies for managing land register and land cadastre and the integration of data contents and improvement of data exchange among land register and land cadastre with the purpose of achieving higher security in real property markets.

Agricultural land registers are also benefiting from this project and a special subproject is producing maps of actual land use based on aerial photos. The reason that the Slovene ministry for agriculture, forestry and food initiated this project is that these maps are needed for better control in the system of direct payments, introduced in Slovenia in accordance with the policy of accepting CAP. These maps will enable the Slovene Agency for Agricultural markets and Rural development to better control the authenticity of farmers applications for subsidies, and so meet the demands of the EU for transparency of financial interventions in agriculture.

The other positive move for agricultural markets is the development of a new property valuation methodology. Part of this methodology will also be the valuation of agricultural land. It is expected that the new methodology will bring more transparency into the agricultural land market and especially that those institutions which are already established (land fund) or are forecast (valuation institute) will provide a better information system on agricultural land values and prices. This will make the market more lively. Together with the anticipated price fall it should also make agricultural land more available for the farmers, which in the long run fulfils one of the main goals of present Slovene agricultural policy – increase in farm size.

Conclusions

As in other CEEC countries, the transformation of land markets and connected land property rights in Slovenia are primarily driven by the logic of transition to market economy. Land is even today still one of basic production factors that can be used in different production processes either directly (agriculture, forestry, natural resources) or indirectly (building land). That makes it a very interesting market commodity, and the policy makers are aware of that. So one of the first measures at the start of the transition was the introduction of the land restitution and privatisation model. EU accession is forcing the deregulation of the market in the sense of accessibility, requiring transparency of the market and the creation or improvement of instruments for property rights protection and security.

For preparing the land markets for equal free access for domestic and foreign customers Slovenia is getting financial help from the EU and the World Bank. This money is used for building up institutions and information systems for supporting effective functioning of the land market. In this process the government is putting in place the right base conditions and supporting framework to allow the land market to develop. The government is becoming aware of over-regulation in some segments and lack of sound legislation in others, which still obstructs the proper functioning of the market. The accession pressure on the government is to provide enough support for market development and to ensure that the regulatory measures are soundly implemented. Inevitably, whichever policies are going to be adopted, they will represent a compromise between the interests of the different parties, and what the government perceives as its political priorities. In particular, the government still has to take into account the demands of the EU. The Union requires that Slovenia concentrates on maximising the potential involvement of the private sector by providing the required base conditions and ensuring that the necessary legal and institutional frameworks are in place to support the buying and selling of land. The Slovenian state is required to dispense with its role as a major landowner, while at the same time the government must assume the responsibility for the initial modernisation and restructuring of the three regulatory pillars of land registration and cadastre, valuation and financial services. It should identify measures necessary to support and encourage an increasing number of participants in the land market and promote accountability, openness and transparency at all levels.

Notes

1 Constitution of Republic of Slovenia, Official gazette of RS 33/1991 (Ljubljana, 1991).
2 UNECE, Land Administration Guidelines: With Special Reference to Countries in Transition, UN ECE/HBP/96 (Geneva, 1996), 94 pp.
3 P. Dale and R. Baldwin, 'Lessons Learnt from the Emerging Land Markets in Central and Eastern Europe', *Quo Vadis: International Conference Proceedings, FIG Working Week 2000*, 21–26 May (Prague, 2000), 44 pp.
4 E. Zavadskas, B. Sloan and, A. Kaklauskus, 'Property Valuation and Investment in Central and Eastern Europe', *Proceedings of the International Conference held in Vilnius, Lithuania* (Vilnius, Gediminas Technical University, 1997), 371 pp.
5 M. van der Velde and F. Snyder, 'Agrarian Land Law in the European Community', in M. R. Grossman and W. Brussaard (eds.), *Agrarian Land Law in the Western World* (Bristol, Cab International, 1992), pp. 1–9.
6 The project was financed under the Action for Co-operation in the field of Economics (ACE) programme of the European Union.
7 ACE, 'The Development of Land Markets in Central and Eastern Europe', Final Report Project P2128R, ACE programme (EC Brussels, 1998), 121 pp. (unpublished).
8 SORS (Statistical Office of the Republic of Slovenia), *Statistical Yearbook of the Republic of Slovenia 2000* (Ljubljana, 2001), 621 pp.
9 A. Udovč and R. Baldwin, 'The Institutional Environment of Land Market in Slovenia', *Research Reports, Biotechnical Faculty, UoL*, 69 (1997), 147–156.
10 Ibid.
11 SMA (Surveying and Mapping Authority of the Republic of Slovenia), *National Report on Slovenia 1996*, CERCO Plenary Session (London, Granada, 1996), 37 pp.
12 Law on Privatisation of Real Estate in Social Ownership, *Official Gazette of RS* 44/1997 (Ljubljana, 1997).
13 Agricultural Land Act, *Official Gazette of RS* 59/1996 (Ljubljana, 1996).
14 Law on Land Cadastre, *Official Gazette of RS* 16/1974 (Ljubljana, 1974); modified: *Official Gazette of RS* 42/1986 (Ljubljana, 1986).
15 Land Registry Act, *Official Gazette of RS* 33/1995 (Ljubljana, 1995).
16 Denationalisation Law, *Official Gazette of RS* 27/1991 (Ljubljana, 1991); modified: *Official Gazette of RS* 42/1997 (Ljubljana, 1997).
17 MAFF (Ministry of Agriculture, Forestry and Food of the Republic of Slovenia), *Report of Agricultural Land and Forests Fund of Republic of Slovenia for the Year 1996* (Ljubljana, 1997), 42 pp.

8

Regional reform in Hungary: does EU enlargement matter?

László Vass

In the course of its preparation for membership in the European Union, in recent years Hungary has made serious efforts to meet the requirements of the EU's structural funds policy. Due to these efforts the capacity of the administrative system has been growing rapidly, but the desired results in terms of establishing stable and empowered regions have not materialised yet.

The factors which should be taken into consideration in the process of setting up administrative regions in Hungary, are a well balanced territorial development of the country, the social-economic and cultural development of its different regions, the regional policy of the European Union and its basic principles. The European Union does not formally require the modification of the administrative division of a country, yet adjustments in regional administration are implicitly required as a condition for participating in the structural and cohesion funds and thus territorial reorganisation has become part of enlargement conditionality.

Comparing the Hungarian situation to the Polish and Czech regional reforms, Hungary seems to lag behind in terms of institutional change and in particular regionalisation. The question arises why the Hungarian public administration has not been able to manage its territorial reorganisation so far? This chapter will address this question and examine the factors which make the creation of new regional institutions and organisation in Hungary difficult despite the pressure and incentives coming through EU enlargement governance.

An idealised tradition: the county system

To answer the question raised at the end of the previous paragraph, we have to discuss the most important aspect of the existing territorial structure of the Hungarian public administration: *the county system*. The territorial level of the Hungarian public administration primarily means counties.

It can be said that the history of regionalism in Hungary consists of the reform endeavours and plans aiming at the alteration of the system of counties developed during feudalism. Nowadays the question of regionalisation boils down to the question of whether the development of the regional units in Hungary should be realised parallel to or instead of the counties. In practice, territorial or more precisely, regional governance, can be called, with only a slight exaggeration, 'rule of the counties', since the system of counties originating in the twelfth century is still in force, with only its name changed in 1945. The main factors accounting for the persistence of the county system will be examined in the following sections. These are historical tradition, cultural and political factors and related reform approaches.

An embedded county system

Historically established counties

After the liberation from the Ottoman occupation at the end of the seventeenth century, there was a Hapsburg initiative to form *three regencies* as a part of a comprehensive repopulating policy for Hungary, which failed to materialise. In 1723, a National Commissioner Office in charge of administrative tasks related to the regiments of the regular army stationed within Hungary was created in four *circles* of the country. The number of these circles was raised up to six and later, in 1738, to seven. Later, the circle division acquired greater significance in the sessions of the parliament members of each circle. Joseph II, Hapsburg Emperor, a reformer aiming to modernise of the Austro-Hungarian empire, entirely rearranged the traditional territorial division of the country, organising *ten circles* beyond the modified and fused counties.[1] It should be noted that traditional Hungarian historical accounts of these reforms introduced by enlightened Hapsburgs, have underestimated their modernising elements and emphasised 'alien' characteristics. The traditional Hungarian counties became the symbol of the national resistance against the Hapsburg power.

After suppressing the revolution of 1848–49, the Hapsburg Emperor divided Hungary into five crown lands, together with their seats of Buda, Kassa (now Kosice, Slovakia), Nagyvárad (now Oradea, Romania), Pozsony (now Bratislava), and Sopron, containing seven to ten counties each. Following the Austro-Hungarian Compromise of 1867, a rationalisation of the system of counties was attempted, but without any attempt for its weakening.

After the First World War, the Trianon Peace Treaty drew new borders for Hungary and the majority of the historical counties were attached to the neighbouring countries. The rest of the counties constituted the basis of the territorial administration of Hungary. After 1945, the counties were reorganised on the basis of the interwar arrangement. Except for some minor corrections of the county borders, they continued playing a central administrative role during the state-socialist period. In fact, communist politics was built on the well-working control over and through the counties.

Cultural identifications and political determinations

As a result of the strong, historically established role of the counties in the administrative system of Hungary, Hungarians cannot easily imagine a different kind of regional set-up of the territorial administration. The findings of a research on the regional identity of the population revealed that the 32.2 per cent of the people think that the counties are necessary, while 22.6 per cent says that the counties are not needed. A relatively high proportion, 34.5 per cent, had no idea about the issue, and 10.7 per cent did not give an answer. The answers to another question are more interesting in terms of determining the possibility of alternative institutional arrangements (see Table 8.1).

Table 8.1   *What kind of middle-level administrative unit would be better than the county? (%)*

Answers	Female	Male	No answer	Average
None	7.2	6.8	12.9	7.2
Province or region	2.3	4.6	6.5	3.6
Province or region with smaller circles	1.5	2.7	–	2.1
Smaller circles or city-and-outskirts	2.7	3.4	3.2	3.1
Free associations of municipalities	20.0	21.5	35.5	21.2
Other	0.6	1.0	–	0.8
Only the current counties	21.5	19.7	6.5	20.1
Do not know	25.1	21.0	22.6	22.9
No answer	19.2	19.1	12.9	19.0
Total	46.1	51.2	2.7	100.0

Source: M. Oláh, 'Közelítési módozatok a regionális identitás térbeliségének megrajzolásához' (Approaches to the Spatial Formation of the Regional Identity) (Budapest: *Comitatus*, February 1998), p. 18.

The finding that 41.9 per cent of the respondents have no idea or interest in the issue and 20.1 per cent want to keep the current system suggests that there is no critical mass of public support behind any reform of the territorial administrative system. The high proportion of the 'liberal' answers is also instructive: 21.2 per cent say that any kind of new territorial structuring of the public administration should be based on the free and voluntary co-operation of the municipalities. The respondents in favour of keeping the counties usually refer to the county as 'historically proven to be good'. The researchers did not find real cohesion factors such as ethnicity, minority, religion, language or dialect, or economic relations mentioned by the respondents as justification of the county identities.

When the elected mayors of the municipalities were asked about the necessity of the counties, the percentages of the answers significantly differed (see Table 8.2).

Table 8.2   *What kind of middle-level administrative unit would be necessary?*

Answers	% of mayors in 1992
None	2.2
The current counties	46.7
Region with smaller circles	2.8
Provinces or regions larger than a county	5.8
Free associations of municipalities	12.1
Other	1.4
No answer	26.1

Source: M. Oláh, 'Közelítési módozatok a regionális identitás térbeliségének megrajzolásához.' (Approaches to the Spatial Formation of the Regional Identity) (Budapest: *Comitatus*, February 1998), p. 12.

These results show that local politicians are very committed to the counties, and this is the essential explanation for the slow process of the regionalisation. National politicians, members of the parliament, government leaders are strongly depended on the local support and the familiar, controlled territorial administrative mechanisms.

The new electoral law prepared at the very beginning of systemic change in Hungary uses the counties as foundations for the electoral system. The mixed electoral mechanism set the constituencies for the individual candidates and national and county lists of party candidates in order to have better expression of the principle of proportionality. The county list is very important for political parties, because some leading politicians have the opportunity of avoiding individual competition, and get elected by the compensation votes. Changing the county system would involve a change of the electoral system as well. It is hard to foresee the consequences of such a change, therefore the parties are very cautious about any change in the county system.

During the electoral campaign, parties have sometimes promised a more significant rearrangement in the territorial administrative system, but after wining the election, they have given it low priority. Governing parties immediately understood the political value of keeping their positions on county and local levels.

It is therefore possible to predict that reform aiming at regionalisation will come up against the county system in Hungary. Regionalists will encounter opposition from the part of counties whether they prefer choosing 'either regions or counties' to 'regions together with counties'.

Reform attempts and theories

Early modern theories of administrative reform in the nineteenth century in Hungary presented proposals for country planning based on the counties rather than any efforts targeting the dissolution or modification of the county system. The next great wave of reform theories raised the idea of radical transformation of the territorial structuring because of the dramatic changes resulting from the Trianon Peace Treaty in 1920. In the 1920s, statistics divided the country into 28 economic units based on 28 regions of agricultural production. There were also other concepts elaborated in this period to be mentioned including the proposal prepared for the Ministry of Interior for 14 planning counties and 162 districts. In the 1930s, the Hungarian Institute of Administrative Sciences led by Zoltán Magyary (the 'Hungarian Luther Gulick') developed the idea of small districts forming one large region. This idea has never been realised, similarly to the districts included in the National Labour Plan of Gyula Gömbös, the Prime Minister, who was a Mussolini supporter.

In 1939, the radical reform concept of Ferenc Erdei aimed to eliminate the system of counties, replacing them by a development of 80 urban centres and 7 regions, but such radical reform had no chance of success. Once again, after the Second World War, Ferenc Erdei, as minister of the interior and with István Bibó, the director of the Department of Public Administration, presented a concept on behalf of the National Peasants Party, which proposed to divide the country into 75–80 'city-counties'. They stressed that the historical (feudal) county system has always been the obstacle to modernisation of the country, symbol of the rule of the conservative Hungarian ruling class, and an irrational configuration by size, economic capacity and social structure. The counties are political creatures, too small to have real integrating power and co-ordinating capacity, easily controlled by the central government, yet they are too big to be able to understand the needs of the municipalities.[2]

After the communist takeover, soviet-type councils were introduced on the basis of the counties. The counties became efficient tools for the government, as administrative offices of the executive. In 1956, the communist party intended to rearrange this system by forming 12 counties instead of the previous 19 ones. Reform concepts presented in the period of the 1960s and 1970s, sought to establish regions beside the counties rather than instead of them. Between 1958 and 1963, the National Concept of Settlement Development was established, dividing Hungary into three central regions and six peripheral ones. In 1960, another plan developed at the University of Economics divided the country into ten economic units. In 1970 the Ministry of Water Management and of Housing marked six planning and economic regions. In 1975, István Bibó elaborated again a further plan based on a system of city-districts of 80–110 units, and put on the agenda a proposal for larger regions as well.

Systemic reform and transformation in the post-communist period

The Hungarian parliament passed the Act LXV/1990 on Local Governments as one of the first 'system-changing' legal regulations. This legislation reflects Hungary's progress in administrative reform.[3] The objective of this reform was the establishment of real local autonomy, and in order to achieve it parliament created a strict separation between the power of the central government and the autonomous local self-governments. Due to this dichotomy, counties lost their strong position, but the administrative system also lost a middle-level structure. The need to re-establish the 'missing middle'[4] provoked discussions about the counties during the transition period.

Also during this period, local government elections were held and won by the parliamentary opposition parties. As I have argued elsewhere,

> this fact motivated the government to establish the system of regional commissioners for 'supervising' the local governments. Partisan candidates were appointed to these administrative positions in order to balance the political composition (opposition) of the local governments. With this move, politicians compromised the issue of the regional reorganisation of public administration for a long time.[5]

The question of regions gradually became overly politicised. From a strictly administrative point of view, the formation of administrative regions with democratic representation and self-government could be accomplished by using the regions of the commissioners of the republic formed on the basis of county boundaries. Because of its background of political interference, the system of regional commissioners could only function until the end of the period 1990–94, and the new government re-established and strengthened the counties.

Regionalisation by stealth?

The first program for modernisation of Hungarian public administration after the start of the systemic change, contained in the Government Resolution 3603/1992, mentioned no regions or regionalisation. Instead, it spoke about the role of the counties, county self-governments, and the perspectives of a county reform under the title 'Administration of Self-Governments'. It also mentioned the role of institutions of special administration under central subordination as well as the commissioners of the republic under the title 'Central Administration'.

In 1996, Government Decree 1100/1996. (X.2) on the reform of public administration discussed the question of regionalisation in connection with county reform and county authorities. Comparing Hungary with other European countries of similar size, this reform program did not consider it necessary to disrupt the counties or to form smaller regional units, but took the establishment of a system of larger counties into account in a longer-term perspective. It did not consider it reasonable to recommend that parliament decide on the fusion of smaller counties without local initiative for this, but incited the free association of the counties. The reform program encouraged the spontaneous association of the smaller counties for specific purposes as and when they would need it. Later these spontaneous associations would serve as a basis for a system of larger counties.

In 1998, the evaluation of the results of the reform process coincided with those written in the program and the original concept did not change.[6]

However, the summary of the first phase and the next tasks of the process of modernisation contained a suggestion to form regional units of the central administration. According to the evaluation, however, there was no need to establish a new organ between the county level and the central level exercising general powers and functions. The region should be constituted on the basis of general elections and form an autonomous level because, as the concept of the reform program says, the spontaneous county associations in co-operation with other organs concerned should perform tasks of a regional character, assuming suitable stimulation of the co-operation between the counties.

Administrative regions and the European Union

As mentioned in the beginning of this chapter, the European Union does not officially or formally require the modification of the administrative division of a country.[7] The establishment of regions conforming to the European Union's regional policy may be done without modifying the actual territorial structure of the public administration. Hungary was required to establish its statistical-measuring units (NUTS), but their establishment did not necessarily belong to the transformation of the administrative structure of the country, even if this would seem inevitable for a longer term. The White Paper outlining the NUTS requirement linked to European integration and accession, contains no indication for changes in administrative division. The focus of the EU and the Commission's attention has been the so called Madrid criterion related to the development of administrative capacity, which according to the interpretation of the Hungarian governments can be handled relatively separately from the problem of the territorial administrative reform.[8]

When the Hungarian government published its Answers to the Questionnaire by the European Commission (used in the preparation of the Agenda 2000 opinions), it contained only a few references to this topic. The Answers state that in Hungary there are no larger units of self-government than the counties although the idea of shaping regional units is planned in the Act XXI/1996, albeit as a recommendation.

Hungary and NUTS

The system of NUTS on local and regional level was to be formed before the accession negotiations on the regional policy chapter could be finalised. The structure of NUTS in Hungary was to be established by creating levels of NUTS2 and 4 between the existing local level (NUTS5) and the national level, and beyond the county level (NUTS3) aiming at statistic planning which represents no administrative units by any means.

In Hungary, the formulation of the great regions at the level of NUTS1 did not seem reasonable due to the size of the country, although the possibility of creating three groups of regions was already raised. Therefore neither the

XXI/1996 Act on Regional Development and Physical Planning, nor the National Concept on Regional Development takes it into consideration. In other words this means that the unit NUTS1 is to represent the whole country as an entity.

Units of NUTS2 have a role of high priority in the programs of regional development which affected the structure of NUTS as well as the closely attached system of country plans. Section 5, point a) of the Act on Regional Development and Physical Planning determines that planning-statistical (so called great) regions are the adjoining planning and statistical territorial units covering the territory of several counties, bordered by the administrative borders of the counties concerned, which are equal to the units of NUTS2. Then, this provision of the Act determines that statistical regions shall cover the territory of several counties.

In March 1998, according to Section 6, point a) of the Act, parliament passed the National Conception of Regional Development in a form of a resolution, which provides for the establishment of the statistical-observing system of regions and, at the same time, determines the seven planning-statistical regions. This means that regional level, units of NUTS2 were established in Hungary. Regions established in this way have an average territory of 13.000 km², an average population of approximately 1.5 million. (These index numbers are similar to the EU average: 15.700 km² and 1.8 million.) Disregarding the region of Central Hungary involving the capital the differences between the regions are not significant. Each region is constituted of three counties (units of NUTS3) except for the above mentioned Central Hungary. Each region consists of 21–22 units of NUTS4 and about 450 units of NUTS5. The largest region, Southern Great Plain has a territory twice as large as the one of the smallest regions, South Transdanubia. The region of the Northern Great Plain has the highest population; it is half as much again than that of Southern Transdanubia, the region having the lowest number of population.

There are greater differences between the regions considering the GDP per capita, but there is something common in them: none of the Hungarian regions has an average as high as 75 per cent of that of the EU average. Neither Northern Great Plain nor Northern Hungary has an average as high as 75 per cent of Hungary's average.

Concerning the units of NUTS3, the counties comply with this level taking either their size or their population into account. The parameters of the 20 units of NUTS3, established in this way, including the capital, are approximately half as much again as that of the EU average (their average territory is 4.700 km², the average population is 510,000 versus the average of EU 3.100 km² and 360,000). In the European Union, there are some smaller as well as larger units of NUTS3 than the smallest and largest county of Hungary.

A hundred and fifty units determined by the Central Statistical Office in 1997 form units of NUTS4.

In summary, we may declare that the establishment of the units of NUTS is an organisational measure, which is based on a special decision made by the central authorities. This decision neither affects directly the structure of public administration nor changes it. That is why a decision of this kind has less political significance than the organisational decisions of territory concerning the administrative division.

Hungary is the first country among the CEE countries to adopt a legal framework suited to the structural policy of the EU. The act specifies the modern institutional system of spatial policy, which was established after the implementation of the act. However, the factual provision of conditions for their operation, and further, regionally differentiated improvement of the institutional system, takes longer. An emphatic claim of the act is the reinforcement of partnership co-operation between ministries and main offices, respectively, between these central and the regional institutions and partakers, including efficient procedures and integrated utilisation of financial resources. Regional co-operation of counties is also a stated objective of the act. As far as the working of the act is concerned – along with the institutional system – the controlling of licensing and resources demands the elaboration of further measures.

Licences are controlled in the act so that the medium-level licences of public control get to county local governments. At the intermediate level, the body of local governments of a county, the so-called General County Assembly is the only body in Hungary that is formed through election, by lists raised by the political parties. Thus the General County Assembly, as a sort of first chamber, gains the licence to approve spatial plans and operate the regional informational system, whereas the role of the regional development council is to elaborate concepts and programs, respectively, and to allocate the decentralised means for regional development. To stimulate national regional development, new institutions have been set up.

Regional development institutions

National Regional Development Council
The modernisation of regional policy in Hungary and in particular the establishment of the institutional system specified in Act XXI/1996 on Regional Development and Physical Planning, requires the creation of a new, higher-level, separate central state administrative organisation: the National Regional Development Council. Apart from this, almost every central state administrative organisation (ministries, national range organisations) administers certain regional development or physical planning functions.[9]

The National Regional Development Council is the governmental body for regional and spatial development. The increased importance of regional development in the past few years in Hungary is reflected in the fact that a separate governmental institution has been created for regional developmental tasks. The National Regional Development Council prepares decisions of parliament and the government, harmonises national and regional development actions, offers suggestions for Governmental Decrees, and participates in the administration of spatial organisations. The composition of this body is specified in the XXI/1996 Act on Regional Development and Physical Planning. Members of the body are: representatives of county development councils, presidents of national economic chambers, representatives of the council for interest conciliation, concerned ministers, the Budapest mayor, a representative of national-local government partnerships. The National Regional Development Centre administers the secretarial functions of the interest conciliation council.

In accordance with principles of the European Union, decentralisation is the main concept underlying the reform of Hungarian spatial policy. In the spirit of decentralisation, Act XXI/1996 started the specification of the institutional system of modern regional development from below.

The smallest spatial category mentioned and governed by the Act XXI/1996 is the sub-region, which has no administrative equivalent, although in its dimensions, it is rather similar to the former district or environs. Sub-regions are basically the institutional frameworks of development activity for mainly settlement- and sub-regional economical and infrastructure development, based on the co-operation of local settlement governments.

Since forced partnership is alien to the Hungarian local government model, the co-operation of sub-regions is voluntary, in the form of so called regional development partnerships, proposed by Act XXI/1996. This partnership is a legal entity which can take on rights and responsibilities, can have own resources, organisations, etc. These voluntary partnerships are established by the local governments, on an area-formation basis and with a number of members that local governments consider optimal for the objectives of the cooperation. However, the Regional Development Act includes an indirect enforcing element so that these partnerships function at optimal number, size and geographical situation, in regional cohesion. According to Act XXI/1996, the number of representatives of sub-region partnerships in county development councils follows the number of so called statistical regions.

As an effect of this regulation, community associations that formed spontaneously in the previous years have formally established their public act type partnerships, adjusting to the statistical regions. However, real activity is still connected to the former partners. This confusion demands some remedy in the near future, which may be provided by the re-examination of the statistical regions.

County Development Councils

In the first PHARE Regional Development Programme, executed between 1993–96 as an experiment, county-level regional development councils were created in two counties in Hungary: Borsod–Abaúj–Zemplén and Szabolcs–Szatmár–Bereg. Observations about their functioning were so positive that a Governmental Decree was issued to provide for the countrywide introduction of the new type of organisations. By 30 June 1996, county development councils had been created in the nineteen counties of Hungary and they became the repository of decentralisation in the decision procedure of regional development.

The county, a level that is important from an administrative perspective as explained above, has a key role in regional development, too. At present, county development councils decide about county regional development plans, and accordingly, the distribution of decentralised governmental development resources.

The county development council organises and unifies the activities of concerned local governments and state administrative organisations in the field of regional development, and co-ordinates their operation. County development councils co-operate with local governments, with regional state administrative organisations that directly participate in the development of the county, with concerned social trade organisations and county councils of labour affairs, which play an important role in employment policy. In accordance with the National Regional Development Plan, they elaborate the long-term regional development strategy of the county, its development programful and sub-programmes, respectively, and financial plans necessary for the realisation. They have at their disposal considerable financial resources, and decide upon the utilisation of their resources.

The county development council is a legal entity, with its own competences. According to the Act, members of the council are: president of the county assembly, mayors of county-right cities in the county, representatives of the government, representatives of the regional economic chambers, representative of the county council of labour affairs. Sectoral ministers can also be invited to participate. The president is the president of the county assembly and a vice-president is also elected. The council determines its rules of operation. Operating costs are provided by the institutions represented. The county development council decides independently on its operational procedures and administrative apparatus.

Regional Development Councils

In Hungary, traditional counties, which represent administrative units, correspond to the so-called NUTS3 spatial level in the European system. However the elaboration of development programmes for much larger regions, the NUTS2 dimension, is a condition of receiving regional development support from the European Union. A fundamental element of Hungary's preparation for accession is the elaboration of dimensions in regional development that can serve as the basis of complex development programmes. This realisation led the leaders of reform of Hungarian spatial policy to develop a regional dimension of several counties, that corresponds to the NUTS2 range. The XXI/1996 Act on Regional Development and Physical Planning indicates the importance of larger regions, but *leaves the formation of the regions to the free decision of the counties.*

In the course of Hungarian history, there have been a few initiatives to form larger regions than the counties (although, never on the basis of representative local governments), but social-political acceptance of the regions could not be secured, thus, they played a role in the system of administration and spatial planning only for shorter periods.

Parliamentary acceptance of the National Regional Development Plan, will establish the following, so-called planning-statistical regions:

• Central Hungary: Budapest, Pest county;
• West Transdanubia: Györ–Moson–Sopron, Vas and Zala counties;
• Central Transdanubia: Komárom–Esztergom, Fejér and Veszprém counties;
• South Transdanubia: Somogy, Tolna and Baranya counties;
• North Hungary: Borsod–Abaúj–Zemplén, Heves and Nógrád counties;
• North Great Plain: Jász-Nagykun–Szolnok, Hajdú–Bihar and Szabolcs–Szatmár–Bereg counties;
• South Great Plain: Bács–Kiskun, Csongrád and Békés counties.

The creation of the planning-statistical regions, equivalent to the European NUTS2 level, is not equal to a process of regionalisation resulting from natural organisational processes. Therefore, it is possible that the territory of the decision-making institutions will differ from statistical items of spatial planning. Full equalisation will not be effected in the near future, since it will only be possible to tell after the modernisation of the administration whether the thousand-year-old counties will continue to be the administrative focal points of the country, or administration will decide to follow the processes of regionalisation.

Nevertheless, through the establishment of the planning-statistical regions and regional development councils, it is possible to form the basis of such a planning and institutional system that is compatible with European structures.

In 1997, regions evolved, including more counties, and covering the whole of Hungary, and by now, they have formed their own regional development councils, too. These are the following regions, in order of their establishment:

• the North-West Hungarian;
• the South Transdanubian;
• the South Great Plain;
• the Balaton; and
• the Budapest Agglomeration regions.

The act only obliged the agglomeration of Budapest and the accentuated recreation area of Lake Balaton to establish regional development councils. It specified the institutional system and rules of operation of these two regional development councils. Members of the regional development councils are the presidents of the county development councils, the Minister of Environment, the Minister of Finance, representatives of the Ministers of the Interior, of Transport, Communication and Water Management, of Agriculture, of Industry and Trade, of Welfare, of Labour, and of Culture and Education, one representative from each economic chamber, a definite number of representatives from the concerned regional developmental local governmental partnerships, etc. The regional development councils rules of operation are set out in their statutes. Members elect its president, and work out its labour methods. Regional development councils work out and accept regional development plans. They organise and co-ordinate the regional developmental process, evaluate the county regional and spatial development plans.

Conclusions: towards further regionalisation?

Hungary is a unified, homogenous nation-state. Considering this, it is evident that a regionalisation on ethnic, linguistic, cultural or historical grounds cannot be realistic since there are no separate regions or territories formed on these bases. Furthermore, one must note that any of the above factors by itself cannot and does not serve as a necessary basis for regionalisation. Given Hungary's geography, there is no possibility for regionalisation based uniquely on geographical factors due to lack of islands, high-mountains, etc.

Regional economic development as well as regional differences including the ones between the centre and the periphery are the most significant factors of regionalisation and could serve as a basis of the regionalisation in Hungary. It cannot be accidental that contemporary theories of regionalisation are of economic or of regional development character.

The necessary conditions required for a regional reorganisation of the territorial administrative system are:[10]

- professionally well-elaborated region policy;
- minimum consensus on reform among the majority of key experts;
- a strong, committed political party;
- this party should win the parliamentary elections in absolute majority;
- support from the administrative elite;
- well-meaning cultural and media elite;
- supporting citizens.

This fortunate combination of the conditions has not so far come into existence in Hungary. Historically, administrative units have been first established in compliance with political power relations, as examples of the development of European regions show. Regions, city-counties, or city-circles never existed in Hungarian practice. Regions can be established, no matter how meaningful and necessary they are from a professional point of view, by a political decision. Since the beginning of the transition period no political actors have wanted or even ventured to make this decision, and so far no significant political force has seemed to plan such a decision for the near future or put it in its political programme.

Currently, analysts and public administration experts point out the contradiction between the legal-functional developments and the stalemate situation with the regional-institutional rearrangement. The real question for the future is whether the statistical-planning regions created so far and lacking administrative and political power have enough capacity for the efficient and economic use of the structural funds? Additionally, whether the doubled and rather confused structure of the statistical regions and the regions of the regional development councils can hinder each other in forming and implementing regional development projects?

The regionalisation of Hungary is one of the most important tasks to complete before EU accession, otherwise the necessary capacity for absorbing EU structural fund resources will be painfully missing later on. The political class has already understood the importance of this issue. Whether the 'critical mass' of political support can emerge in time to make the crucial decisions on regional restructuring is a question that still needs an answer.

Notes

1 I. Temesi, 'Integration to the EU: Tendencies of Regionalization in Hungary', in K. A. Wojtaszczyk and M. Jarosinska (eds.), *EU-Enlargement to the East: Public Administration in Eastern Europe and European Standards* (Warsaw: Fundacja Politeja, 2000), p. 249.

2 I. Pálné Kovács, *Regionális politika és közigazgatás* (Regional Policy and Public Administration) (Budapest-Pécs, Dialog Campus, 1999), p. 143.

3 A. J. G. Verheijen, *Administrative Capacity Development: A Race Against Time?*, Working Document 107 (The Hague, WRR, 2000), p. 25.

4 A. Ágh, *The Actors of Systemic Change: The Political Context of Public Sector Reform in Central Europe*, Discussion Papers, 19 (Berlin, European Centre for Comparative Government and Public Policy, 1997).

5 L. Vass, 'Hungarian Public Administration: Reform and EU Accession', in Wojtaszczyk and Jarosinka, *EU-Enlargement to the East*.

6 I. Verebélyi, *Összefoglaló a közigazgatási reformfolyamat elsö szakaszáról és a soron következö feladatairól.* (Summary on the First Phase of the Administrative Reform Process and on the Next Tasks) (Budapest, PMO, 1998).

7 'Agenda 2000 for a Stronger and Wider Union', *Bulletin of the European Union*, Supplement 5/97.

8 A. J. G. Verheijen, 'Administrative Capacity Development: A Race Against Time?', p. 28; and also L. Vass, 'Hungarian Public Administration: Reform and EU-Accession', p. 219.

9 N. Horcher (ed.), *Regional Development in Hungary* (Budapest, Hungarian Institute for Town and Regional Planning, 1999), p. 45.

10 M. Oláh, 'Közelítési módozatok a regionális identitás térbeliségének megrajzolásához' (Approaches to the Spatial Formation of the Regional Identity) (Budapest, *Comitatus*, February 1998), p. 31.

9

Administrative reform in Romania and the European Union

Călin Hințea, Sorin Dan Șandor and Veronica Junjan

The issue of public administration reform is a debated one for professional literature. It has always been at the core of an important theoretical debate that started with the idea of compatibility between the concepts of 'public administration' and 'reform'. The arguments in this debate[1] have been confronted with the challenges of social practice in Central and Eastern European countries, which have been faced with an acute need for reform after the crash of the communist regimes and the painful exposure of the inefficiency of previous bureaucratic models.

In this context, institutional change, seen both as a change at institutional and policy level, quickly became an important topic both for political debates and academic research. Beyond the need for changing the rules, structuring new institutions and modifying old ones, institutional change has been motivated by the requirement of first building and afterwards maintaining the operational capacity of implementing policies and regulations. For Romania this challenge was, and still is, a particularly important one, since administrative institutions, as has been repeatedly stressed in the Commission's Progress Reports, have not been able to respond to European Union requirements set in the context of enlargement, especially those concerning programme implementation.

Recent experiences of Romanian public administration show that an equally important challenge in the context of reform is related to communication with citizens. In fact, the shifting expectations of citizens are a major source of pressure for change in post-communist countries. In Romania this was best illustrated with the changes brought by the elections in 1996 and 2000, when citizen disappointment with political parties have led to major swings in votes. Although bureaucrats might believe – especially in countries with recent anti-democratic experience – that citizen expectations are of lesser importance compared to changes at infrastructure level, the change in citizen's expectations (based on various factors, from the influence of market mechanisms to generational change) can influence significantly the functioning of administrative structures.

Obviously, administrative reform cannot be conceived separately from its political environment and political decision making. Strong political will for change is definitely able to influence the direction, strength and implementation of administrative reform. In addition to these factors, external factors have exerted, in the context of globalisation, pressures linked to economic interdependence[2] and the rise of information technology. This situation has led to an increased circulation of political and administrative ideas and choices, models and 'success stories' of reform adopted and implemented in other countries.

For many countries of the former Eastern bloc, reforms have to overcome realities that are difficult to imagine by Western administrators. Things that are taken for granted by the latter can, sometimes, be objectives difficult to reach by the administration of a state in transformation. For example, nowadays some well-known reform objectives belong to a functional bureaucratic model inspired by New Public Management (NPM). It should be enough to remember that administrations in many post-communist states have not achieved some primary objectives like professionalisation of civil service (public function), stability of the civil service, guaranteed status of the civil servant, reduction of the influence of politics in administrative work, decentralisation and others, to realise that change does not even come close to the ambitious objectives of the NPM approach.[3] The environment in which public administration is placed in the post-communist countries is not particularly stimulating for change and reform. This environment is characterised by a precarious economic situation, market mechanisms functioning in a rather random manner, ubiquitous corruption, citizens who are not always aware of their rights and the nature of the relationship that should exist with public administration structures (perceived as a factor promoting a unilateral authoritative approach), political elites that are not always able to provide clear, strong and coherent political decisions concerning administrative change and dangerous political instability. In Romania, the consequences of this environment are evident in examples showing the slow introduction of the various components of reform in the development of a professional body of civil servants. This reform has known numerous changes and adjustments reflected in the Law concerning the Status of the Civil Servant, the National Agency of Public Servant, and the Regional Centres for Local Public Administration.

This chapter will try to assess the importance of the EU enlargement process in the reform of Romanian administration. The first section aims to identify the main challenges for the administration in the post-communist period. The second section will deal with the role of European integration as an impetus for administrative reform. In the third section reforms and developments that have already taken place will be discussed, such as the new legal framework, implementation problems, the fight against corruption, human resources. The section will also address the accomplishments and failures in each domain. The next section will evaluate these developments from the point of the relationship with the EU. Finally, the conclusion will stress that public administration reform in Romania is the key to the country's accession to the EU, but it cannot succeed without serious help from the European Union.

We will argue that the European Union can be perceived as a distinct factor influencing not only the direction of reforms in Romania but also the depth and rhythm of implementation. The conditions and requirements coming from EU regarding the adoption of the *acquis communautaire* have a significant impact in motivating the rhythm of administrative reform. Furthermore, the chapter argues that in the specific case of Romania, sometimes the EU conditions represent the only real pressure towards reform, due to an acute lack of clear policies and strategies of successive Romanian cabinets. Many of the necessary and natural steps for building a modern public administration (like the voting of the Law concerning the Status of the Civil Servant) have been taken due to the pressure exerted for fulfilling the requirements of European integration.

The challenges for public administration reform in Romania in the post-communist period

The revolution of 1989 found the Romanian administrative system in a deadlock caused by centralisation, politicisation of structures and a complete lack of communication with the citizen. In the period that followed the fall of the communist regime, political declarations and speeches referring to the issue of reform have stressed the need for modernisation, decentralisation, 'citizen as client', de-politicisation, etc. The new democratic Constitution, adopted in 1991, set decentralisation and local autonomy as its basic concepts. The objective of creating a professionalised public service, free from political interferences, can be found in the electoral platforms of all political parties.[4] Governing cabinets after 1989 have shown, at least at declaration level, a wish to conduct a significant change concerning public administration. However, this wish has been supported neither by expert knowledge and vision, nor by the means necessary for a successful implementation of reform.

Starting from these observations we come to the main problem related to the reform of public administration in Romania: the continuing absence of a comprehensive reform programme for public administration.[5] In addition, no significant progress has been accomplished towards reducing the corruption level and the co-ordination of institutional development in the fight against corruption.

Although it has been repeatedly asserted that administrative reform is a priority for government,[6] the painful reality is that in recent years its current status is far from advanced despite all formal declarations and strategies.

Establishing an effective and efficient administrative system without which a real democratic evolution cannot be conceived represents the main objective of transition in the field of public administration reform. The development of public administration is of vital importance in shaping the European future of Romania, a future that cannot be imagined without a clear relationship between the citizens and the state, represented among others by administrative institutions. Administrative reforms today are facing important issues, which need to be urgently addressed.

There are a large variety of obstacles influencing the poor performance of Romanian public administration, ranging from legislative to managerial ones. Education and training for civil servants are still marked by old bureaucratic traditions that lead to a lack of flexibility and imagination. Professional literature is not easily accessible, while Romanian professional analyses are still timid. Although technology is sometimes available in certain administrative structures, the opportunities offered by it cannot be used in the absence of the necessary knowledge and expertise. New legislation in the field finds administrative personnel unable to implement it in appropriate ways. At managerial level there is a serious lack of effort to introduce a new approach in the decision-making process. The lack of visible results can influence in a negative way the overall systemic transformation and the European integration process.

An illustrative example of implementation problems is provided by the two-year delay in setting up the agency for managing the EU funds under the SAPARD programme, which has led to inability on Romania's part to run the programme and major delays in agricultural reform in Romania.[7]

Administrative reform in Romania has suffered throughout the years from a chronic lack of strategic vision at central governmental levels. There is a lack of clear criteria to guide and evaluate the medium and long-term evolution of administrative institutions and practices. Various governing cabinets have often appeared to be acting only due to immediate stimuli (either internal or external) in decision making concerning public administration reform. This was the case in the adoption of the Law of the Status of the Civil Servant, of the Law concerning the Demilitarisation of Police, and in the establishing of regional policy.[8] Even when certain steps have been taken by adopting various documents (usually laws) of strategic importance, they seemed to serve a decorative purpose rather than offer clear reference points concerning the desired future of Romanian public administration. From this point of view it should be safe to say that European Union pressure has often been the only factor pushing towards the creation of coherent strategic documents.

The co-ordination of activities in the field of public administration still needs a significant level of improvement. The relationship existing among various types of institutions is not clearly defined. In addition, a lack of a real managerial capacity has led to major deficiencies related to aspects such as supervision, control, evaluation, etc. A good example illustrating this is the way in which National Agency for Regional Development was created and is currently functioning.[9]

The influence of the political realm upon the administration represents another obstacle in the way of building operational administrative structures. In a country still marked by the reflexes of the communist system, where the ruling party and the administrative structures overlapped almost completely and where political loyalty was necessary to occupy administrative positions, political interference tends to go beyond all acceptable limits and marks in a negative way the effective functioning of administrative structures.[10] The selection of civil servants based on political criteria and the use of administrative positions as rewards for political clients have significantly affected administrative capacities. The regular tsunami sweeping away administrative structures after each election has led to a lack of continuity and certainty visible for the civil servant body. Furthermore, the re-distribution of high-level administrative positions according to political party preferences has led, logically, to gridlock in administrative co-ordination and co-operation processes. Decision making processes are often driven by political criteria, even at local government level, where it is much easier to identify objectives related to community well being. The substitution of administrative logic with political logic has unfortunately become current practice for administrative institutions.

The role of European integration as an impetus for administrative reform

All major political parties in Romania have expressed their commitment to European integration. None of these political forces has presented in public a view opposed to European integration. Furthermore, following the disappointment and dissatisfaction related to the exclusion of Romania from the first wave of Eastern European countries invited to join NATO, the focus of all discussions referring to options for foreign policy has moved increasingly towards Euro-Atlantic integration. During various electoral campaigns (1992, 1996 and 2000), the issue of European integration and attachment to European values became an essential element in electoral debates, even contributing to the split in the political scene between 'real Europeans' and 'fake ones'. Both in 1996 and 2000, the parties that had highest rankings as 'European' in voter preferences won the elections. Even in 2003, political opposition attacked governmental policies for being just a "facade" and accused the government of promoting different policies inside the country from those promoted outside the country.

Popular support towards European integration has been located at very high levels, with 78 per cent of the population agreeing with the assertion that 'EU membership is a good thing'[11] and the same percentage declaring that they would vote 'yes' in a referendum about joining the EU.[12] These high rankings were achieved in spite of the lack of a clear governmental policy designed to inform the public about what the integration effort requires from an operational point of view. For the Romanian public, European integration is related to the ideas of prosperity (although this link is relatively unclear), and to the motion of coming back to the family of European nations. Unfortunately, public declarations referring to Romania's integration goal have been paired with unsatisfactory results in terms of real steps taken in order to accomplish this objective. The slow progress made by governments in reaching the integration objective has the potential to lead to a backlash in public opinion and the emergence of different ideas regarding the anticipated positive consequences of the integration process.[13]

The European integration of Romania as well as the other candidates has been driven by the decisions of the European Council in Copenhagen in June 1993. In addition, the European Council held in Madrid in December 1995 referred to the need, in the context of the pre-accession strategy:

> To create the conditions for the gradual, harmonious integration of the applicant countries, particularly through:
> • The development of the market economy,
> • The adjustment of their administrative structure,
> • The creation of a stable economic and monetary environment.[14]

Romania, like Bulgaria, adopted civil service laws in response to EU requirements, which were one of the final conditions to be fulfilled before it started negotiations. Following a process of evaluation according to these criteria and the yearly progress reports, accession negotiations were opened with Romania in February 2000, and by September 2002 negotiations on twenty-seven chapters had been launched and thirteen chapters had been provisionally closed.[15]

Romania, like the other candidate states, is required to strengthen and adjust administrative structures in order to create the conditions for a harmonious integration in the EU. This is a complex effort, especially because clear measurement criteria for progress in administrative reform have not been defined yet. From this point of view, institutional change should be seen as a complex process aimed at changing rules and norms. The creation of new institutions is considered not only necessary but also unavoidable.

Romania realised the importance of public administration for accession quite late in the process. The Copenhagen political criteria were considered to be fulfilled mainly on the basis of the political change that occurred at the end of 1996. The regular reports by the European Commission identified the administration as one of the weakest points of Romania, a sector that was reformed to a very small extent. For example, in the 1998 Regular Report on Romania, the European Commission concluded that:

> There has been little progress in strengthening the Romanian public administration. While in many areas steps have been taken to establish the legal framework for setting up the institutions responsible for the application of the *acquis*, there has been little progress in actually creating these institutions. The provision of the financial and human resources to permit the functioning of these institutions, once established, has not been ensured.[16]

Subsequently, several key issues regarding public administration were addressed in the Commission's Regular Reports and almost all of them were included in Romania's National Programme for the Adoption of the Acquis, but serious reforms were made at a very slow pace and not in the shape intended.

The way in which some very necessary reforms have been proposed and the results they yielded after implementation has been a source of disappointment.

New measures such as Law 161/2003, concerning the declaring of personal property/estate of the political leaders, the Law concerning the free access to public information, Law 544/2001, and the Law 52/2003 concerning transparency in decision-making processes in public administration were announced with considerable optimism as part of a package that would lead to reducing corruption, but after they were voted they did not accomplished the intended results.[17]

European requirements have increasingly become strategic goals in the general reform process of the administrative system. Obviously, Romania's lack of a strategic vision of its own has negatively influenced the process of administrative capacity building. The lack of clear and coherent objectives has led to a 'reform' process organised in a completely illogical manner, seemingly based on the whims of various Cabinets. The developments that have already taken place were mostly linked to the adoption of new legislation.

Progress and problems in Romanian public administration reform

Legal reforms (introducing new rules)

There has been some progress already made at legislation level as part of the effort of reforming the Romanian public administration.[18] Thus, the *Law of Local Public Administration* from 1991 (amended in 1996), established the general framework of local government autonomy. This piece of legislation has had a number of positive effects.

It ensures the functional autonomy for local authorities, due to the fact that they can issue decisions, which have the authority of the law for local administrative structure;

It stipulates the direct election (according to the *Law of Local Elections* of 1991) of local councils, county council and the mayor, which in turn ensures the necessary legitimacy for an autonomous leadership of local affairs. This is supported by the right of local governments to hire their own civil servants.

The law provides for the most liberal type of control of legality known in comparative law, the so called 'control of legality from central to local authority', that does not allow the controlling institution (in this case the prefect) to cancel or modify the decisions issued by local governments, but only to ask the administrative court for a ruling on the legality of the decision.

The law provides for the establishment of a system of 'administrative descentration' combining the local governments autonomy (decentralisation) with deconcentration of ministerial public services.

The new law also introduces an action of administrative judicial review concerning power abuse of local authorities. This action can be taken upon by every citizen in order to determine in the court the annulment of local council decisions adopted by councillors who had a conflict of interest in the issue.

In spite of these positive aspects, this new law has also brought some less positive effects from the perspective of developing administrative capacity. For example, prefects have legal control only upon administrative decisions, but not upon administrative contracts signed by local governments. This is linked to another problem, concerning the willingness of the prefect to send for legal control documents signed by the mayor, concerning the fact that both have political positions (the prefect being nominated based on political criteria from central level, once the mayor is elected). Thus, either the prefect is constantly 'pestering' the mayor (if they belong to different political parties) using his/her right to control for legality to the maximum, or the opposite, namely he/she waits for the expiration date when these documents can be sent for control to the court, covering in this way the mayor's illegalities (if they are in the same political party).

The lack of a clear deadline when the prefect has (under the sanction of decay) to send for control the illegal documents allows after an unspecified amount of time, these documents to be considered legal. In addition, when a new prefect is nominated, he or she can start a campaign attacking the decisions issued during the previous administration.

Another piece of legislation, the *Law Concerning Payments towards Public Employees and Public Dignitaries* that was adopted in 1998, has led to a limitation of local autonomy by establishing a range for salaries of local government civil servants. Local and county councils can establish the salaries for local government personnel, but within the limits imposed by the law. Another sensitive point of this law relates to ensuring the transparency of this payment system.

The *Law of Local Finances* of 1998 meant a step forward for initiating the financial autonomy of local governments. This Law allows local governments to vote local budget, and to establish local taxes and fees. Another sources for local revenues, according to this law, are personal income taxes and appropriations from annual national budget. The Law also provides for the possibility of borrowing from the market (either internal or external) using local government or state guarantees. This right is limited, though, both by this very Law and by other normative documents that impose both a financial and administrative control, given that the act of borrowing has to be approved by certain central authorities.

The *Law of the Status of the Civil Servant* of 1999 has brought significant progress for the effort of professionalisation of the civil servant body. This is a piece of legislation adopted at the specific request of the European Union. It is worth remembering that this law has been finally passed very quickly after eight years of delays, in a short time before the European Council meeting in Helsinki in 1999, that debated the issue of opening negotiations with a group of accession candidates, among which was Romania.

One important point to note in relation to this law is that the job stability of public servants is not considered as a right, but is defended as a principle of civil service status. As a consequence, it cannot be defended through recourse to administrative judicial review. This aspect slows down the process of creating a professionalised body of career civil servants. However, the statute brings a useful distinction among career civil servants, public dignitaries and employees according to the Labour Code.

Several other laws, adopted as part of the legal framework which contribute to the effort of developing a public administration based upon modern principles, are:

- The *Law on Referendums* makes it compulsory to organise a referendum if the territory of the county, municipality or commune is to be modified, and the referendum can be called for in other situations of particular local interest as well.
- The *Law of Public Ownership* clarifies the Constitutional provisions for public ownership, establishing the goods that belong to the state and local governments.
- The *Law of Concession of Public Goods, Services and Activities* establishes the procedures for concession and the public goods and services that can be included in this procedure.
- The *Law of Romanian Fund for Social Development* provides for the possibility of financing by grants obtained through projects aiming at reducing poverty for less developed local communities, disadvantaged social groups, and productive social groups coming from these communities.
- The *Law on Regional Development* provides for various means for fostering regional cooperation.

Despite the progress made with this legislation, a number of problems remain. Similarly to other European countries, administrative reform has been conceived in Romania as meaning exclusively the adoption of laws and regulation.[19] Often, laws have been considered as the *only* instrument leading to administrative change. Complete neglect for implementation stimulated the maintenance of rigid administrative structures, unprepared to work with the required efficiency. These structures have little interest in operating under new conditions and with a new attitude towards the citizen. The bureaucratic logic, assuming a clear distinction between the decision makers and the executors of decisions, strict respect towards procedures, lack of initiative of the executors and very strong separations (both on the horizontal and vertical levels) of administrative structures, is acutely present in administrative institutions. Obviously, this type of logic is not able to provide for institutions capable of fulfilling citizens' expectations about the simplification of administrative procedures, a quick and effective service, and a more personalised relationship between the citizen and the administration.

Implementation issues and the need for a managerial logic

The change from the juridical rationality[20] based strictly upon respect for procedures to a managerial rationality, based on effectiveness and efficiency is not only desirable, but also necessary in order to build administrative capacity. The problems in this field are visible not only at the level of the organisation and management of Romanian administration, but also at the decision-making level, where actors often promote narrow political and group interests.

In terms of increasing the efficiency and effectiveness of administrative structures[21] problems persist and need continuing attention. The implementation of the principle of decentralisation of responsibilities is a good example. Although this principle is constantly referred to in political speeches on public administration reform, its implementation so far has shown an incomplete (if not biased) understanding of its meaning. More often it has included decentralisation of responsibilities towards local authorities without ensuring proper support at financial and human resource level. However, this situation seemed to have been addressed by the new Law on Local Public Administration adopted by Parliament in 2001.

On the whole and despite some progress, we can consider that the Romanian administrative system as still suffering from a lack of managerial, strategic thinking at leadership levels. Sometimes, public management is seen as a sort of fashion, not as a proven way for improving efficiency at administrative level; at other times, it is considered rather as a cookbook able to offer universally valid recipes for solving various issues. This is the reason why the development of managerial skills in a general frame of managerial thinking based upon flexibility and effectiveness in structuring administrative reform is of crucial importance for Romania's future.

Policy evaluation problems

Up to now, the development of significant administrative capacity has been negatively influenced by a lack of attention to policy evaluation, which leads to considerable difficulties in estimating their success.[22]

Little attention has been paid to the role of evaluation. A number of factors account for the neglect of policy evaluation, for example: the acute lack of awareness of the real position of administration towards the citizen, the monopoly/quasi-monopoly position of the state in many fields and the administration's perception of the citizen as subject, not as client. It is understandable, within this context, that an approach based upon the idea of respecting citizens' rights does not engender particular enthusiasm among bureaucrats.

There is also an insufficient understanding of the role of evaluation as a managerial instrument. In the Romanian administrative environment, still marked by juridical influences, public management is situated at declaration level and attention towards specific evaluation techniques remains limited.

There are also problems related to the widespread misunderstanding of the evaluation concept. Often, evaluation is viewed as an instrument for authoritarian control, having a punishing finality (like managerial control), not as it should be, as an instrument able to improve the activity and the results of the institution.

Training and human resources management

The whole reform process after 1989 has been characterised by an orientation towards changing the infrastructure, legislation, increasing financial and technical resources, and less towards the proper usage of human resources. Human resource management has been almost completely neglected as a component of the strengthening of administrative capacity. This neglect constitutes a major impediment for administrative reform.[23] Obviously, there are few chances for implementing a substantive change in the administrative system in the absence of a quality body of civil servants. Several problems hinder progress in this area starting from the low level of human-resource development in public institutions and including deficiencies in the education and training of civil servants.

Civil servants training is still at a very early stage and a relatively low number of universities have approached this field seriously. The schools of public administration rely, to a significant extent, on an exclusively juridical approach, without a 'European' component of public administration. Several generations of civil servants have been unable to go beyond the components of a traditional bureaucratic administration. However, there are positive signs as well: there are several university-level programmes based on an interdisciplinary approach, able to educate a modern civil servant, attached to European values and approaches. Although few, these programmes seem to be on the rise and they place their graduates with surprising efficiency on the job market. Unfortunately, the level of co-operation between universities and governmental structures aiming to develop a critical mass of modern, well prepared civil servants, able to act as change agents for Romanian public administration needs substantial improvement.

Further progress has been made as parliament has approved the establishment of the National Institute for Administration. The institute is subordinate to the Ministry of Public Administration and will provide intensive training for new recruits as well as continuous training for existing civil servants. The institute will also be responsible for managing the existing network of eight regional centres that are providing training for local officials and civil servants. It has been charged with preparing and implementing a national training strategy and started training activities during the 2002/3 academic year. The institute is envisaged to play a similar role to the national Administration School (the ENA) in France.

In spite of the development of continuous training, there are still issues that have to be dealt with. Among these one can count:

- A lack of coherent policies at governmental level for this field.
- A distorted image of continuous training, either as an unimportant element (illustrated by the low budgets allocated for this item) or as a miracle solution for every organisational problem.
- Still insufficient development of the curricula and of training programs. This lack of training for civil servants has led to paradoxical situations when some

public authorities have the information technology needed to improve their activities but they do not have the skills and abilities necessary to use this material support properly.

- Extremely strong political pressures put on civil service. Both at central and local level, after each election, there have been massive changes in political criteria in the civil service. This fact had negative consequences upon personnel selection on competence criteria, professionalisation of public administration, results of implemented policies, etc.

Despite these deficiencies, the Law on the Status of Civil Servant and the National Agency of Civil Servant have brought a positive signal in terms of professional stability of civil servants, selection based on competence criteria, and decrease of political influence. There have been, however, significant issues concerning the implementation of the Law and the start of the actual work of the agency. The implementation of the Law can be strongly improved and, in spite of the fact that many civil servants took certification exams and the oath, there have been fierce debates concerning changes in administrative institutions after the 2000 elections. The agency was for a long time in a construction phase characterised by the lack of clear policies and strategies, its placement under uncertain autonomy, and political disputes related to the control upon it. Now its mandate is still unclear and its influence over the ministries is very small.

Obviously, this lack of proper use for human resource had negative consequences like: maintenance of negative values, based upon rigidity and lack of initiative specific to the communist regimes, problems related to the professionalisation of public service, major communication issues both at internal (inside the organisation) and external (towards the citizens) level, the low quality of the service provided in the public administration structures, lack of corporate spirit at the level of the civil servants body.[24] This latter issue is directly related to the low development of co-operation between local governments in defending and promoting local interests and initiating activities aiming to influence central government decisions referring to local public administration.

However, there are certain positive signs in this field; in particular the constitution of professional associations of these authorities, such as associations of mayors, associations of the presidents of county councils, or associations of secretaries of local councils. Although at an early stage, these associations have started to represent a significant voice for debates related to public administration reform. For instance, in a debate on the bill on local public administration, a provision allowing the prefect to suspend the mayor if the latter was under criminal charges was cancelled at the mayors association request.

Battling corruption

Corruption is one of the major problems facing Romanian public administration. According to the definition adopted in Resolution 99/1999 of the Council of Europe ratified by Romania in 1999 (establishing of the Group of States against Corruption: GRECO), corruption is a 'a very serious threat against the state of law, democracy, human rights, equity and social justice'. Corruption is viewed as impeding social and economic development, threatening the stability of democratic institutions and, last but not least, undermining the moral principles of society.

In spite of previous attempts (at least at declaration level) to deal with this phenomenon, corruption continues to be a widespread and systemic problem. It undermines not only the functioning of the legal system, but also the economy. In addition, corruption has led to a loss of confidence in public authorities, that has negative long-term effects on the development of Romanian democracy.

It is interesting to note the evolution of the corruption issue in the governmental programmes since 1992. The first cabinet that included extensively in its programme the issue of the fight against corruption was the Ciorbea cabinet. The fight against corruption was considered as a high-priority policy emergency. To address this issue the Ciorbea cabinet set up an anticorruption department, directly subordinated to the prime minister. That particular cabinet programme also included an extensive legislative programme to organise the fight against corruption including: drafting a law on ministerial responsibility, creating new organisational structures specially dedicated to the preventing and combating corruption inside the justice system, and forming an institute dedicated to studying the corruption phenomenon. Beyond laying out this generous programme, few of its provisions have been implemented.

Political instability led to the forming of a new cabinet (led by Radu Vasile) at the beginning of 1998. Its programme mentioned only in passing the issue of corruption, although it started considering the draft Law on Prevention and Combating Corruption, which eventually became Law in May 2000. For the first time in a cabinet programme, emphasis was placed on strengthening regional co-operation for combating organised crime and corruption. A year later, the next cabinet (led by Mugur Isarescu) included in its programme the goal of 'zero tolerance towards corruption', without, however, referring to means of accomplishing it. In addition, the adoption of the Law on Civil Servants was considered a good instrument for reducing corruption within the civil service.

Finally, the cabinet of Adrian Nastase listed in its programme the objectives of 'reducing red tape, combating corruption and criminal behaviour' as its priority number four, closely related to improving the state's and state's institutions' authority. There is an extensive part of the cabinet programme dedicated to improving the fight against corruption. Various means for accomplishing this goal have already been laid out, from clarifying the responsibilities of various institutions from the justice system (an issue of great importance, due to overlapping responsibilities that have burdened the justice system so far), to improving co-ordination among various institutions of the justice system and involving Romania more in international organisations dedicated to fighting corruption. Another effective tool for reducing corruption is considered to be the institution of the Instruction Judge. The Instruction Judge benefits from the advantages of the status as judge and has a greater degree of freedom from political influence in doing his/her work than the previously existing district attorney. Some additional measures were also implemented, such as the establishment of an electronic public procurement system in April 2002.

A major step towards organising efforts to tackle the real problem of corruption is the adoption of the new Law on the Prevention and Punishment of Acts of Corruption which entered into force in May 2000. This new law initiated a reorganisation of the bodies responsible for dealing with the problem of corruption. Two major institutional changes brought by this law are: establishing a special anti-corruption and organised crime unit within the general prosecutor's office and the reorganisation of the squad for countering organised crime and corruption, which is the central structure specialised in fighting against organised crime and corruption. In 1999 The National Office for the Prevention and Fight against Money Laundering was established. It has assumed its duties by processing an important number of cases and delivering them to the general prosecutor's office for further investigation. The evolution of sentences for corruption in the 1998–2000 period came out as follows: 534 in 1998, 381 in 1999[25] and 168 in the first half of 2000[26] and 343 in 2001.[27]

In 2002 the major institutional development was the setting up of the national anti-corruption prosecutor's office. This new body replaces the existing anticorruption section of the general prosecutor's office. The national office only investigates corruption cases involving sums over 100,000 euros and relating to high-ranking officials. There are also regional branches of the office attached to each of the fifteen Courts of Appeal.

Developing a strategy for reform

With regard to giving Romanian public administration reform a new start, in 2002 the prime minister established an interministerial committee on administrative reform under his personal authority. A central unit for public administration reform has been created within the Ministry of Public Administration and an interministerial structure has been set up at working level in order to develop reform proposals. Preparations are also underway to develop a fast-track programme to recruit young professional managers to the Romanian civil service. There is still progress to be made in reducing the levels of corruption and improved co-ordination is needed between the various anti-corruption initiatives that have been launched.

Reforms and the role of European integration

The developments and problems discussed in the previous section affect the ability of Romanian administrative institutions to respond to EU requirements for the development of administrative capacity. The difficulties arising in the management of funds coming from the European Union sources are a visible and negative consequence of this inability. Major deficiencies shown at project management level range from a lack of information and initiative to relation to EU-funded projects to only partial accomplishment of objectives.

The transition from an administrative approach based on a centrally established budget to an approach based on project management is not easy. The difficulties of the process have led to a certain lack of trust on behalf of European structures concerning the Romanian authorities' capacity of absorption and usage of EU funds. A recent example of problems regarding Romania's administrative capacity is the limited ability of the Romanian administration to establish priority areas for European investments, which has considerably impeded the implementation of programmes such as the EU's pre-accession support programmes, SAPARD and ISPA.[28]

In contrast to these difficulties, training has seen significant developments in recent years, based on both governmental training programmes and offers coming from universities and NGOs with the benefit of EU funding. There has been a strong European support for this field, with a wide beneficial influence. The PHARE programme funded the a network of training centres for public administration and some twinning programmes were launched for transportation, finance and border police.

Regarding the implementation of laws related to human resource management, the Law of the Statute of Civil Servant and the National Agency of the Civil Servant are the two examples of rule making most representative for the state of capacity-building efforts and administrative reform in Romania. They are extremely important measures adopted after long delays under direct pressure from the European Union. However, they suffer serious deficiencies at implementation level.

The fight against corruption was and still is a distinct sub-chapter in each Commission regular report on Romania and in the National Accession Programme. Alongside other major priorities listed in the 2000 Regular Report on Romania such as child protection and Roma integration, anti-corruption measures occupied a prominent place.[29] The 1999 Accession Partnership between the European Union and Romania (outlining a number of short, medium and long-term priorities in the area of administrative reform), also focuses on corruption.

The new legislation targeting corruption is a first step towards a comprehensive approach to this issue. There is still need to adopt several international instruments designed to fight corruption, and to ratify the Council of Europe Convention on Laundering, Search, Seizure and Confiscation of the Proceeds from Crime, or the Council of Europe Criminal and Civil Law Conventions on Corruption, OECD Conventions on Combating Bribery of Foreign Policy Officials in International Business Transactions, and on Bribery in International Business Transactions. The other short-term priorities of the 1999 Accession

Partnership – establishment of an independent anti-corruption department, ratification of both the European Convention on Laundering of Proceeds of Crime and the European Criminal Law Convention on Corruption, and signing of the OECD Convention on Bribery are still to be accomplished.

It remains to be seen whether new measures will be implemented and have any impact upon the functioning of the Romanian institutions. However, within the context of the negotiations with the EU it is expected that significant steps will be taken in order to deal with the issue of corruption. As a recent EU evaluation report says: 'Corruption remains a common aspect of commercial operations but is also widely reported in dealings with public bodies as well as at the political level. Such high levels of corruption undermine economic development and erode popular trust in state institutions'.[30]

Conclusions

The problems facing Romanian public administration after 1989 vary from the lack of political will for reform to the lack of the necessary managerial capacity. Beyond these elements we can argue that the main issue of administrative reform is the limited capacity to implement the *acquis* of the Union. From this point of view, the European Union represents a reform factor requiring adjustments distinct from the processes of post-communist change. Far too often, the only clear policies of Romanian authorities for public administration have arisen as answers to the stimuli coming from European structures. The overcoming of deadlock on certain reform issues, the initiation of a more dynamic approach concerning the implementation of the *acquis* of the Union, and increasing efficiency and effectiveness of the Romanian administrative structures are required to ensure the following of the only viable path of evolution for Romania: European integration.

Notes

1 See for example C. Pollitt and Bouckaert G., *Public Management Reform: A Comparative Analysis* (Oxford, Oxford University Press, 2000); G. Caiden, *Administrative Reform Comes of Age* (New York, Walter de Gruyter, 1991); W. S. Pierce *Bureaucratic Failure and Public Expenditure* (New York, Academic Press, Harcourt Brace Jovanovich Publishers, 1981).
2 Pollitt and Bouckaert, *Public Management Reform*, p. 28.
3 W. J. M. Kickert, *Public Management and Administrative Reform in Western Europe* (Cheltenham, Edward Elgar Publishing, 1997), p. 35.
4 M. Balogh, 'Public Administration in the Political Parties Electoral Platforms in Romania', *Transylvanian Journal of Administrative Science*, 5 (2000), 81–83.
5 EU Commission, *Regular Report from the EU Commission on Romania's Progress Towards Accession* (November 2000), p. 37.
6 www.guv.ro/obiective/map/reforma-admin-public.pdf
7 M. Balogh, I. Hosu, D. Pop and F. Pop, Report of the project titled 'Map of the Actors

and Problems of the Adheration Process', financed by the Foundation for Open Society, pp. 54–56.

8　For the case of regional policy, a heated debate developed when the cabinet announced a proposal of establishing regions as an intermediary administrative level between the county-level administration and national-level administration. The proposal was abandoned, because it would only have introduced a supplemental administrative layer in the institutional organisation, without any real decision-making authority.

9　The National Agency for Regional Development was established as the agency responsible for implementing regional policy after the Law promoting Romania's division into eight regions according to European standards was passed in 1998, after pressure from EU institutions. Due to the vague formulation of the Law, the agency became functional much later.

10　S. D. Şandor and C. E. Hinţea, 'Professionalisation of Civil Servants', *Transylvanian Journal of Administrative Science*, 2 (1999), 62–63. In addition, one of the big issues relates to the replacement of the civil servants after the elections in 2000.

11　European Commission, 'Candidate Countries Eurobarometer: Public Opinion in the Countries Applying for European Union Membership', Report Number 2002.2 This represents the highest support for joining the EU registered among the candidate countries.

12　*Public Opinion Barometer*, October 2002: www.gov.ro/objective/afis-index-diversedoc-o.php?idrubrica=2.

13　It would suffice to recall here that Romania was one of the last countries of the communist bloc included on the 'blacklist' of states whose citizens needed visas to enter the Schengen area (until 1 January 2002), a real reason for frustration for every Romanian citizen travelling to a Western European country. It is perhaps, significant to remember that the 2000 elections brought an unprecedented and, until few years ago, unimagined rise of extremist political parties, promoting an authoritarian discourse less oriented towards western democratic ideals.

14　European Commission, DG 1A, Commission Opinion on Romania's Application for Membership of the European Union, 1997, p. 1.

15　These were: Company Law, Fisheries, Economic and Monetary Union, Statistics, Social Policy and Employment, Industrial Policy, Small and Medium-sized Enterprises, Science and Research, Education and Training, Consumers and Health Protection, External Relations, Common Foreign and Security Policy and Institutions.

16　European Commission, *Regular Report* (1998), p. 63: www.infoeuropa.ro/infoeuropa/insidePage.jsp?webPageId=77&id=6628.

17　The Law concerning the declaring of personal property of political leaders led to hilarious declarations by some leaders who transferred their personal property to the names of close relatives or declared items such as their personal dog.

18　We thank Prof. Dacian Dragoş, Babeş Bolyai University, Cluj Napoca, for his keen observations on Romanian administrative legislation after 1989.

19　T. Verheijen, 'Dix Ans de Reformes en Europe Centrale et Orientale: Toujours les memes Problemes', *Revue Francaise d'Administration Publique*, 87 (1998), 401.

20　J. Chevallier and D. Loschak, 'Rationalite Juridique et rationalite manageriale dans l'Administration Francaise', *Revue Francaise d'Administration Publique*, 24 (1982), 14.

21　F. J. Auby, *Management Public* (Paris, Sirey, 1996), p. 4.

22 C. Hinţea, and L. Radu, 'Programme Evaluation and Romanian Public Administration', *Transylvanian Journal of Administrative Sciences*, 5 (2000), 11–19. Budgets allocated for evaluation in governmental programmes are very small, and 'evaluation' has a negative connotation, being associated with hierarchical control and punishment.

23 C. Hinţea and S. D. Şandor, 'Reform and Public Administration', *Transylvanian Journal of Administrative Science*, 3 (2000), 42–43.

24 S. D. Şandor and C. E. Hinţea, 'Professionalisation of Civil Servants', *Transylvanian Journal of Administrative Science*, 2 (1999), 62–64.

25 European Commission, *Regular Report from the Commission on Romania's Progress Towards Accession* (Brussels, 1999), p. 28.

26 EU Commission, *Regular Report from the EU Commission on Romania's Progress* (2000), p. 18.

27 EU Commission, *Regular Report from the EU Commission on Romania's Progress* (2000), p. 27.

28 The SAPARD National Agency was accredited as late as June 2002.

29 Romanian Government, *National Program for Accession* (Bucharest, 2000), p. 22.

30 EU Commission *Regular Report from the EU Commission on Romania's Progress* (2000), p. 26.

10

Challenges for Latvian public administration in the European integration process

Iveta Reinholde

Since the establishment of independence at the beginning of the 1990s, public administration in Latvia has faced important changes. In order to be able to function in the European Union, Latvia has to fulfil one of the most crucial and challenging conditions for accession – to improve its administrative capacity to the level required for implementation of the *acquis*. At the same time, in the context of the multiple post-communist transformations, Latvia has to build an administration capable of performing the tasks of democratic and economic development of the country.

The aim of this chapter is to evaluate changes in Latvian public administration related to the European integration process. The analysis will focus on the relationship between Latvian public administration reform and the requirements for the development of administrative capacity necessary for integration, implementation of the *acquis* and overall development.

The first section will outline the challenges to Latvian public administration as part of its post-communist reform. In order to analyse the institutional aspect of integration in detail, the comparison between the EU integration process and public administration reform process in Latvia will be conducted, and the reforms will be analysed in more detail in the next section. Finally, the Latvian National Programme for Adoption of Acquis (NPAA) and management of the integration process will be analysed in order to describe the real situation regarding Latvia's administrative reform today.

The Public administration reform process since independence: goals, challenges and political will

Reform in stops and starts

On 4 May, 1990, Latvia adopted its declaration of independence from the USSR and reinstated the constitution (Satversme) already approved in 1922. To ensure the development of modern and effective public administration the necessary institutional framework of public administration (i.e. ministries, subordinated and supervised organisations) was designed, based on Western models and its own experience. In particular, when developing the system of ministries and subordinated organisations, Latvia took into account the experience of Germany and the Anglo-Saxon countries: the UK, Australia and New Zealand. Regarding the functioning of public administration, the constitution requires that all public administration organisations should be under the supervision of the Cabinet of Ministers. The decision on institutional details like establishment or reorganisation of the ministry is left to the cabinet of ministers.

In 1993 the Ministry of State Reforms (1993–95) was established with the main functions of designing and implementing governmental policy in the area of public administration.[1] In December 1993 the State Civil Service Administration was established to carry out the development of civil service, and the School of Public Administration was established to provide training for civil servants.[2] In the course of one year, the institutional framework for the civil service was defined. The next tasks were to resolve substantive and legal issues of public administration development.

In 1995, the Public Administration Reform concept paper was approved which specified the objectives of public administration development, namely to develop an administration which is 'fair, effective and impartial'.[3] In 1997, the Bureau of Public Administration Reform attempted to issue an updated version of the concept paper and even elaborate a new one, but those attempts were not sufficiently targeted and specific to maintain the interest of the government. However, one of the tasks defined for the bureau at its establishment was to elaborate a new vision for public administration reforms.

Responsibility for public administration reforms was shifted between different institutions in the course of time: the Ministry of State Reforms (1993–95), the Ministry of Welfare (1996–97), the State Chancellery (1995–96), Deputy Prime Minister and Bureau of Public Administration reform (1997–99). Since January 2000 the Secretariat to the Minister on Special Assignment of Public Administration is responsible for coordination and implementation of reform.

Analysing public administration reform development in the 1990s, two visible trends should be mentioned. The reform speed increased between 1993 and 1995, but from 1995 onwards governments appeared to have lost interest, putting public administration issue at the bottom of their political agendas.

There are several factors accounting for this slowdown. First, governments were expecting to achieve long-term results with instruments of short-term planning and implementation. As they were unsuccessful, societal expectations were not fulfilled and the public started to lose confidence in reforms. Second, governments lost the motivation for reform, because the partners (internal and international) accepted the existing system. Also, the emotional euphoria linked to recently established independence was dampened by real economic problems, especially the banking crisis in the summer of 1995. Facing the banking crisis, the government was forced to focus its attention on economic and financial policy in the country. Therefore, this was a period in which there was little political will to reform public administration, not just because successive governments would not make public administration reform their priority, but because society was more concerned with social and economic issues.

The requirements of the European Union and public administration reform

Alongside the goal of making public administration efficient and effective, Latvian public administration had to prepare for effective membership in the European Union structures, a factor which became even more important after Latvia received an invitation to join the EU in Copenhagen in 2002. This determines the need to develop such an administrative system in Latvia, which could succesfully handle EU requirements and ensure the suitable representation of Latvia's national interest in EU structures.

The European Union enlargement criteria and in particular the so called 'Madrid' criterion on administrative capacity from 1995 require the development of Latvian administrative capacity to implement and enforce the *acquis*. This means that after including the rules and norms of the Union acquis into Latvian legislation, administrative implementation is required. This necessitates the development of the capacity to design and implement sectoral reforms and public administration reform in general. The sectors of a national economy do not develop in isolation and any particular sector will not be able to function effectively, if it is not supported by the general public administration.

There is no *acquis* in the public administration area; therefore, there are no legally defined EU requirements. At the same time, most of the administrative principles created for regulation of public administration in the member states have turned out to be an unwritten *acquis* with diffuse borders. Latvian public administration is expected to be ready to become a part of the European administrative space, based on the following principles: public administration functions according to the law, legal certainty, proportionality and responsibility of administration.[4] While these are clearly defined, current EU administrative environment is highly multiform and changing; it consists of different administrative traditions, management methods and cultures of member states. Candidate countries such as Latvia are expected to implement European administrative standards while developing their own administrative system. The more administrative systems in EU countries are based on the same principles, the more the performance of those countries will be qualitative, reliable and foreseeable.

As Agenda 2000, containing the Commission's Opinion on Latvia came out in 1997, Latvian public administration reform was in need of a re-start. In the summer of 1997, the Bureau of Public Administration Reform and the post of deputy prime minister responsible for public administration reform were created, to demonstrate the political will to speed up reform process. These events can be linked to the impact of the Commission Opinions published in the Agenda 2000 document, even if a direct link between Agenda 2000 and the creation of a political body responsible for reform is difficult to prove.

The European integration process: speeding reforms?

The relationship between reform and integration has become a complex one: it may be stated that public administration reform has been an important part of Latvia's pre-accession strategy, but at the same time it aims to deal with the possible impact of the European integration process. The preparation for integration is a complex task in terms of cost minimisation, people and institutions involved. Latvia has attempted to make the link between public administration reform and integration in its National Programme for Adoption of the Acquis, however it is hard to evaluate to what extent integration into EU and public administration reform go hand in hand in practice.

Thus, the modernisation of Latvian public administration has been strongly influenced by the demands of the European Union. To illustrate this, Table 10.1 provides an overview of the chronological development of public administration reform and the EU integration process. Table 10.1 explicitly shows the effects of EU's enlargement governance but also illustrates what has been a desperate search for a public administration identity within the framework of political and social reform in Latvia. The reform slowdown is also evident. In order to establish the reasons for the slow progress in the public administration reform and to highlight the role of the European integration process, a more detailed analysis of the reform history is required.

Table 10.1   *Public administration reforms in Latvia*

Public administration reform	*European integration*
1993 • Ministry of State Reforms was established • The law 'On structure of cabinet of ministers' was approved	• Council of EU on Copenhagen approved the criteria (so called Copenhagen criteria) for the new candidate countries
1994 • The law 'On civil service' was approved	• Council of EU in Essen approved the pre-accession strategy for candidate countries
1995 • March 28: The Cabinet of Ministers approved the Latvian Public Administration Reform Concept • July 1: The Ministry of State Reforms was abolished as well as the post of minister • December: The post of the state minister for self-government affairs was created in the framework of the Ministry of Environmental Protection and Regional Development	• June 12: Association (European) Agreement was signed • October 27: The Government of Latvia presented an application to EU presidency – Spain expressing will to join EU • December: Council of EU in Madrid set to prepare the European Commission the views on candidate countries and decided to organise the IGC for evaluation of EU Treaty

Table 10.1 *Public administration reforms in Latvia (continued)*

Public administration reform	European integration
1997	
• January–July: Ministry of Welfare is responsible for reforms politically • July 1: Bureau of Public Administration Reform and the post of Deputy Prime minister were created	• June 26: The European Commission published 'Agenda 2000' that includes opinions on candidate countries and recommendations • December 12: Council of EU in Luxembourg decided to involve in the negotiation process all 11 candidate countries
1998	
• March 10: the Cabinet of Ministers approved the 'Strategy for Public Administration Development till 2000' • May 8: the post of Deputy Prime Ministers was abolished	• February 1: Association (European) agreement came into force
1999	
• Mid 1999: The post of Minister on Special Assignment on Public Administration Reform and Local Self-government Affairs was created	• October 13: European Commission proposed to start the accession negotiations with Latvia mentioned in the summary on the progress of candidate countries to participation in EU • December 11–12: Council of EU in Helsinki invited Latvia to start the accession negotiations
2000	
• January 1: The Bureau of Public Administration Reform and Secretariat to Minister on Special Assignment of Public Administration were merged together • September 7: The new law 'On civil service' was adopted by parliament	• February 9: Strategy for integration into EU was adopted by parliament. • February 15: Accession negotiations officially started
2001	• Accession negotiations are underway
• March 22: Law 'On public agencies' adopted by parliament • July 10: The government approved public administration reform strategy for the years 2001–6 • October 25: parliament adopted the law 'On administrative procedure'	
2002	
• June 6: Law 'On public administration structure' adopted by parliament	• 27 of 31 negotiation chapters are closed • Negotiations were closed by the end of the year

Table 10.1   *Public administration reforms in Latvia (continued)*

Public administration reform	*European integration*
2003	
• March: State Chancellery is nominated as responsible for public administration reform	• 20 September: Referendum on accession into the EU took place with a positive result
• July: Council of Public Administration is established	

Source: The author prepared the table based on official information provided by the European Integration Bureau www.eib.lv, the Ministry of Foreign Affairs www.am.gov.lv, Bureau of Public Administration Reform, Secretariat to Minister on Special Assignment of Public Administration Reform, the State Chancellery www.mk.gov.lv.

The dynamics of reform

At the beginning of the 1990s, Latvia could be characterised as one of the leading post-socialist countries in the sphere of public administration reforms. The government set goals to establish a professional civil service, to separate politics and administration, and to decentralise the public administration system.[5]

The establishment of the Ministry of State Reforms, State Civil Service Administration and Latvian School of Public Administration explicitly emphasised a need for institutional structures driving the reform process. The adoption of a number of legal acts to provide the framework of reform also demonstrated a certain willingness of politicians to move forward with public administration reform. The law 'On the civil service' of 21 April 1994, was a starting point for the development of a professional civil service. Following the law, the attestation of civil service candidates started. The newly established School of Public Administration provided specialised training for civil service entrants. In 1994, 7,824 people passed the exam for status of candidate civil servant; in 1995, 6,246 people.[6] The next step for candidate civil servants according to the civil service law was a civil servant position. Till the year 2000 training programmes for new civil servants and candidate civil servants were based on the four basic building-blocks of the courses – introduction to market economy, management skills, introduction to legislation and communication IT skills.[7]

At that time, EU matters were not included in the training programmes. The co-ordinated training on EU matters started after the 'Training strategy of Latvian public officials in EU matters' was approved at 1999.[8]

From 1993 to 1995, the deputy prime minister, later the minister of state reforms, guided reforms politically. In July 1995 the Ministry of State Reforms was abolished and reforms were left without political leadership. Abolition of the ministry was a response to the pre-electoral promise by one political party, 'Latvian Way', which was fulfilled after Latvian Way found itself in government.

From the point of view of continuing the reforms, this step can be evaluated as improvident and ill considered. The rapid development till 1995 can be explained in the context of a need to start reforms in public administration and a will to demonstrate to Europe excellent achievement in so short period of time. However, as mentioned above, the banking crisis in 1995 forced the government to concentrate primarily on economic and financial issues, rather than continue the search for the most appropriate reform model.

As the primary focus in public administration reforms was the establishment of a civil service system, the structural and functional aspects of public administration organisation were left unco-ordinated for a long time. The lack of unified principles in the territorial location of public administration institutions created a complex public service delivery system, which was, and still is, time consuming and irrational from the point of view of citizens. Therefore, the development of public administration was aimed to create a rational division of competencies between state government and self-government authorities, clear definition of responsibility and public accountability mechanisms, effective vertical and horizontal co-ordination, professional and ethical civil service, efficient public finance management system and the predictable performance of public institutions.[9]

Given this clear realisation of the reform needs, the Latvian Public Administration Concept (approved by the government on 28 March, 1995) was elaborated. The concept provided an overview of the reforms in several directions in relations between state and society; and in functions, structures and the fundamental principles of public administration.[10] In order to achieve the stated goals the main instruments in public administration were defined – use of financial and human resources and development of the legislative system.[11]

The concept did not mention anything about EU integration and Latvia's commitments to this goal. Till 1995 Latvia was on its way to signing the European agreement as well as applying for membership, and till that moment and even longer integration into the EU was a matter of foreign policy, without any deeper impact on internal policy. Basically, public administration reform was a priority till 1995 due to the interest of the government. During that period, by accepting relevant documents and establishing institutions, the government created the basic structure of public administration.

Following the chronology, the year 1996 brought nothing special regarding the strengthening of public administration. Any relevant event in public administration, which could influence the development, cannot be mentioned. Due to the bank crises in the summer of 1995, public administration reforms and EU integration were left aside, waiting for recovery of economic and financial problems in the country. The period from 1995 to 1997 was uncertain too in terms of political leadership. Political leadership was shifted from one institution to another after nearly every six months, creating chaos and a lack of co-ordination between public administration institutions.

Coming back to the chronology of public administration reforms, it is useful to focus on the year 1997. The Bureau of Public Administration reforms was established in July 1997 to prepare a new reform strategy, to implement the existing public administration reform concept and to support technically the activities of the Council of Public Administration Reform.[12] The post of deputy prime minister was also created and the Council of Public Administration Reform was established to ensure political supervision and co-ordination of the reform process.[13] However after a year the Council stopped its activities and the Bureau lost political support, which altogether resulted in an inability to achieve significant reform goals.

At the end of 1997, the Bureau developed a 'Strategy for Public Administration Development till year 2000', which was approved by the government on 23 December, 1997.[14] In March 1998, the government also approved the implementation plan for the strategy.[15] The strategy and its implementation plan by nature were a fragmented list of activities giving some impulse for speeding up reforms. Some activities included in the implementation plan were too detailed and operational, but others were oriented towards the fulfilment of EU requirements on administrative capacity in a particular sector (e.g. environmental protection or education).[16] Activities regarding the Strategy for Public Administration Development till year 2000 became necessary also because of Agenda 2000, which pointed out the need to promote structural reforms.[17]

In 1998, a report, 'Latvian Civil Service: Problems and Perspectives', was prepared by a group of experts invited to Latvia by the Bureau of Public Administration Reform.[18] On the basis of this report, the main problems of the civil service were identified: lack of motivation and career development, low civil servant status and the negative consequences of the remuneration system. Following the report, the elaboration of the new law 'On civil service' was started. In its 1998 Regular Report, the Commission also concluded that 'important steps have been taken to create an efficient and professional civil service' so forcing attention towards the need for an elaboration of the civil service law.[19] As more attention was turned to institutional aspects, the preparatory work for new laws on public administration structure and agencies was completed. However, the public administration issue, despite its importance in the context of EU integration, was not recognised as a priority by the politicians.

It should be mentioned that the Latvian public administration reform was quite strongly influenced by the New Public Management theory reform model. The establishment of executive agencies, introduction of the quality management system based on the ISO 9001 standard, and the introduction of performance management instruments clearly illustrates the impact of new management ideas. In contrast, the European Commission analyses and requirements have been inspired by the classical model of public administration, and have focused on administrative capacity and contained limited NPM elements.

The year 1999 can be described as the new wave of the public administration reform process. It came with new ideas regarding the introduction of human resource management in public administration and the huge preparatory work, the 'Law on civil service'. Moreover, the 1999 Regular report concluded, 'many priority actions, outlined in the 1995 Concept, the Strategy of March 1998 and the Government Declaration of November 1998 have not yet been completed'.[20]

At the end of year, Latvia was invited to start accession negotiations. Therefore, Latvia was compelled by external forces to look at administrative capacity issues in order to reach EU expectations.

Finally, the year 2000 brought the adoption of the new law *On civil service* on 7 September. Accession negotiations started at the beginning of the same year. There were more and more voices claiming that public administration reform should become one of the priorities of state development. In its Regular Report of 2000, the Commission emphasised that 'the new government has demonstrated its commitment by continuing the reform process by according the issue a prominent place in its declaration of May 2000'.[21] As the relatively stable institution established in the process of public administration reform we can mention that the Bureau of Public Administration Reform was transformed into a Secretariat to the Minister on Special Assignment of Public Administration at the beginning of the year 2000.

For the purposes of accelerating reform, the new Public Administration Reform Strategy for the year 2001–6 was prepared and approved by the government in July 2001. The strategy defines five medium-term reform objectives, namely: 'to ensure single, stable and future oriented public administration, to ensure effective management of public finances, to ensure public participation in the administration, to provide qualitative public service delivery and to ensure professional and ethical civil service'.[22] The law *On public agencies* was approved on 22 March 2001, clarifying the status of semi-autonomous agencies.

Finally, the year 2002 in the reform process can be considered significant, because the most fundamental law for public administration, the law *On public administration structure* was adopted by parliament on 6 June 2002. The law *On public administration structure* defines the institutional framework of public administration and its basic performance criteria.[23] The *Law On administrative procedures* (approved on 25 October 2001) together with the *Law On civil service* defines the scope of civil service and regulates the actions of civil servants as well as providing the appeal mechanism for misadministration. Thus, by implementing the principles of reliability, transparency, accountability and efficiency embodied in the laws, Latvia should fulfil all preconditions for successful integration into the European Union. Regarding the future, the Regular Report 2002 states that 'further improvements have been achieved in setting up the framework for policy co-ordination and strategic planning'.[24]

The management of the European integration process

An important prerequisite in the successsful integration process is effective co-ordination among the institutions. The key institutions in the management of the integration process are the Committee of European Affairs at the parliament (Saeima), the Ministry of Foreign Affairs, the European Integration Council, the European Integration Bureau and the Secretariat to the Minister on Special Assignment of Public Administration (see Figure 10.1).

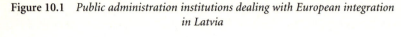

Figure 10.1   *Public administration institutions dealing with European integration in Latvia*

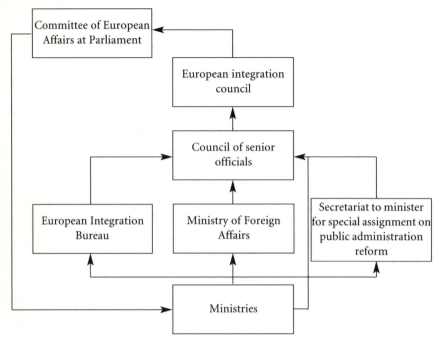

Source: Based on information in 'Saeima (2000) Strategy of the Republic of Latvia for the Integration into the European Union', Riga, 2000: www.eib.lv, pp. 5–6.

The main institution politically responsible for supervision of the process in Latvia is the Committee of European Affairs at the parliament, consisting of members of parliament.[25] The European Integration Council is politically responsible for co-ordinating EU integration since it consists of ministers.[26] The council co-ordinates elaboration and implementation of a single national policy regarding integration into the EU, as well as co-ordinating the elaboration of a national policy regarding public administration to ensure fulfilment of EU requirements after accession.[27] The European Integration Council also makes decisions regarding public administration reform. This logically provides a close link between the European integration process and public administration reform.

The European Integration Bureau monitors the decentralised sectoral integration process within ministries, prepares proposals on EU integration issues, provides information to society and institutions as well as the National Programme for the Adoption of the Acquis.[28]

The Ministry of Foreign Affairs ensures co-operation between Latvia and the EU as well as overseeing preparations for the accession negotiations.[29] The Ministry of Foreign Affairs together with the European Integration Bureau reports on progress to the European Commission and Latvian government and ensures a response to Commission opinions and reports. The Secretariat of the Delegation of Accession Negotiations and the Delegation of Accession Negotiations were established within the structure of the Ministry of Foreign Affairs with the task of working on negotiations.[30]

The Secretariat to the Minister for Special Assignments on Public Administration is indirectly involved in the integration process – mostly through co-ordination of public administration reforms responding to requirements on the part of the EU. Thus the European Integration Council and the Secretariat to the Minister on Special Assignment of Public Administration are involved in the management of public administration reform. Due to the extra high interest of the Council in the acquis and accession negotiations, public administration is not an issue to be frequently discussed during the meetings of the Council.

In general, European matters affect the majority of issues in the agenda of the Council, while those of public administration are left aside, without the necessary minimum of attention. This indicates a persistent lack of political willingness to accelerate reforms and look at the reform globally.

Finally, ministries are responsible for the legal approximation and implementation of their sectoral part of the *acquis*.[31] Therefore, implementation of the *acquis* and fulfilment of accession criteria is a task for each sectoral ministry and their subordinate institutions. It should be noted that the Secretariat was integrated into the State Chancellery in March 2003. This is a short description of the role of institutions involved in the integration process, but a more detailed overview can be found in the strategy for integration into the European Union as well.

The National Programme for Adoption of the Acquis (NPAA) and public administration reform

Latvia's National Programme for Adoption of the Acquis (NPAA) is a single planning document with strong strategic elements to establish mechanisms for undertaking membership obligations expressed by EU. Therefore, the programme covers the policy, legislative and institutional requirements for adoption of the *acquis*.

Actually, the programme represents a starting point for setting priorities on how to assume the membership obligations. The programme describes the current status in each sector of the national economy, the tasks to be achieved, and the responsible institutions, inputs, outputs and time schedule. Therefore, the programme turns out to be a simple planning document, but one extremely necessary for the development of reforms in all sectors.

The present NPAA sets out the commitments of Latvia regarding weaknesses identified in the Commission's Regular Reports and Opinion. In addition, the NPAA opens the priorities identified in the Accession Partnership.[32] Since the European Commission's assessment of Latvia is expressed with reference to the

Copenhagen and Madrid criteria, Latvia is using the same structure in defining strategic priorities. Therefore, the structure of NPAA is almost identical to the European Commission's Opinions and the Regular Progress Reports reflecting the above-mentioned four criteria: preparing Latvian society for membership, the economy for membership, meeting the obligations of membership, and preparing the administration for membership. These are interconnected. As the 1999 Commission regular report noted in relation to public administration reform, 'delays in public administration reform have weakened policy co-ordination and impact assessment and risk undermining the ability of Latvian administration and subordinated bodies to implement and enforce the acquis with efficiency and effectiveness'.[33]

It would be interesting to look in more detail at the part of NPAA, which deals with improving the public administration institutional system in 2000 and 2002. In year 2000, the NPAA envisaged the development of the *Law on public administration structure*, *Law on public agencies* and the *Law on public and private institutions*.[34] The NPAA also planned the conducting of functional reviews in the Ministry of Defence, the Ministry of Interior, the Ministry of Foreign Affairs, the Ministry of Culture, the Ministry of Welfare, the Ministry of Regional Development and Environmental Protection and the Ministry of Transport until the end of 2000. Due to a lack of financial resources, the functional reviews were not conducted. Only the Ministry of Welfare carried out a functional review on its own.

The NPAA also envisaged work on administrative procedures making them effective and transparent, inspection (regulatory body) reform and activities aiming at improving of the quality of public administration are also included as priorities.

In the year 2002, the priority theme 'Preparing the administration for membership', provides several activities relevant both to integration into the EU and to public administration reform. Among these activities are: preparing all necessary secondary legislation for implementation of the *Law On public agencies;* implementing the inspectorate improvement programme; elaborating a unified remuneration system for civil servants, as well as developing training programmes for civil servants on EU and public administration matters.[35] Part of these activities have already been introduced, some are under implementation. By comparing priority themes for both years, the continuity of activities should be mentioned, which requires the NPAA to be realistic in budgetary terms. It should be noted that activities included in the NPAA have to be implemented within the frameworks of the existing budget. The NPAA defines the functions, which should be implemented following acquis as well as resources for the implementation required.

Finally, it should be recognised, that the NPAA is impressive by its volume and detail, but nevertheless it gives a complete view of what kind of activities and tasks which are planned and should be implemented for achieving a goal – integration into EU.

Other reform priorities

Regarding the increase of specialised knowledge in every sector of the national economy, Latvia should plan to raise the level of knowledge on EU issues among civil servants. The School of Public Administration is continuing to work on the training modules on EU matters. Generally, the training programme on EU matters includes the following issues: basic knowledge of EU history and institutions, the principles of EC law, the internal market etc. During the year 2000, approximately 2,400 (from a total of approximately 8,000) civil servants attended basic courses on EU matters.[36] Altogether, since 1999, 4,341 civil servants attended courses on the basics of the EU.[37] Since 2000, the more specialised EU courses on regional policy, pre-structural funds, budgeting and finances are offered by the School of Public Administration, and 579 civil servants have already attended those courses.[38] The Strategy 'On training of civil servants in EU matters' sets up the main principles for training management and the co-ordination process taking into account the factor that almost all public institutions and civil servants are involved in the integration process and that the speed of the integration process depends on the professional skills of the civil servants involved.[39] The strategy also emphasises information and the education of society as relevant components of the EU integration process.[40] It should be mentioned that training takes place in Riga as well as in regional training centres, and is financed by the state budget and external financial assistance.

In addition, the task of the administration is to ensure that all interests are taken into account in formulating national positions. Latvia just started to work on this process. There is increasing communication with interest groups and professional associations in the work related to the elaboration of legislation provided by the law *On public administration structure* and Regulations No. 111 *On internal order of the Cabinet of Ministers.*[41]

Conclusions

The operation of the Latvian administration since the early 1990s has been strongly influenced by the European integration process and the requirements and administrative criteria that Latvia has to fulfil for accession. Latvian administration has to develop institutions that implement and enforce the Union *acquis*, and at the same time achieve the public administration reform goals.

The driving force for reforms in the period of 1992–95 was national interest in creating a rational public administration, but after 1995 when the Ministry of the State Reforms was abolished, external pressure was a main factor accelerating public administration reform. Therefore, the whole process of public administration reform can be divided into two main stages. The first stage can be characterised by response and acting according to the national interest, but the second is related to the EU integration process and the implementation of EU requirements.

At present, the National Programme for Adoption of the Acquis is serving as a planning document till the time when Latvia becomes a member of EU. In addition, the NPAA is updated regularly, so that purposeful implementation of all pre-accession requirements is provided and monitored. Despite its shortcomings, the NPAA prescribes how Latvia will take the commitments of the EU, step by step, defining each activity: transposition of *acquis*, law approximation and institution building. As a planning document NPAA remains the most important, because of its unique ability to look at all sectors of national economy and what should be done to achieve certain goals originating from EU.

Latvia expects to be a part of the EU in 2004. The NPAA is not intended to be a planning document after accession. This fact eventually might create problems in EU-oriented policy making as well as removing policy advice at the period just after the accession.

It is essential to establish a close link between NPAA and public administration reform strategy. The most rational way could be to use the same system and tools for implementation of both programmes. There are some incentives in Latvian administration for this. In future, Latvia should purposefully implement public administration reform moving towards qualitative and rational public administration system since this is the only way to provide the representation of the national interest in the international arena and manage the development of the national economy. For such a purpose, Latvia should overcome uncertainty in political leadership, and should choose one single reform approach. The consequent and well-elaborated public administration reform strategy is a precondition for successful international relations and for internal functioning of the Latvian administration. Regarding political leadership, it is necessary to provide continuity in the reform, which could be achieved by nominating a single responsible political official working on the issues over more than one government. The public administration reform should result in the establishment of a structure of public administration that is capable of implementing the *acquis*.

The scope of the task for the Latvian administration is growing proportionally to the volume of transposed *acquis* and technical assistance programmes. It creates an additional demand, because of the huge amount of preparatory work to be done in Latvia. This process requires an administrative capacity that is not available at the moment. Recently, the European Commission critically evaluated a situation in public administration highlighting its weak points.[42] However, it is a phenomenon of the transition period. The problem of administrative capacity should be and will be solved, together with such issues as remuneration reform, the civil service and the status of administration. Certainly, all problems will be resolved in time, but transition years are hard for both administration and society.

Notes

1 Cabinet of Ministers, Decision No. 46 Temporary statutes of the Ministry of State Reforms, *The Latvian Herald*, 111, 25 November 1993, p. 1.
2 Cabinet of Ministers, Decision No. 63 On establishment of the State Civil Service administration and the School of Public Administration, *The Latvian Herald*, 126, 17 December 1993, p. 1.
3 Cabinet of Ministers, Public Administration Reform Concept, approved at 28 March 1995, pp. 1–3: www.lv-laiks.lv.
4 For all principles see OECD, *SIGMA Paper No. 27 European Administrative Principles for Public Administration* (Paris, Sigma, 1999).
5 Cabinet of Ministers, Report on formation of the Cabinet of Ministers and Declaration on planned activities of the government, *The Latvian Herald*, 153, 21 July 1993.
6 A. Kalnins, *Public Administration and State Civil Service: Achievements, Problems and Perspectives* (Riga, State Civil Service Administration, 2000), pp. 2–5.
7 U. Rusmanis, 'Priorities of Civil Servants Training' *New Administration*, 10 (October 2000), p. 7.
8 European Integration Council: The Strategy on Training of Latvian Public Officials in EU Matters (Riga, 1999).
9 Kalnins, *Public Administration and State Civil Service*, pp. 3–4.
10 Cabinet of Ministers, Public Administration Reform Concept, pp. 1–2.
11 Ibid., pp. 1–2.
12 Cabinet of Ministers, Regulation No. 213, Statutes of the Bureau of Public Administration Reform, 10 June 1997.
13 Cabinet of Ministers, Regulation No. 191, Statutes of the Council of Public Administration Reform, 27 May 1997.
14 Cabinet of Ministers, Strategy for Public Administration Development till Year 2000, 23 December 1997.
15 Cabinet of Ministers, Implementation Plan for Strategy on Public Administration Development till Year 2000, 10 March 1998, p. 2.
16 Ibid., pp. 2–3.
17 European Commission, Agenda 2000: Commission Opinion on Latvia's Application for Membership of the European Union: www.europa.eu.int/comm/enlargement/dwn/opinions/latvia/la_op_en.pdf, 1997, p. 104.
18 Bureau of Public Administration Reform, *Latvian Civil Service: Problems and Perspectives'* (internal archive of the Bureau of Public Administration Reform, 1998).
19 European Commission, Regular Report from the Commission on Latvia's progress towards accession: www.europa.eu.int/comm/enlargement/report_11_98/pdf/latvia_en.pdf, 1998, p. 8.
20 European Commission, Regular Report from the Commission on Latvia's progress towards accession: www.europa.eu.int/comm/enlargement/report_10_99/pdf/en/Latvia_en.pdf, 1999, p. 59.
21 European Commission, Regular Report from the Commission on Latvia's progress towards accession: www.europa.eu.int/comm/enlargement/report_11_00/pdf/en/lv_en.pdf, 2000), p. 15.
22 Cabinet of Ministers, Public Administration Reform Strategy 2001–2006, 10 July 2001, pp. 12–17.

23 Law on public administration structure, approved 6 June 2002 at www.likumi.lv.
24 European Commission, Regular Report on Latvia's progress towards accession: www.europa.eu.int/comm/enlargement/report2002/lv_en.pdf, 2002, pp. 20–21.
25 Ministry of Foreign Affairs, *Latvia's Integration into European Union:* www.mfa.gov.lv/lv, 2002, p. 1.
26 Cabinet of Ministers, Regulation No. 389, Statutes of the European Integration Council, 16 November 1999, pp. 1–2.
27 Ibid., p. 1.
28 Cabinet of Ministers, Regulation No. 327, Statutes of European Integration Bureau, 16 September 1997, pp. 1–2.
29 Strategy of the Republic of Latvia for the integration into the European Union, adopted by Saeima 2000: www.eib.lv, pp. 7–8.
30 Ministry of Foreign Affairs, *Latvia's Integration into the European Union*, p. 1.
31 Strategy of the Republic of Latvia for the integration into the European Union, pp. 6–7.
32 European Commission, Accession Partnership, www.europa.eu.int/comm/ enlargement/report2001/aplv_en.pdf, 2001, pp. 4–13.
33 European Commission, Regular Report from the Commission on Latvia's progress towards accession (1999), p. 60.
34 Cabinet of Ministers, National Programme for Adoption of Acquis (NPAA) (Riga: www.eib.lv, 2000), annex 4.
35 Cabinet of Ministers, National Programme for Adoption of the Acquis (Riga: www.eib.lv, 2002), pp. 882–897.
36 European Commission, Regular Report from the Commission on Latvia's Progress towards Accession (2000), pp. 16–17.
37 School of Public Administration, 'Training of Civil Servants on EU Issues' (*New Administration*, 3, March 2002), pp. 4–5.
38 Ibid., p. 5.
39 European Integration Council, The Strategy on Training of Latvian Public Officials in EU Matters, p. 3.
40 Ibid., p. 5.
41 Law on public administration structure, 20 June 2002, www.likumi.lv.
42 European Commission, Regular Report from the Commission on Latvia's Progress towards Accession (2000), pp. 15–16.

11

Conclusions: the 'end of history' of enlargement or the beginning of a new research agenda?

Antoaneta L. Dimitrova and Bernard Steunenberg

Historical change

In the last decade of the twentieth century and the first of the twenty-first, the European Union has launched two political projects, which, if completed, have the potential to bring to the continent the biggest changes since the end of the Second World War and the Cold War. These are the 'future of Europe', constitutional project aiming to redesign the existing European Union and bring it closer to its citizens and the enlargement to the East, expanding the Union geographically and unifying an unjustly divided continent. Neither of these projects can be postponed and succeed on its own. The obstacles standing in the way of the successful completion of both projects have been formidable and yet not to complete them would mean missing the chances for the consolidation of a peaceful and democratic Europe with institutions that empower its citizens and bring them stability and prosperity. This realisation and the determined efforts of policy makers in the East and West of Europe, as well as the openness of citizens in adjusting to an ever-faster pace of reform have brought the European Union's enlargement closer and closer.

The European Council meeting in Copenhagen in December 2002 took a decisive step towards completing the formal part of the accession process by declaring ten of the negotiating candidates ready to join in 2004. With the exception of Cyprus, which was held up by the complex negotiations to unite the north and the south of the island with a peace deal that would allow both parts to accede to the EU, the rest of these prospective members concluded their final accession negotiations. Some, such as Poland, bargained hard, literally until the last hour and minute while others found acceptable solutions and deals before the Copenhagen summit. Bulgaria and Romania, still in the process of preparation, have been accepted for accession in 2007, provided they continue their reforms in accordance with the enlargement criteria.[1] Turkey has received a provisional date for the start of negotiations, based again on progress made in complying with the Copenhagen criteria until that date.

Given these events, it is tempting to announce that the 2002 Copenhagen decisions have marked the end of enlargement history – thirteen years after the fall of communism and nine years after the first cautious invitation to join extended again in Copenhagen in June 1993. For political leaders such as the Czech president Vaclav Havel, who has dreamed and worked for the 'return to Europe' to become a reality for a long time, 2004 may certainly seem like the end of history. For social scientists, however, the formal accession of ten candidates may be regarded as a continuation of processes set in motion by enlargement preparation and the development of changing patterns of enlargement governance. Whatever the deals negotiated in this long marathon of accession, their impact will come to be felt in future years and continue to influence the institutions and societies of the new members. Thus the question of enlargement-driven institutional change remains as topical as ever.

The chapters of this book provide us with a variety of examples illustrating the complexity of enlargement-driven change and the need for further research into the interaction between post-communist transformation and accession adjustment. Based on the authors' research into various aspects of change in post-communist institutions, several preliminary conclusions can be drawn which set us on a path for further exploration.

What we know so far: from enlargement governance to Europeanisation

Enlargement governance and adaptation pressure

The process of accession to the EU and this enlargement in particular puts candidate states and their institutions and policies under tremendous adaptation pressure. While EU member states are also influenced by the appearance of structures, rules and policies at the European level, setting off a number of processes nowadays studied under the broad term Europeanisation, the adaptation pressures on the candidates have been of a different, and greater magnitude. As introduced in the first chapter of this book and the chapters by Maniokas and Rybar and Malova, key features of the EU's enlargement governance, such as asymmetry and conditionality, have ensured that the EU has influenced the political process in candidate states in a very substantial way. In chapter 2, Maniokas speaks of the emergence of 'a consistent logic of control' as a result of the increased conditionality, complexity, asymmetry and differentiation in this enlargement. This logic of control, he argues, has been created by the need to provide a template of the transition target for the candidates as well as to delay the process. The effects of enlargement governance are, therefore, far reaching and affect the very foundation of the polities in question. They are also, however, limited in time, since the enlargement mode of governance may disappear for those candidates which become new members.

Changing the rules of the political game

The European Union's goal of providing a template for the post-communist transformations in addition to preparing the candidates for adoption of the *acquis* is crucial for understanding the impact the enlargement process has on institutions and societies. As we have pointed out in chapter 1, enlargement governance has meant that the EU has influenced basic institutional choices setting the rules of the political game (in other words, constitutional changes) and the day-to-day political process in the candidates – to an extent unseen in the member states themselves. This is very clearly illustrated by the chapters by Popławska, on constitutional change in Poland and by Rybár and Malová, on political change in Slovakia.

The Slovak case can be now cited as a textbook one of successful conditionality – the European Union, acting through a multiplicity of channels and in parallel with other international actors, succeeded in exerting influence on Slovakia's 'contentious polity' whose new democratic institutions were under strain under Vladimir Mečiar. Marek Rybár and Darina Malová convince us that external conditionality can be successful not only in influencing the choices of the electorate, as was the case in the Slovak elections in 1998 and 2002 when Slovaks were convinced they would be left out of the EU if they re-elected Meciar, but also, ultimately, in changing the basic rules of the political game. Unfortunately, the Slovak case may not be easy to replicate – as the authors point out the emergence of a viable political opposition working for popular mobilisation has to accompany the EU's threat of exclusion for conditionality to be successful.[2]

While the Slovak case may stand out in other ways, the effects of conditionality in Slovakia fit well with the proposition claiming that conditionality can act not only through governments but can also change the domestic opportunities structure and empower certain domestic actors.[3] In almost all of the enlargement period, Slovakia was a highly polarised polity, split between those supporting Mečiar's nationalistic authoritarianism and the new democratic elites.[4] As Rybár and Malová show, several democratic institutions and the opposition were weakened by the cabinet's actions and by constitutional provisions, which created deadlock in the system. Between 1994 and 1998 in particular, the majority coalition government led by Mečiar was able to marginalise parliamentary opposition and to weaken other institutions such as the presidency. The Slovak opposition, the Hungarian minority, and the president soon learned to use EU demands for more democracy in the domestic political arena.

In contrast to Slovakia, the story of constitutional changes in Poland, as told by Ewa Popławska, hardly features any conditionality, but seems to be a case of forward looking adaptation of elites to the demands of future membership. European Union institutions, possibly aware of the sensitivity of an issue that goes to the very heart of a polity, have not applied very much overt conditionality to constitution making or amendment in the candidates, except in cases where constitutions have directly contradicted basic tenets of the *acquis* of the Union such as the free movement of capital. Several of the candidate states, furthermore, had adopted their post-communist constitutions before enlargement governance could make an impact. Poland, however, as Popławska notes, adopted its constitution fairly late, in 1997. As a result, the European clause and other provisions related to Polish EU membership had to anticipate and adjust to the forthcoming accession.

The chapter by Popławska captures the complexity of arguments and forces involved in this constitution-building process. Even though changes were not made under EU pressure, debates about loss of sovereignty or the acceptance of the supremacy of EC law were vigorous and reflected dissenting views in Polish society. Learning from the experience of other states who had joined the EU and emulating features of the fundamental laws of EU member states such as France and Germany seems to have played a central role in shaping the new rules. Popławska's detailed case study suggests that several mechanisms may have been at play – from simple learning, where Polish constitution makers recognised the utility of rules in certain EU member states and emulated them, to socialisation mechanisms driving those who made strong arguments in favour of joining the EU and making the necessary constitutional adjustments limiting Polish sovereignty.

Thus the profound changes in the basic rules of the political game in Poland and Slovakia highlighted by Popławska and Rybár and Malová leave us with a puzzle as to the mechanisms at play behind these changes. While the changes in Slovakia seem to have been driven mostly by the EU's relentless conditionality and thus to be the result of logic of consequences, the Polish case suggests learning and socialisation mechanisms were at play, driven by a logic of appropriateness. Thus a clear question for further research emerges, namely under what conditions do the different logics play a role in the enlargement adaptation process.

Asymmetry and a need for flexibility

The chapters on Bulgaria and Estonia, focusing on economic adaptation, present a similar contrast between adjustment in anticipation and responses to EU pressures. The chapter on socio-economic problems linked to enlargement by Reijlan and Toming analyses the costs and benefits of accession from the perspective of a small open economy. It is a timely reminder that for some candidates, enlargement has no alternative if they are to ensure growth and competitiveness. The economic benefits which enlargement is expected to bring, however, do not obscure the fact that the changes will also bring challenges, especially in adjusting to EU environmental, health and consumer protection levels. The adjustment is, as the authors reflect, inevitable given the asymmetry of enlargement governance and is in response to EU pressures: requirements set in the Copenhagen criteria and the need for new members to accept fully the *acquis*. Nevertheless the chapter strongly argues for a continued need for more flexibility and compromise in applying EU rules if the new members are to be able to survive inside the EU.

The removal of the remaining trade barriers with EU member states and anticipated increase of FDI represent only half the story for Estonia or other new members. The other half is the need to establish new institutions to increase Estonia's absorption capacity of structural funds and other EU funds and the need for serious investment to reach EU standards in environment, worker and consumer protection. While the benefits still outweigh the costs in economic terms, Reijlan and Toming stress that adjustments to membership have a deeper societal dimension and require a strengthening of the rule of law. They also argue that in order to go beyond the technical side of adopting new legislation, a change of social attitudes is essential. How and under what conditions such changes might or might not follow the change of formal rules is another key question for future research.

A further issue which will inevitably attract more attention in the coming years is whether, post-accession, the new member states economies will be adversely affected by the uniformity and inflexibility of EU legal rules as anticipated by Scharpf and suggested by Reijlan and Toming.[5] This question's relevance is also evident from the analysis by Andronova Vincelette of Bulgaria's options in the run-up to accession with regard to its monetary policy and the currency board operating in the country.

Reform versus enlargement driven changes: contradictory or complementary?
While the changes in Estonia were evaluated from the perspective of enlargement, the other two chapters dealing with aspects of economic change start from the analysis of reforms, which are so crucial for the functioning of economies of markets of transition countries that they have to be implemented with or without the EU, while still subject to enlargement driven changes. For Bulgaria this is the establishment of a stable monetary policy and the currency board and for Slovenia, the creation of a market for land.

The transition developments described by Andronova Vincelette in her chapter on Bulgaria were driven by the need to respond to the economic and financial crisis of 1996, stop hyperinflation and restore the credibility of the banking system. Andronova Vincelette shows that the measures taken to restore financial stability and create an independent market-based system of financial intermediation were not driven by the European Union, but they appeared complementary to accession requirements for the establishment of a functioning market economy and potential EMU membership. As Bulgaria comes closer to its goal of accession, however, it is faced with the dilemma of whether it should preserve its currency board institutions until EU and EMU entry or abolish the board beforehand in order to comply with formal EU requirements for EMU entry. Andronova Vincelette highlights the challenge that a possible compliance with EMU second-stage requirements and the potential abolition of the currency board may present to the fragile stability of the Bulgarian monetary system. This potential scenario of having to undermine a working institution (the currency board) to comply with rules created for a different context and actors underscores again the need for more flexibility in EU economic governance before and after accession. As the chapter explores the options for a monetary regime strategy for Bulgaria in the pre-accession period she concludes that prescribed institutional forms predetermined by the path of others to EMU may bring instability in the Bulgarian monetary system prior to accession. The question what is more important, adopting EU rules or reacting to them in a way that preserves stability is given new dimension by the discussion in this chapter.

The chapter by Udovč and Baldwin follows the establishment of institutions supporting the agricultural land market in Slovenia. The authors stress that Slovenia's inherited structure of the land market and the changes starting in 1990 meant that the process of establishing the land market in the country was not EU driven. Nevertheless challenges related to the fear of foreigners buying land in Slovenia emerged already with the signing of Slovenia's Association agreement. The debate led to the signing of the so-called Spanish compromise and the changes in the Slovene constitution in 1997 allowing foreigners to buy land in Slovenia under certain conditions. In contrast, Udovč and Baldwin show that an even more important set of changes, the development of Slovenia's system of land and other real estate registration, has been driven by complementary transformation and enlargement objectives.

The Bulgarian and the Slovenian cases are clear-cut instances of adjustment in anticipation, but one that was not primarily EU driven. Yet, as both chapters illustrate, post-communist transformation and enlargement adaptation are far from identical. Enlargement-driven changes complement and strengthen but also sometimes challenge the reforms that are already in progress.

Administrative conditionality

As the following chapter shows, there are also cases when EU driven changes simply do not take root and domestic institutions persevere. Vass's discussion of regionalisation in Hungary is important and instructive as it reminds us that it is possible that enlargement governance fails to make an impact despite the conditionality and asymmetry of the enlargement process. The fact that, as Vass points out, Hungary seems to lag behind other candidates such as Poland and the Czech republic in terms of installing the institutional arrangements required by the EU for the utilisation of its structural funds does not mean that Hungary does not have a regional policy. On the contrary, Vass shows that Hungary's long-standing institutional arrangement placing the counties at the center of its administrative division has been so long established that uprooting it has proven very difficult. He singles out factors such as historical path dependency, the commitment of local actors and the embeddedness of the counties system into other sets of rules such as the electoral law to explain their stability.

Vass raises important questions regarding the limits of EU conditionality and enlargement governance in general. When faced with the option of replacing the system of counties with EU style regions, Hungarian governments have hesitated. Their reluctance can be explained with the fact that the old system has not been discredited and even, as Vass states, continued to function successfully in another guise during the socialist period. Furthermore, being a small, unitary state Hungary has never had strong regions. Their formal establishment is only the result of EU presented incentives in the form of structural funds. Whether these will be sufficient for changes in the established administrative structures to occur, remains to be seen.

In contrast to the Hungarian case, in Latvia and Romania EU-driven administrative reform appears to have given an impetus for transforming rules and policies, which were discredited and perceived as in need of modernisation. According to Reinholde and Hinţea, Şandor and Junjan, what was lacking in both the Latvian and Romanian cases, was political will. This is a common enough diagnosis, which can explain the lack of much progress in administrative reform in other candidate states such as the Czech republic as well.

More importantly, cases like these illustrate the real impact of enlargement governance in general and administrative conditionality in particular. When no significant political actor has a preference for reform, it can still happen, as governments perform their own analysis of costs and benefits and agree to reform as a way to stay in the EU accession process. Hinţea, Şandor and Junjan's conclusion that in Romania's case the EU conditions sometimes represented the only real pressure for reform, illustrates this point well. The Latvian case is more nuanced, but ultimately also Reinholde reaches the conclusion that the accession process made the difference between reform rhetoric and practice in the Latvian administration.

The impact of the European Union enlargement process

The analysis so far shows us that, broadly speaking, the European Union matters. Yet we do not know how and under what conditions enlargement governance makes the most significant impact. If we employ the useful division between polity, the political and state institutions within a given territory, policy, the sets of specific decisions and their implementation and politics as the institutions and actors that define a particular regime, we can establish that the EU influences all of these. The effects on polity appear to be particularly remarkable and farther reaching than Europeanisation effects in the current member states, although a systematic comparison is needed to confirm this proposition. In particular, the EU has had more of an influence on basic institutions and rules of the political game: an impact on the balance of power in Slovakia and on the basic constitutional arrangements in Slovakia, Poland and Slovenia. The Union's ability to affect administrative reform in Romania and Latvia has been considerable. Yet there are also cases, such as land reform in Slovenia, financial reform in Bulgaria and regional policy in Hungary when the EU influence and institution-building efforts have not had much of an effect.

What are we to make of this picture? And should it matter, given that once the candidates have joined the EU, the enlargement mode of governance would disappear – after all, current EU member states restrict the possibilities for the Commission to impose conditionalities on them and asymmetry in rule making would no longer be a problem. The potential disappearance of the enlargement governance mode, however, will not eliminate processes of Europeanisation, defined as the influence of the Union structures and policies on domestic politics, polity and policies. Furthermore, Europeanisation in the new members will take place under significantly different conditions than in the old members. Thus we have to examine whether Europeanisation approaches can be applied to study the continuing changes in the post-communist states, soon to be EU members.

In search of theoretical explanations

When searching for theoretical frameworks that could serve as a basis for future research into the changes discussed above, the literature on Europeanisation[6] seems an obvious starting point, since it deals, under various guises, with the impact of European Union on domestic structures.[7] As was argued at the beginning of this book, insights from the Europeanisation literature are not always applicable to the post-communist candidate states, since most Europeanisation studies disregard the character of EU enlargement governance and the importance of the post-communist transformations – both factors absent in the existing EU member states. In agreement with this, Leonardo Morlino stresses that the assumption by Green Cowles, Caporaso and Risse, shared by much of the Europeanisation literature, that domestic institutions are well established and actors strategies correspondingly well defined does not hold for democracies which are or have been in a long transition.[8] Instead, in countries in transition (in this case the post-communist states), 'main institutions are discussed and debated and suffer from a lack of legitimacy.'[9]

This is obviously the case with the states from Central and Eastern Europe whose democratic transitions are very recent and in some cases not complete. To illustrate this it is enough to mention that accession requires constitutional amendments still to be made in several of the candidates and in some cases, such as Bulgaria, these may be more substantial than the required adjustment in rules on the purchase of land. In her analysis of constitutional change in chapter 4 of this book, Ewa Popławska also stresses that she anticipates more changes in Poland. She notes the concerns among the creators of the 1997 Polish constitution who aimed to ensure the greatest possible stability of this document but are faced with the need to make further constitutional amendments to adjust to further requirements linked to the entry of a quasi-federal polity with pooled sovereignty.

Another reason why Europeanisation[10] may be expected to proceed in the new members differently from many of the EU's current members is the often-quoted issue of adjustment costs. Despite having negotiated some transitional arrangements in the area of environmental policies, for example, governments of the countries expecting to join in 2004 and in 2007 are well aware that they may not be able to comply with these even at a later date. The costs related to an adjustment to EU process regulation (difficult and potentially disastrous for the weaker EU economies as Fritz Scharpf argues)[11] for the economies of the transforming countries and to their new democracies should be investigated carefully. The social cost of complying with the Union *acquis* will be imposed on populations, which have been driven to change since the late 1980s. Pro-European and pro-democratic elites may find themselves in an impossible stranglehold between measures they have no choice but to implement, and populations which hold them accountable for the effects of these measures. Unless the EU finds a way to bargain for compensatory or support payments, a new democratic deficit can be created.

As for the Europeanisation of policies, existing research frameworks should be able to capture the dynamic of policy adjustment in the new members once the 'distorting effects' of enlargement governance have disappeared. Héritier *et al.*[12] use an actor-driven institutional approach incorporating actors, institutions[13] and ideas. The ideal-type responses to EU driven change in policy, which they find in the existing EU member states, can be expected to come up in the new members. One significant difference would be that some institutional structures such as competition boards and accompanying antitrust rules in the new members will be recently established. However, in terms of administrative rules and structures created to implement a policy the difference between old and new member states would not be as pronounced as in the case of basic polity rules, given that the EU member states have also established new institutions to cope with the implementation of new EU policies.

Can institutionalist theories provide some insights that are more general than the findings of the Europeanisation literature? Will the new institutions, established under the pressure of enlargement governance, endure?

Understanding the new institutions

Institutions, even in the most minimalist definitions, consist not only of rules but also, at the very least, of underlying norms. A broader definition would also include values, practices, and ways of doing things. While it is easy even at this early stage of enlargement-driven changes to pinpoint the changes in rules, changes in norms and other underlying structures that make up viable institutions are difficult to discern. Nevertheless, we have to ask ourselves whether all the rules which the European Union enlargement governance and, in some cases, domestic elites, have introduced in the candidate states will endure, whether all the institutions created will become effective and legitimate. Given that the effects of Europeanisation resemble a patchwork in the Union itself, we can expect that not all the enlargement driven changes will endure, even if the

EU's influence on candidates has been found to be much greater than on its member states.

This is a crucial question both from social scientific and practical points of view. From a practical point of view, institutional instability is highly undesirable in new democracies. The dangers of institutional instability have far-reaching consequences in Central and Eastern Europe. The alternative to a lack of its institutionalisation is, at worst, violence, at best a 'pathology of permanent ad hoc tinkering' with institutional change.[14]

From a theoretical point of view, the emergence and endurance of institutions is a major challenge for two different and competing perspectives, for which these issues are both central: *rational choice* institutionalism and *sociological* institutionalism. These approaches start from different assumptions about how to explain social reality.

Reform as a result of political actors and their interests

From a *rational choice perspective*, the political actors involved as well as their interests are crucial elements in explaining the outcome of the transformation processes in Central and Eastern Europe. The importance of interests has been stressed in several contributions to this volume referring to the political will of elites to introduce reforms. The basic hypothesis here is that if actors share the same views – or have homogeneous preferences – it will be rather easy to reach agreement on changing current institutions and policies. Or, to put it differently, when both the interests of the EU and the candidate members are the same, no complications will arise in adapting and implementing reform. In most instances, however, these preferences differ, which result in difficulties in reaching agreement. In view of *preference heterogeneity*, two separate hypotheses arise with regard to institutional reform in Central and Eastern Europe, which, taken together, stress the importance of the multi-level nature of governing in Europe.[15]

First, when the interests of the EU *and* the candidate country differ, more resistance against the proposed reforms arises and the adaptation process slows down. Many of the authors of this book who have been able to observe reforms and their course at first hand speak of the importance of political will for reform. This is a very important reminder that reform is not simply a techno-cratic operation but depends on actors and decisions, which are driven by preferences. In order to respond to enlargement conditionality, and particularly when the interests substantially differ, national government may introduce 'symbolic' changes, which will not have a substantial effect on policy-making structures in the country. Moreover, these 'symbolic' changes can easily be reversed when the imposed obligation for reform is reduced.

Second, when the *national interests* are divided, the resistance against reform also increases, which slows down the transformation process. Not only disagreement with the Union, but also conflict within the national political arena has an impact on the reform process in the candidate countries. Taken together, both hypotheses indicate that reform will slow down when differences in view exist between the EU and the national government and/or between the different fractions within the national political arena. In other words, delays in the reform, different interpretations of the EU requirements, and partial or even 'symbolic' changes of national policy-making structures might be the most likely outcomes of the current transformations. Only when all domestic actors more or less support the EU requirements for reform, is a rather smooth and unproblematic transformation process expected.

A second explanatory factor in institutional rational choice is the *multitude of actors*, which may further complicate the introduction of change. The basic hypothesis is that when the number of actors involved in the decision-making process increases, it becomes more difficult to find solutions that are preferred by all. Political actors are often labelled as 'veto players' in this context, since these actors have the possibility of 'blocking' decision making and thus preventing change from occurring.[16] Following this logic, multiparty systems may allow for more 'veto players' than bipartisan systems, which makes the introduction of institutional change and policy adaptations more difficult. Similarly, a federal political system, in which the national government shares power with rather autonomous regions, also allows for more 'veto players' than centralised or unitary ones, which again may hinder the transformation process. Combined with the hypotheses on heterogeneous preferences, a multitude of actors may further worsen the introduction of change when these actors have rather different views on the matter. In that case, change may be almost impossible, at least based on the current conceptions of who has to be consulted and who needs to be part of a political coalition to introduce reform. Only when these more fundamental conceptions are challenged and altered in the national political arena, might a slowdown of reform be prevented.

At this point, we should also bear in mind the proposition used in the Europeanisation literature, among others, that external pressure changes the domestic structure of opportunities. In other words, to further develop research into the influence of the EU on reforms, we might want to further examine how the European Union influences the configuration of political actors through enlargement governance. If enlargement governance empowers those actors whose preferences are in favour of reform, it may prove an alternative means of pushing for reform in the new member states.

Reform as a result of shared understandings and a search for identity

The other potential source of explanations and hypotheses regarding the enlargement driven changes we have observed is sociological institutionalism, which does not focus so much on political actors and their interests, but suggests that mutual expectations, norms, and constructed identities are key factors to understanding social behaviour.[17] In this view, institutions are approached as structures that shape behaviour and influence actors' preferences. As March and Olsen indicate, institutions define a 'logic of appropriateness' that provides guidance to group members in making choices.[18]

Based on this approach, the transformation process as imposed by the European Union can be seen as one in which the candidate countries aim to change their norms to those advocated by the Union. The construction of a common European identity by elites would also play a role in such a process. Of course, when these countries are already part of the same 'policy community', both sets of norms would be more or less the same and no problems would arise. However, in the case of the candidate countries, this is not yet the case. This leads to the basic hypothesis that differences in the mutual expectations and norms between the Union and a candidate country – in other words, *heterogeneity* in underlying norms – may lead to problems with regard to the contents and speed of reform. Focusing on the differences between the Union and the 'national' political elite, shared understandings might not exist, possibly leading to an unwillingness to transform the 'national' view into that proposed by the Union. The more substantive these differences, the more a process of change will be delayed and lead to outcomes that will differ from the proposed changes. Here, again, the possibility of 'symbolic' or rather instrumental adaptations may easily arise out of the conflicting sets of values and the necessity to comply with some of the EU's wishes.

A second possibility is that a division may occur between 'national' elites and other groups in society. When 'national' elites somehow share the views and understandings of their counterparts in the Union and identify themselves as 'European', sharing for example the values of democratic governance within a market economy, this may bring about a division between these groups in power and the population. The population may not share the same norms or understandings already constructed by the 'avant-garde' in their society, and may instead possess more traditional, older norms and values, remnants of previous institutional structures. Such a divide may not immediately reveal a slowdown in the progress of reform, but could easily disrupt the reform process at either national elections or the stage of implementation. The public may punish reformers: as we know most reformist governments in Central and Eastern Europe have not been elected for a second term. Furthermore, even after the formal introduction of new institutions or policies, the resistance against these changes may only become apparent when these new structures or policies have to be implemented. The institutions created by elites as a response to EU requirements will encounter a discrepancy between the new rules and the underlying norms, practices and ways of doing things and may be unstable. Alternatively, the difference in the normative frameworks between those introducing the changes and those who have to work with them on a daily basis may require much more attention and effort than simply the passing of law.

Sociological institutionalism provides the opportunity to develop a different but equally promising research agenda around the notion that the European Union plays a role in – as Reinholde aptly names it in her chapter on Latvian administrative reform – the 'desperate search for identity of reforms'.

Sociological institutionalism could help us formulate hypotheses regarding the way in which the EU might serve as a model in setting new norms or understandings in the candidate countries, or might shape the identity of those dealing with reforms in Central and Eastern Europe.

The challenge ahead

Both rational choice and sociological institutionalism approaches thus seem suitable for research in the large-scale institutional changes in post- communist states participating in this enlargement, while Europeanisation approaches seem applicable but narrower. Research based on the Europeanisation approach, however, should guard against teleological assumptions, which can easily replace the 'transition' paradigm, which used to dominate research into post-communist societies, with a Europeanisation one. As this book has shown, the diversity of responses to pressure from the EU precludes an automatic process of convergence towards one European model. The Europeanisation of polities in the new members may be hindered by the very weakness of the institutions and by the weak states, where institutions are in competition with a variety of networks, some of which may actively oppose European rules. A research programme which aims to explore the impact of Europe on Central and Eastern Europe has to take into account weak statehood, contested institutions, a great variety of informal rules and networks which interact with actors and institutions at the European Union level. One should not forget that the nature of post-communist change makes this enlargement significantly different from all previous ones with the possible exception of the accession of Spain and Portugal. In other words, enlargement looks different viewed from the East.

Enlargement viewed from the East

Enlargement viewed from the East looks inevitably different than from the perspective of the European Union as this book has endeavoured to show. In terms of research agenda, the crucial question has proven to be not how the EU can export or stabilise its rules in CEE but whether these rules are compatible with reform on a large scale and what effects the EU's pressure for change might have on reforms. In terms of future research agenda, the stability of the institutions established under the influence of the EU's enlargement governance should be explored. And, last but not least, the societal implications of this enlargement loom much larger in societies that have been driven to change for a number of years now. It is easy for those inside the Union to forget the future shock to which many of the citizens have been subjected when their societies changed at a pace unthinkable in the West of Europe. We should give credit to the patient, but not passive agents of change in every country that has striven since the early 1990s to catch up with a more prosperous and stable European Union.

Notes

1 European Council, Conclusions of the Presidency, Copenhagen, 12–13 December 2002, pp. 4–5.

2 It is also worth noting that in Slovakia the EU has applied the pressure of conditionality in combination with other, consensual mechanisms and in a very consistent way, which it has not replicated with other states such as Bulgaria or Romania. Thus the Slovak case remains difficult to generalise from.

3 T. A. Börzel and T. Risse, 'When Europe Hits Home: Europeanisation and Domestic Change', European Integration Papers Online, 4:15 (2000), at http://eiop.or.at/eiop/texte/2000-015a.htm.

4 See J. Dryzek, L. Holmes, S. Auer and A. Dimitrova, 'Slovakia', in J. Dryzek and L. Holmes (eds.), *Post-communist Democratization: Political Discourses across Thirteen Countries* (Cambridge and Canberra, Cambridge University Press, 2002).

5 F. W. Scharpf, 'European Governance: Common Concerns versus the Challenge of Diversity', Jean Monnet Working Paper 6/01, Symposium: Response to the European Commission's White Paper on Governance at www.jeanmonnetprogram.org/papers/01/010701.html (Harvard, 2001).

6 See for example, A. Héritier, 'Differential Europe: The European Union Impact on National Policy Making', in A. Héritier, D. Kerwer, C. Knill, D. Lehmkuhl, M. Teutsch and A. C. Douillet, *Differential Europe: The European Union Impact on National Policy Making* (Lanham: Rowman and Littlefield, 2001), pp. 1–13. For a different, broader definition of Europeanisation, see C. M. Radaelli, 'Whither Europeanisation: Concept Stretching and Substantive Change', *European Integration Online Paper* (EioP) 4:8: http://eiop.or.at/eiop/texte/2000-008a.htm.

7 See T. Risse, M. G. Cowles and J. Caporaso, 'Europeanisation and Domestic Change: Introduction', in M. Green Cowles, J. Caporaso and T. Risse (eds.), *Transforming Europe: Europeanisation and Domestic Change* (Ithaca and London, Cornell University Press, 2001).

8 L. Morlino, 'What We Know and What We Should Know on Europeanization and the Reshaping of Representation in SE Democracies', paper delivered at the conference on 'EU and Democracy in Southern Europe' (University of California, Berkeley, 31 October–2 November 2002), p. 6.

9 Morlino, 'What We Know', p. 9.

10 Defined here in accordance with Risse, Green Cowles and Caporaso, *Transforming Europe,* pp. 4–5, as the adjustment of domestic structures to the emerging structures at European level.

11 F. W. Scharpf, *Governing in Europe: Effective and Democratic?* (Oxford, Oxford University Press, 1999).

12 A. Héritier *et al.,* 'Differential Europe'.

13 On institutional veto points see E. Immergut, *Health Politics: Interests and Institutions in Western Europe* (Cambridge, Cambridge University Press, 1992), G. Tsebelis, 'Decision Making in Political Systems: Veto Players in Presidentialism, Parliamentarism, Multicameralism and Multipartism', *British Journal of Political Science,* 25 (1995), 289–325, and M. Haverland, 'National Adaptation to European Integration: The Importance of Institutional Veto Points', *Journal of Public Policy,* 20:1 (2001), 83–103.

14 J. Elster, C. Offe and U. K. Preuss, *Institutional Design in Post-communist Societies:*

Rebuilding the Ship at Sea (Cambridge, Cambridge University Press, 1998), pp. 27, 34.

15 See G. Marks, L. Hooghe and K. Blank, 'European Integration from the 1980s: State-centric v. Multi-level Governance', *Journal of Common Market Studies*, 34 (1996), 341–378.

16 See Tsebelis,'Decision Making in Political Systems'; Immergut, *Health Politics, Interests and Institutions*; and Haverland 'National Adaptation to European Integration'.

17 See, for instance, P. J. DiMaggio and W. W. Powell, 'Introduction', in W. W. Powell and P. J. DiMaggio (eds.), *The New Institutionalism in Organizational Analysis* (Chicago, University of Chicago Press, 1991), and P. A. Hall and R. Taylor, 'Political Science and the Three Institutionalisms', *Political Studies*, 44 (1996), 936–957.

18 J. G. March and J. P. Olsen, *Rediscovering Institutions: The Organizational Basis of Politics* (London, Macmillan, 1989).

Select bibliography

Documentary sources

Bulgaria

Bulgarian Foreign Exchange Law, at www.bnb.bg.
Law on the Bulgarian National Bank, at www.bnb.bg.

Estonia

Bank of Estonia (2002). Statistical database at www.ee/epbe/et/statistika.html.
Elanikkonna monitooringu aruanne (Report on Public Opinion) (2001, 2002), at www.elis.ee/est/index.html.
Estonian Ministry of Finance 2002. Database. At www.fin.ee/dokumendid/8_1_yl_2001_abi_tabel.pdf.
Põllumajandussaadusi töötleva tööstuse ülevaade ('Overview of the food processing industry in Estonia') Estonian Ministry Of Agriculture (Tallinn, 2002) at www.agri.ee.
Riigikogu EL teabekeskuse küsitlus 2002 (Enquiry by the European Union Information Secretariat to the Estonian Parliament) web.elis.ee/data/content/majandushinnangud06.02.pdf.

Hungary

Act on the Local Governments (LXV/1990).
Act on Regional Development and Physical Planning (XXI/1996).
Act on the Shaping and Protection of the Built-Up Environment (LXXVIII/1997).
Act on the Amendment of the Act XXI/1996 (XCII/1999).
Governmental Decree on the formulae of establishment and operation of enterprise zones (189/1996; XII.17).
Governmental Decree on the challenges of ministers and leaders of country-wide organisations, connected to regional development and physical planning (193/1996; XII.19).
Governmental Decree on the registry of beneficiary communities of regional development (219/1996; XII.24).
Governmental Decree on the reform of public administration (1100/1996; X.2).

Government Decree on the order of the harmonisation and authorisation of regional development plans and programmes, respectively, plans about physical planning (*184/1996; XII.11*).

Government Decree on the 1997–1998 action plan implementing the public administration reform (*2039/1997; II.12*).

Government Decree on the detailed conditions of the utilisation of the Spatial Equalisation Financial Assistance in 1997 (*80/1997; V.14*).

Government Decree on the detailed conditions of the utilisation of the Regional Development Expenditure Approximation in 1997 (*81/1997; V.16*).

Government Decree on the county-level allocation of the Regional Development Expenditure Approximation and Spatial Equalisation Financial Assistance in (*1997105/1997; VI.18*).

Government Decree on the registry of beneficiary regions of regional development (*106/1997; VI.18*).

Government Decree on the informational system of regional development and physical planning, and on the order of compulsory publication of information (*112/1997; VI.27*).

Government Decree on the register for municipalities disadvantaged economically and being below the average unemployment rate (*215/1997; XII.1*).

Government Decree on the requirements of national settlement and building development (*253/1997; XII.20*).

Government Decree on the rules of harmonised utilisation of chapter-level controlled expenditure approximations and separated state funds with related targets or functions (*263/1997; XII.21*).

Government Decree on the register for the beneficiary areas of the regional development (*19/1998; II.4*).

Government Decree on the tasks related to the preparation for the Structural Funds and the Cohesion Fund (*2073/1999; IV.21*).

Government Decree on EU-compatible alignment of the state aid system (*2134/1999; VI.11*).

Government Decree on the establishment of an Inter-ministerial Co-ordination Committee of Development Policy (*2171/1999; VII.8*).

Government Decree on tasks related to the preparation for the Structural Funds and the Cohesion Fund (*2273/1999; X.22*).

Government Decree on the 1999–2000 action plan implementing the public administration reform (*1052/1999; V.21*).

Government Decree on the 2001–2002 action plan implementing the public administration reform (*1057/2001; VI.21*).

Parliamentary Resolution on the principles of regional development support and decentralisation, on the conditional basis of the classification of beneficiary regions (*30/1997; IV.18*, modified by the 70/1997; XI.06 Parliamentary Decision).

Parliamentary Resolution on the National Concept of Regional Development (*35/1998; III.20*).

Parliamentary Resolution on the Regional Development Policies and the Principles of Decentralization (*30/1997; IV.18*).

Latvia

Bureau of Public Administration Reform, *Latvian Civil Service: Problems and Perspectives* (internal archive of the Bureau of Public Administration Reform, 1998).

Cabinet of Ministers, 'Report on formation of the Cabinet of Ministers and Declaration on planned activities of the government', *The Latvian Herald*, 153 (21 July 1993).

Cabinet of Ministers, Decision No. 46 'Temporary statutes of The Ministry of State Reforms', *The Latvian Herald*, 111 (25 November 1993).

Cabinet of Ministers, Decision No. 63 'On the establishment of the State Civil Service administration and the School of Public Administration', *The Latvian Herald*, 126 (17 December 1993).

Cabinet of Ministers, Public Administration Reform Concept (28 March 1995) at www.lv-laiks.lv.

Cabinet of Ministers, Regulations No. 191 Statutes of the Council of Public Administration Reform (27 May 1997).

Cabinet of Ministers, Regulations No. 213 Statutes of the Bureau of Public Administration Reform (10 June 1997).

Cabinet of Ministers, Regulations No. 327 Statutes of European Integration Bureau (16 September 1997.

Cabinet of Ministers, Strategy for public administration development till year 2000 (23 December 1997).

Cabinet of Ministers, Implementation Plan for Strategy on public administration development till year 2000 (10 March 1998).

Cabinet of Ministers, Regulations No. 389 Statutes of the European Integration Council (16 November 1999).

Cabinet of Ministers, Public administration reform strategy 2001–2006 (10 July 2001).

Cabinet of Ministers, Regulations No. 111 On internal order of the Cabinet of Ministers (12 March 2002).

Cabinet of Ministers, National Programme for Adoption of the Acquis (NPAA) (Riga, www.eib.lv, 2000), annex 4.

Cabinet of Ministers, National Programme for Adoption of the Acquis, at www.eib.lv (Riga, 2002), pp. 882–897.

European Integration Council, The Strategy on training of Latvian public officials in EU matters (Riga, 1999).

Law on public administration structure (20 June 2002) at www.likumi.lv.

Ministry of Foreign Affairs, *Latvia's integration into the European Union,* at www.mfa.gov.lv/lv (2002).

Strategy of the Republic of Latvia for the integration into the European Union (Saeima, 2000) at www.eib.lv, pp. 7–8.

School of Public Administration, 'Training of Civil Servants on EU Issues' (bulletin *New Administration*, 3, March 2002), pp. 4–5.

Slovenia

Agricultural Land Act, *Official Gazette of RS 59/1996* (Ljubljana, 1996).

Constitution of Republic of Slovenia, *Official Gazette of RS 33/1991* (Ljubljana, 1991); modified: *Official Gazette of RS 42/1997* (Ljubljana, 1997).

Denationalisation Law, *Official Gazette of RS 27/1991* (Ljubljana, 1991).

Land Registry Act, *Official Gazette of RS 33/1995* (Ljubljana, 1995).

Law on Land Cadastre, *Official Gazette of RS 16/1974* (Ljubljana, 1974); modified: *Official Gazette of RS 42/1986* (Ljubljana, 1986).

Law on Privatisation of Real Estate in Social Ownership, *Official Gazette of RS 44/1997* (Ljubljana, 1997).

MAFF (Ministry of Agriculture, Forestry and Food of the Republic of Slovenia), *Report of Agricultural Land and Forests Fund of Republic of Slovenia for the Year 1996* (Ljubljana, 1997).

SORS (Statistical Office of the Republic of Slovenia), *Statistical Yearbook of the Republic of Slovenia, 2000* (Ljubljana, 2001).

SMA (Surveying and Mapping Authority of the Republic of Slovenia), *National Report on Slovenia, 1996,* CERCO Plenary Session (Granada, 1996).

Romania

Romanian Government, National Programme for Accession (Bucharest, 2000): www.guv.ro/obiective/map/reforma-admin-public.pdf.

www.electoral2000.ro/platforme.php.

General

ACE, 'The Development of Land Markets in Central and Eastern Europe', Final Report Project P2128R, ACE programme (Brussels, EC, 1998), 121 pp. (unpublished).

European Bank for Reconstruction and Development, 'Transition Report 2002: Agriculture and Rural Transition' (London, European Bank for Reconstruction and Development, 2002).

European Commission. White Paper: 'Preparation of the Associated Countries of Central and Eastern Europe for Integration into the Internal Market of the Union,' COM(95)163 (Brussels, May 1995).

European Commission. 'Agenda 2000: For a Stronger and Wider Union', *Bulletin of the European Union, Supplement* 5/97 (Brussels, 1997).

European Commission, Agenda 2000: Commission Opinion on Latvia's Application for Membership of the European Union (Brussels, 1997).

European Commission, Agenda 2000: Commission Opinion on Romania's Application for Membership of the European Union (Brussels, 1997).

European Commission, Regular Report from the Commission on Latvia's progress towards accession (Brussels, 1998).

European Commission, Regular Report from the Commission on Slovakia's progress towards accession (Brussels, 1998).

European Commission, Regular Report from the Commission on Latvia's progress towards accession (Brussels, 1999).

European Commission, Regular Report from the Commission on Romania's progress towards accession (Brussels, 1999).

European Commission, Regular Report from the Commission on Slovakia's progress towards accession (Brussels, 1999).

European Commission, Regular Report from the Commission on Latvia's progress towards accession (Brussels, 2000).

European Commission, Regular Report from the Commission on Romania's progress towards accession (Brussels, 2000).

European Commission, Regular Report from the Commission on Slovakia's progress towards accession (Brussels, 2000).

European Commission, 'Exchange Rate Strategies for EU Candidate Countries' (Brussels, 22 August, 2000), ECFIN/521/2000.

European Commission, Accession Partnership with the republic of Latvia (Brussels, 2001).

European Commission, 'Candidate Countries Eurobarometer. Public Opinion in the Countries Applying for European Union Membership', Report No. 2002/2 *Public Opinion Barometer*, October 2002.

Eurostat database, www.europa.eu.int/comm/eurostat/Public/datashop.

Enlargement argumentaire. DG for Economic and Financial Affairs, European Commission, *Enlargement Paper* 5 (2001).

European Commission, Regular Report from the Commission on Latvia's progress towards accession (Brussels, 2002).

European Council in Copenhagen, 21–22 June 1993, Conclusions of the Presidency (DN: DOC/93/3, of 22 June 1993).

European Council, Presidency Conclusions, Copenhagen, 12–13 December 2002, at www.ue.eu.int/pressData/en/ec/73774.pdf.

IMF, 'The Baltics: Medium-Term Fiscal Issues Related to EU and NATO Accession', *IMF Country Report* No. 02/7 (January 2002), p. 39.

OECD database, 2002: www.oecd.org.

OECD, SIGMA Paper No. 27 *European Administrative Principles for Public Administration* (Paris, Sigma, 1999.)

Trade Policy Review. European Union. WT/TRP/S/30. WTO, 1997.

UNECE, *Land Administration Guidelines: With Special Reference to Countries in Transition*, UN ECE/HBP/96 (Geneva, 1996), 94 pp.

World Bank. World Human Development Report 2000 (Washington, 2000), pp. 157–158, 202–203.

Books and articles

Ágh, A., *The Actors of Systemic Change: The Political Context of Public Sector Reform in Central Europe*, Discussion Papers 19 (Berlin: European Centre for Comparative Government and Public Policy, 1997).

Amato, G. and J. Batt, 'Final Report of the Reflection Group on the Long Term Implications of EU Enlargement: The Nature of the New Border', *RSC/EUI Working Papers*, 12 (Florence: EUI, 1999).

Angerjärv, J., 'Madal palk ajab ajud Eestist' (Low Salaries Lead to Brain Drain from Estonia) *Äripäev* (20 June 2001).

Auby, F. J., *Management Public* (Paris: Sirey, 1996).

Avery, G. and F. Cameron, *The Enlargement of the European Union* (Sheffield: Sheffield Academic Press, 1998).

Avramov, R., 'The Introduction of the Euro: A Make-Believe Solution', *Capital Newspaper*, 20 (Sofia, 2000).

Balogh M., 'Public Administration in the Political Parties' Electoral Platforms in Romania', *Transylvanian Journal of Administrative Science*, 5 (2000), 81–83.

Balogh M., I. Hosu, D. Pop and F. Pop, Research Report 'Map of the Actors and Problems of the Process of Accession to the EU', pp. 54–56.

Bake, P., 'Exchange Rate Regimes in Central and Eastern Europe: A Brief Review of Recent Changes, Current Issues, and Future Challenges', *Focus on Transition*, 2 (Vienna: Austrian National Bank, 1999).

Barcz, J., 'Akt integracyjny Polski z Unią Europejską w świetle Konstytucji RP' (Act of Poland's Integration with the European Union in the light of the Constitution of the Republic of Poland), *Państwo i Prawo*, 4 (1998).

Barilari, A., *La Modernisation de l'Administration* (Paris: Librarie Generale de Droit et de Jurisprudence, 1994).

Baun, M. J., *A Wider Europe: The Process and Politics of European Union Enlargement* (Maryland: Rowman and Littlefield, 2000).

Bilčík, V., M. Bruncko, A. Duleba, P. Lukáč and I. Samson, 'Foreign and Defence policy of the Slovak Republic', in G. Mesežnikov, M. Kollár and T. Nicholson (eds.), *Slovakia 2000* (Bratislava: Institute for Public Affairs, 2001), pp. 233–296.

Böckenförde, E. W., *Państwo prawa w jednoczącej się Europie* (The State of Law in the United Europe) (Warsaw, Instytut Studiów Politycznych Polskiej Akademii Nauk, 2000).

Caiden, G., *Administrative Reform Comes of Age* (New York: Walter de Gruyter, 1991).

Caprio Jr., G., M. Dooley, D. Leipziger and C. Walsh, 'The Lender of Last Resort Function Under a Currency Board: The Case of Argentina', *World Bank Policy Research Working Papers*, 1326 (Washington, 1996).

Cecchini, P., M. Catinat and A. Jacquemin *The European Challenge 1992: The Benefits of a Single Market* (Aldershot, Wildwood House, 1988).

Checkel, J., 'Why Comply? Social Learning and European Identity Change', *International Organization*, 55 (summer 2001), 553–588.

Cheung, A., 'La Comprehension des Reformes du Secteur Public: Tendances Mondiales est Questions Diverses', *Revue Internationale des Sciences Administratives*, 4 (1997), 511–537.

Chevallier J. and D. Loschak, 'Rationalite Juridique et rationalite manageriale dans l'Administration Francaise', *Revue Francaise d' Administration Publique*, 24 (1982), 53–94.

Czapliński, W., 'L'intégration européenne dans la Constitution polonaise de 1997', *Revue du Marché commun et de l'Union européenne*, 436 (2000), 168–172.

Czapliński, W., I. Lipowicz , M. Wyrzykowski and T. Skoczny (eds.), *Suwerenność i integracja europejska. Materiały pokonferencyjne* (Sovereignty and European integration. Conference Materials) (Warsaw, Centrum Europejskie Uniwersytetu Warszawskiego, 1999).

Dale, P. and R. Baldwin, 'Lessons Learnt from the Emerging Land Markets in Central and Eastern Europe', *Quo Vadis: International Conference Proceedings, FIG Working Week 2000* (Prague, 21–26 May, 2000).

Di Palma, G., *To Craft Democracies: An Essay on Democratic Transitions* (Berkeley: University of California Press, 1990).

Dimitrova, A. L., 'The Role of the European Union in the Process of Democratization in Central and Eastern Europe: Lessons from Bulgaria and Slovakia', doctoral thesis (Limerick: University of Limerick, 1998).

Dimitrova, A. L., 'Enlargement, Institution Building and the EU's Administrative Capacity Requirement', *West European Politics*, 25:4 (2002), 171–190.

Dobrev, D., 'The Currency Board in Bulgaria: Design, Peculiarities and Management of Foreign Exchange Cover', *Bulgarian National Bank Discussion Paper*, 9 (Sofia, 1999).

Dostál, O., 'Menšiny' (Minorities), in M. Bútora and P. Hunčík (eds.), *Slovensko1995: Súhrnná správa o stave spoločnosti*. (Bratislava: Nadácia Sándora Máraiho, 1996), 51–60.

Duisenberg, W. F. and C. Noyer, 'Introductory Statement', European Central Bank Press Conference, at www.ecb.int/key/00/sp000413.htm (Frankfurt am Main, 13 April 2000).

Duleba, A., 'Democratic Consolidation and the Conflict over Slovak International Alignment', in S. Szomolányi and J. A. Gould (eds.), *Slovakia: Problems of Democratic Consolidation* (Bratislava: Slovak Political Science Association, 1997), 209–230.

Eising, R. and B. Kohler-Koch (eds.), *The Transformation of Governance in the European Union* (London and New York: Routledge/ECPR Studies in European Political Science, 1999).

Elster, J., C. Offe and U. K. Preuss (with F. Boenker, U. Goetting and F. W. Rueb), *Institutional Design in Post-communist Societies: Rebuilding the Ship at Sea* (Cambridge: Cambridge University Press, 1998).

Friis, L., 'The End of the Beginning of Eastern Enlargement: Luxembourg Summit and Agenda Setting', *European Integration Online Papers*, 2/7, www.eiop.or.at/eiop/texte/198-007a.htm (1998a).

Friis, L., 'Approaching the "Third Half" of EU Grand Bargaining: The Post Negotiation Phase of the Europe Agreement Game', *Journal of European Public Policy*, 5:2 (1998b), 322–338.

Friis, L. and A. Murphy, 'The European Union and Central and Eastern Europe: Governance and Boundaries', *Journal of Common Market Studies*, 37:2 (1999), 211–232.

Friis, L. and A. Murphy, 'Enlargement: A Complex Juggling Act', in M. Green Cowles and M. Smith (eds.), *The State of the European Union: Risks, Reform, Resistance and Revival*, Vol. 5 (Oxford: Oxford University Press, 2000), pp. 186–207.

Ganev, V. I., 'Dysfunctional Sinews of Power: Problems of Bureaucracy Building in Post-Communist Balkans', paper presented at the conference on 'Civil Society, Political Society and the State: A Fresh Look at the Problems of Governance in the Balkan Region' (Split, Croatia, 23–24 November, 2001).

Gavriisky, S., 'Currency Boards and EMU: A Bulgarian Perspective', presentation at the seminar on the 'Accession Process' organised by the ECB and the Bank of Finland (Helsinki, 10–12 November 1999). At www.bnb.bg.

Gavriisky, S., 'Statement of the BNB's Governor, Press Conference Held at the Central Bank (Sofia, 11 May 2000). At www.bnb.bg.

Ghosh, A. R., A.-M. Gulde and H. C. Wolf, 'Currency Boards: The Ultimate Fix?', *IMF Working Paper* 8 (1998).

Goodin, R. E., 'Institutions and Their Design', in R. E. Goodin (ed.), *The Theory of Institutional Design* (Cambridge, New York and Melbourne: Cambridge University Press, 1998), pp. 1–54.

Goodin, R. E. (ed.), *The Theory of Institutional Design* (Cambridge, New York and Melbourne: Cambridge University Press, 1998).

Grabbe, H., 'A Partnership for Accession? The Implications of EU Conditionality for the Central and Eastern European Applicants', EUI/RSC Working Papers, 12 (Florence: EUI, 1999).

Grabbe, H., 'How Does Europeanisation Affect CEE Governance? Conditionality, Diffusion and Diversity', *Journal of European Public, Policy* 8:6 (2001), 1013–1031.

Grabbe, H., 'Europeanisation Goes East: Power and Uncertainty in EU Accession Politics', paper presented at the ECPR workshop 'Enlargement and European Governance', ECPR Joint Sessions of Workshops (Turin Italy, 22–27 March 2002).

Grabbe H. and K. Hughes, *Enlarging the EU Eastwards* (London: Royal Institute of International Affairs, 1998).

Green Cowles, M., J. Caporaso and T. Risse (eds.), *Transforming Europe: Europeanisation and Domestic Change* (Ithaca and London: Cornell University Press, 2001).

Gulde, A.-M., 'The Role of the Currency Board in Bulgaria's Stabilization', *IMF Policy Discussion Papers PDP/99/3* (1999).

Gulde, A.-M., J. Kahkonen and P. M. Keller, 'Pros and Cons of Currency Board Arrangements in the Lead-Up to EU Accession and Participation in the Euro Zone', *IMF Policy Discussion Papers PDP/00/1.9* (2000).

Hanke, S., L. Joung and K. Schuler, *Russian Currency and Finance* (London: Routledge, 1993).

Hanson, S. E., 'Defining Democratic Consolidation', in R. D. Anderson, Jr., M. Steven Fish, S. E. Hanson and P. G. Roeder, *Postcommunism and the Theory of Democracy* (Princeton and Oxford: Princeton University Press, 2001), pp. 152–169.

Haverland, M., 'National Adaptation to European Integration: The Importance of Institutional Veto Points', *Journal of Public Policy*, 20:1 (2001), 83–103.

Henderson, K. (ed.), *Back to Europe: Central and Eastern Europe and the European Union* (London: UCL Press, 1999).

Héritier, A., 'The Accommodation of Diversity in European Policy Making and Its Outcomes: Regulatory Policy as a Patchwork', *Journal of European Public Policy*, 3:2 (1996), 149–167.

Héritier, A., 'Differential Europe: The European Union Impact on National Policy Making', in Héritier, A., D. Kerwer, C. Knill, D. Lehmkuhl, M. Teutsch and A. C. Douillet (eds.), *Differential Europe: The European Union Impact on National Policy Making* (Lanham: Rowman and Littlefield, 2001), pp. 1–13.

Héritier, A. and C. Knill, 'Differential Reponses to European policies: A Comparison', in A. Héritier, D. Kerwer, C. Knill, D. Lehmkuhl, M. Teutsch and A. C. Douillet (eds.), *Differential Europe: The European Union Impact on National Policy Making* (Lanham: Rowman and Littlefield, 2001), pp. 257–295.

Hintea C. and L. Radu L, 'Program Evaluation and Romanian Public Administration', *Transylvanian Journal of Administrative Sciences*, 5 (2000), 11–19.

Hooghe, L. and G. Marks, *Multi Level Governance and European Integration* (Lanham: Rowman and Littlefield, 2001).

Horcher, N. (ed.), *Regional Development in Hungary* (Budapest: Hungarian Institute for Town and Regional Planning, 1999).

Jachtenfuchs, M., 'The Governance Approach to European Integration', *Journal of Common Market Studies*, 39:2 (2001), 249–264.

Jyränki, A. (ed.), *National Constitutions in the Era of Integration* (The Hague, London and Boston: Kluwer Law International, 1999).

Kalnins A., *Public Administration and State Civil Service: Achievements, Problems and Perspectives* (Riga: State Civil Service Administration, 2000), 2–5.

Karl, T. L. and P. C. Schmitter, 'Models of Transition in Latin America, Southern and Eastern Europe', *International Social Science Journal*, 128 (1991), 269–284.

King, R. and R. Levine, 'Finance, Entrepreneurship, and Growth: Theory and Evidence', *Journal of Monetary Economics*, 32 (December 1993), 513–542.

Kolarska-Bobińska, L. (ed.), *Polska Eurodebata* (The Polish Eurodebate) (Warsaw, Instytut Spraw Publicznych, 1999).

Kramer, H., 'The European Community's Response to the "New Eastern Europe"', *Journal of Common Market Studies*, 31:2 (1993), 212–244.

Kranz, J. and J. Reiter (eds.), *Drogi do Europy* (Roads to Europe) (Warsaw: Centrum Stosunków Międzynarodowych, 1998).

Krastev, I., 'The Inflexibility Trap: Frustrated Societies, Weak States and Democracy', *Report on the State of Democracy in the Balkans* (Sofia: Center for Liberal Strategies, February 2002).

Kruk, M. (ed.), *Prawo międzynarodowe i wspólnotowe w krajowym porządku prawnym* (International and European Law in National Legal Order) (Parliaments and the European integration) (Warsaw: Wydawnictwo Sejmowe, 1998).

Kruk, M. and E. Popławska (eds.), *Parlamenty a integracja europejska* (Warsaw: Wydawnictwo Sejmowe, 2002).

Kucia, M., 'Public Opinion in Central Europe on EU Accession: The Czech Republic and Poland', *Journal of Common Market Studies*, 37:1 (1999), 143–152.

Levine, R., 'Financial Development and Economic Growth: Views and Agenda', *World Bank Policy Research Working Paper*, 1678 (Washington, World Bank, 1996).

Levine, R., N. Loayza and T. Beck, 'Financial Intermediation and Growth: Causality and Causes', *World Bank Policy Research Working Paper*, 2059 (Washington, World Bank, 1999).

Linz, J. J. and A. Stepan, *Problems of Democratic Transition and Consolidation: Southern Europe, South America, and Post-Communist Europe* (Baltimore and London: Johns Hopkins University Press, 1996).

Lippert, B., 'Shaping and Evaluating the Europe Agreements: The Community Side', in B. Lippert and H. Schneider (eds.), *Monitoring Association and Beyond: The European Union and the Visegrád States* (Bonn: Europa Union Verlag, 1995), pp. 217–248.

Made, V., 'Elu- ja töötingimused Euroopa Liidus' (Living and Working Conditions in the European Union) *ELIS teabeleht*, 13 (January 2002) at www.elis.ee.

Malová, D., 'Slovakia: From the Ambiguous Constitution to the Dominance of Informal Rules', in J. Zielonka (ed.), *Democratic Consolidation in Eastern Europe, Volume 1: Institutional Engineering* (Oxford: Oxford University Press, 2001), pp. 347–377.

Malová, D. and M. Rybář, 'The Troubled Institutionalization of Parliamentary Democracy in Slovakia', *Politicka misao. Croatian Political Science Review*, 37:2 (2000), 99–115.

Maresceau, M. and E. Montaguti, 'The Relations between the European Union and Central and Eastern Europe: A Legal Appraisal', *Common Market Law Review*, 32 (1995), 1327–1367.

Maresceau, M. (ed.), *Enlarging the European Union: Relations between the EU and Central and Eastern Europe* (London and New York: Longman, 1997).

Mayhew, A., *Recreating Europe: The European Union's Policy Towards Central and Eastern Europe* (Cambridge: Cambridge University Press, 1998).

Mayhew, A., 'Enlargement of the European Union: An Analysis of the Negotiations with the Central and Eastern European Candidate Countries', *Sussex European Institute Working Paper*, 39 (Sussex, 2000).

Mayhew, A., The Negotiating Position of the European Union on Agriculture, the Structural Funds and the EU Budget', *SEI Working Paper*, No. 52 (Sussex, 2002), p. 15.

Mesežnikov G. and M. Bútora (eds.), *Slovenské referendum '97: Zrod, priebeh, dôsledky* (The Slovak Referendum 1997: Origins, Course of Events, and Consequences) (Bratislava: Inštitút pre verejné otázky, 1997).

Michalski, A. and H. Wallace, *The European Community: The Challenge of Enlargement* (London: Royal Institute of International Affairs, 1992).

Mik, C. (ed.), *Polska w Unii Europejskiej. Perspektywy, warunki, szanse i zagrożenia* (Poland in the European Union: Prospects, Preconditions, Chances and Threats) (Toruń, TNOiK, 1997).

Mik, C. (ed.), *Implementacja prawa integracji europejskiej w krajowych porządkach prawnych* (The Implementation of the Law of the European Integration in National Legal Orders) (Toruń, TNOiK, 1998).

Mik, C. (ed.), *Konstytucja Rzeczypospolitej Polskiej z 1997 roku a członkostwo w Unii Europejskiej* (The Constitution of the Republic of Poland of 1997 and Poland's Membership in the European Union) (Toruń, TNOiK, 1999).

Mik, C. (ed.), *Europeizacja prawa krajowego. Wpływ integracji europejskiej na klasyczne dziedziny prawa* (The Implementation of the Law of the European Integration in National Legal Orders) (Toruń: TNOiK, 2000).

North, D. C., *Institutions, Institutional Change and Economic Performance* (Cambridge: Cambridge University Press, 1990).

Offe, C., 'Capitalism by Democratic Design? Democratic Theory Facing the Triple Transition in East Central Europe', *Social Research*, 58:4 (1991), 865–892.

Offe, C., *Varieties of Transition: The East European and East German Experience* (Cambridge: Polity Press, 1996).

Offe, C., 'Designing Institutions in East European Transitions', in R. E. Goodin (ed.), *The Theory of Institutional Design* (Cambridge: Cambridge University Press, 1998).

Oláh, M., 'Közelítési módozatok a regionális identitás térbeliségének megrajzolásához' (Way of Approaches to the Spatial Formation of the Regional Identity), *Comitatus*, 8:2 (1998), 6–34.

Osband, K. and D. Villanueva, 'Independent Currency Authorities', *IMF Working Papers*, 50 (1992).

Palk, P., *Euroopa ühendamise lugu* (The Story of European Integration) (Tallinn, Tumm, 1999) 1–206.

Pálné Kovács, I., *Regionális politika és közigazgatás* (Regional Policy and Public Administration) (Budapest-Pécs: Dialog Campus, 1999).

Pelkmans, J. and A. Murphy, 'Catapulted into Leadership: The Community's Trade and Aid Policies vis-à-vis Eastern Europe', *Journal of European Integration*, 14:2–3 (1991), 125–151.

Pierce, W. S. *Bureaucratic Failure and Public Expenditure* (New York: Academic Press, Harcourt Brace Jovanovich, 1981).

Plesu, A., 'Towards a European Patriotism: Obstacles as Seen from the East', *East European Constitutional Review*, Budapest: Central European University (spring/summer 1997), 53–56.

Pogany, I., 'Constitution Making or Constitutional Transformation in Post-Communist Societies?', *Political Studies*, 44 (1995), 568–591.

Pollitt, C. and G. Bouckaert, *Public Management Reform: A Comparative Analysis* (Oxford: Oxford University Press, 2000).

Popławska, E. (ed.), *The National Constitutions and European Integration* (Warsaw: Scholar, 1995).

Popławska, E. (ed.), *Konstytucja dla rozszerzającej się Europy* (Constitution for the Expanding Europe) (Warsaw: Instytut Spraw Publicznych, 2000).

Posavac E. J. and R. G. Carey, *Program Evaluation: Methods and Case Studies* (New Jersey: Prentice Hall, 1997).

Preston, C., *Enlargement and Integration in the European Union* (London and New York: Routledge, 1997).

Pridham, G., *Encouraging Democracy: The International Context of Regime Transition in Southern Europe* (Leicester: Leicester University Press, 1991).

Pridham, G., 'Complying with the European Union's Democratic Conditionality: Transnational Party Linkages and Regime Change in Slovakia, 1993–1998', *Europe–Asia Studies*, 51:7 (1999), 1211–1244.

Quermonne, J.-L., 'L'adaptation de l'Etat à l'intégration européenne', *Revue du droit public en France et à l'étranger,* 5–6 (1998), 1405–1420.

Risse, T., M. Green Cowles and J. Caporaso, 'Europeanisation and Domestic Change: Introduction', in M. Green Cowles, J. Caporaso and T. Risse (eds.), *Transforming Europe: Europeanisation and Domestic Change* (Ithaca and London: Cornell University Press, 2001), pp. 1–19.

Rollo, J., 'Economic Aspects of EU Enlargement to the East', in M. Maresceau (ed.), *Enlarging the European Union: Relations between the EU and Central and Eastern Europe* (London, New York, 1997).

Rusmanis, U., 'Priorities of Civil Servants Training', *New Administration*, 10 (October 2000), 5–7.

Saganek, P. and T. Skoczny (eds.), *Wybrane problemy i obszary dostosowania prawa polskiego do prawa Unii Europejskiej* (Selected Problems and Areas of the Adjustment of Polish Law to the Law of the European Union) (Warsaw: Centrum Europejskie Uniwersytetu Warszawskiego, 1999).

Şandor S. D. and C. E. Hinţea, 'Professionalisation of Civil Servants', *Transylvanian Journal of Administrative Science*, 2 (1999), 62–63.

Saron, T., 'The Impact of Technical Measures on Estonian Dairy and Meat Industry', MBA project (University of Tartu, 2002), appendices 11–14.

Scharpf, F. W., *Governing in Europe: Effective and Democratic?* (Oxford: Oxford University Press, 1999).

Scharpf, F. W., 'European Governance: Common concerns versus the Challenge of Diversity', *Jean Monnet Working Paper*, 6/01, Symposium: Response to the European Commission's White Paper on Governance at www.jeanmonnetprogram.org/papers/01/010701.html (2001).

Schimmelfennig, F., 'The Double Puzzle of EU Enlargement: Liberal Norms, Rhetorical Action and the Decision to Expand to the East', paper presented at ECSA Sixth International Conference (Pittsburgh, 3–5 June 1999).

Schimmelfennig, F., 'The Enlargement of European Regional Organisations: Questions, Theories, Hypotheses and the State of Research', paper presented at the workshop on 'Governance by Enlargement' (Darmstadt University of Technology, 23–25 June 2000).

Schimmelfennig, F., 'The Community Trap: Liberal Norms, Rhetorical Action, and the Eastern Enlargement of the European Union', *International Organization*, 55:1 (2001), 47–80.

Schmitter, P. C., 'The Influence of the International Context upon the Choice of National Institutions and Policies in Neo-Democracies', in L. Whitehead (ed.), *The*

International Dimensions of Democratization: Europe and the Americas (Oxford: Oxford University Press, 1998), pp. 26–55.

Schmitter P. C. and T. L. Karl, 'The Conceptual Travels of Transitologists and Consolidologists: How Far East Should They Attempt to Go?', *Slavic Review*, 53:1 (1994), 173–185.

Schuler, K., *Should Developing Countries Have Central Banks?* (Baltimore: Institute of Economic Affairs, Johns Hopkins University Press, 1996).

Schwartz, A., 'Currency Boards: Their Past, Present and Possible Future Role', *Carnegie–Rochester Conference Series on Public Policy*, 39 (1993).

Stark, D. and L. Bruszt, *Postsocialist Pathways: Transforming Politics and Property in East Central Europe* (Cambridge: Cambridge University Press, 1998).

Thelen, K., 'Historical Institutionalism in Comparative Politics', *Annual Review of Political Science*, 2 (1999), 369–404.

Temesi, I., 'Integration to the EU: Tendencies of Regionalization in Hungary', in K. A. Wojtaszczyk and M. Jarosinska (eds.), *EU Enlargement to the East: Public Administration in Eastern Europe and European Standards* (Warsaw: Fundacja Politeja, 2000), pp. 247–259.

Tismaneanu, V., 'Discomforts of Victory: Democracy, Liberal Values and Nationalism in Post-Communist Europe', *West European Politics*, 25:2 (April 2002), 81–101.

Toming, K., 'Euroopa Liiduga liitumise väliskaubanduspoliitiline mõju Eesti majandusele', MA thesis (University of Tartu, 2002).

Toming, K., 'Estonia's Accession to the EU: What Effect on Agricultural Imports and Economic Welfare?', *Kiel Institute of World Economics Advanced Studies Working Paper*, 382 (Kiel, 2002).

Toonen, T. A., 'Analysing Institutional Change and Administrative Transformation: A Comparative View', *Public Administration*, 71 (1993), 151–168.

Traks, K., 'Segadus ekspordikvootidega' (Confusion about Export Quotas), *Äripäev* (7 August 2002).

Učeň, P., 'Implications of Party System Development for Slovakia's Performance in European Integration' unpublished manuscript (Florence: European University Institute, 1998).

Udovč, A. and R. Baldwin, 'The Institutional Environment of Land Market in Slovenia', *Research Reports Biotechnological Faculty, UoL*, 69 (1997), 147–156.

Ulgenerk, E. and L. Zlaoui, 'From Transition to Accession: Developing Stable and Competitive Financial Markets in Bulgaria', *World Bank Technical Paper*, 473 (Washington, 2000).

Varblane, U., K. Toming, H. Riik., R. Selliov and D. Tamm, 'Võimalikud majanduspoliitilised instrumendid Eesti põllumajandussaaduste jatoodete hindade ühtlustamiseks Euroopa Liidu hindadega' (Economic Policy Instruments to Equalize the Prices of Estonian Agricultural and Food Products with the EU Prices) (Tallinn, Estonian Ministry of Agriculture, 2001).

Vass, L., 'Hungarian Public Administration: Reform and EU-Accession', in K. A. Wojtaszczyk and M. Jarosinska (eds.), *EU-Enlargement to the East: Public Administration in Eastern Europe and European Standards* (Warsaw: Fundacja Politeja, 2000), pp. 217–235.

Vass, László, 'A támogatáspolitika változása' (Changes in the Structural Fund Policy), in Ferenc Csefko (ed.), *EU-Integráció: Önkormányzatok II* (EU-Integration: Local Governments II) (Budapest: Magyar Önkormányzati Szövetségek Társulása, 2001), pp. 101–115.

Verebélyi, I., *Public Administration Reform Program of Republic of Hungary* (Budapest: Prime Minister's Office, 1996).

Verebélyi, I., *Összefoglaló a közigazgatási reformfolyamat elsö szakaszáról és a soron következö feladatairól* (Summary of the First Phase of the Administrative Reform Process and of the Next Tasks) (Budapest: Prime Minister's Office, 1998).

van der Velde, M. and F. Snyder, 'Agrarian Land Law in the European Community', in M. R. Grossman and W. Brussaard (eds.), *Agrarian Land Law in the Western World* (Bristol, Cab International, 1992), 1–280.

Verheijen, T., 'Dix Ans de Reformes en Europe Centrale et Orientale: Toujours les memes Problemes', *Revue Francaise d'Administration Publique*, 87 (1998), 393–403.

Verheijen, A. J. G., *Administrative Capacity Development: A Race Against Time?* Working Document 107 (The Hague: WRR, 2000).

Wagener, H.-J. and H. Fritz, 'Die Erweiterung der Europäischen Union und die Transformation in Mittel- und Osteuropa', *Policy Paper* (Frankfurt/Oder, Europa-Universitt Viadrina, 1996).

Wallace, H. and W. Wallace, *Policy-Making in the European Union* (3rd edn) (Oxford: Oxford University Press, 1996).

Whitehead, L. (ed.), *The International Dimensions of Democratization: Europe and the Americas* (Oxford: Oxford University Press, 1998).

Whitehead, L., 'The Enlargement of the European Union: A "Risky" Form of Democracy Promotion', *Central European Political Science Review*, 1:1 (September 2000), 16–42.

Yankova, E. A., 'Governed by Enlargement? Dynamics of Central and Eastern Europe's Accession to the European Union', paper presented at the workshop on 'Governance by Enlargement' (Darmstadt: Darmstadt University of Technology, 23–25 June 2000).

Zavadskas, E., B. Sloan and A. Kaklauskus, *Property Valuation and Investment in Central and Eastern Europe*. Proceedings of the International Conference held in Vilnius, Lithuania (Vilnius, Gediminas Technical University, 1997).

Zielonka, J and P. Mair, 'Introduction: Diversity and Adaptation in the Enlarged European Union', *West European Politics*, 25:2 (April 2002), 1–19.

Index